Time Decay of 2- and 3-Year Options

Time value premium

3 Years | 2 Years | 1 Year | 4 Months | 0

LEAPS ™ | 9 Months | 1 Month

Short-term option

Time remaining until expiration

LEAPS (LONG-TERM EQUITY ANTICIPATION SECURITIES)

WHAT THEY ARE AND HOW TO USE THEM FOR PROFIT AND PROTECTION

LEAPS (LONG-TERM EQUITY ANTICIPATION SECURITIES)

WHAT THEY ARE AND HOW TO USE THEM FOR PROFIT AND PROTECTION

Harrison Roth

McGraw-Hill

New York ◆ San Francisco ◆ Washington, D.C. ◆ Auckland
Bogotá ◆ Caracas ◆ Lisbon ◆ London ◆ Madrid ◆ Mexico City
Milan ◆ Montreal ◆ New Delhi ◆ San Juan ◆ Singapore
Sydney ◆ Tokyo ◆ Toronto

McGraw-Hill

A Division of The McGraw-Hill Companies

© RICHARD D. IRWIN INC., 1994

This publication is designed to provide accurate and authoritative information in regard to the subject matter covered. It is sold with the understanding that neither the author nor the publisher is engaged in rendering legal, accounting, or other professional service. If legal advice or other expert assistance is required, the services of a competent professional person should be sought.

From a Declaration of Principles jointly adopted by a Committee of the American Bar Association and a Committee of Publishers.

Library of Congress Cataloging-in-Publication Data

Roth, Harrison.
    LEAPS (long-term equity anticipation securities) : what they are and how to use them for profit and protection / [Harrison Roth].
      p.   cm.
    Includes index.
    ISBN 1-55623-819-3
    1. Stock options.   I. Title.
HG6042.R67 1994
332.63'228—dc20   93-15266

Printed in the United States of America
      13 14 15 16 17 18 19 20 QWF 02 01 00

*Dedicated to all those
—including my family and friends; colleagues
on Wall, LaSalle, Pine, and Market Streets as
well as those at The Options Institute; Drexel,
Burnham, Lambert; Cowen & Co.; and the publisher—
who believed in me.*

FOREWORD

In April 1973 the Chicago Board Options Exchange (CBOE) had the privilege of starting the listed options market. During the intervening 20 years the options universe has exploded many times over. It has gone from an initial 16 stocks with listed options to over 1,000. Options are now traded on 5 securities exchanges in the United States and over 30 additional exchanges elsewhere in the world.

In this increasingly competitive environment the CBOE has had to work hard to maintain its position as a pioneer and innovator. In 1983 we had the good fortune to introduce OEX and SPX. These options on the Standard & Poor's (S&P's) 100 and 500 stock indices triggered a whole new wave of growth in the options markets. More recently, in October 1990 CBOE introduced LEAPS—the most successful new option product since index options.

LEAPS—Long-term Equity AnticiPation Securities—is the name CBOE created, trademarked, and licensed, for longer-term options. We started with 2-year LEAPS on the stocks of 14 "blue chip" U.S. companies. They were an immediate success, appealing both to existing options users and to investors who had not previously traded in our marketplace. By June 1991 the open interest in LEAPS exceeded 100,000 contracts, the equivalent of 10 million shares of stock. Today CBOE lists LEAPS on 44 underlying equities, and the open interest is in excess of 600,000 contracts.

Prompted by investors' favorable reaction to equity LEAPS, the CBOE also introduced LEAPS on the S&P 100 (OEX) and the S&P 500 (SPX). Three-year LEAPS have been added as well as options based on one-tenth the value of these indices. This allows an investor to act on his or her longer-term view of the market with a low-cost basis.

From its beginning the CBOE has been totally dedicated to fostering a greater understanding of options. Toward this end we maintain a full-time marketing department and operate a separate educational arm, The Options Institute. Over the past 20 years we have provided extensive educational programs for account executives, branch office managers, institutions and individual public customers, the staffs of the Securities and Exchange Commission (SEC) and the Federal Reserve Board, new members of the exchange, and our counterparts at option exchanges around the world.

Over the past two years, one of the most frequently requested topics for teaching is LEAPS. These have been extremely popular and the demand for information on them appears insatiable. Fortunately, a valuable new resource is now at hand—the book you are holding. This book is unparalleled and in many ways unprecedented. While written on a single subject—LEAPS—it subsumes strategies applicable to ordinary options as well. It is written in a unique manner covering both theory and practice. The subject matter, of necessity, is technical at times, and there is the danger of the reader's interest flagging. That becomes impossible, however, because the author interjects with his *gentle note to the reader*. This provides both a respite and a reassurance; the reader can then continue without feeling overwhelmed.

The author also makes effective use of a second device: interruptions by a heckler. As I read over the manuscript, I had questions at certain points. To my amazement, the next thing I encountered was that very question, posed as an objection by characters with names like Mr. Scoffer. The question would then be adroitly answered, the heckler routed, and the lesson painlessly learned. Through this method the author successfully used humor as an educational device. I found this clever, instructional, and quite satisfying.

The book's merit is by no means limited to humor, however. It contains sound strategies for bullish outlooks, bearish stances, and neutral expectations. Perhaps its strongest point is that it shows how each and every strategy and technique discussed can be implemented in more than one way. Specifically, it explains and documents how each method can be used from a viewpoint that is conservative, moderate, or aggressive. The book walks the reader through each strategy very smoothly. It gives the theory behind the technique, describes the workings with options, and then makes the translation to LEAPS. The transitions are seamless; at no point will the reader feel overwhelmed.

There is something in this book for everybody in the market. Participants from the novice to the experienced trader will find appropriate and attractive expositions. There is also something for those who are afraid to enter the market. The author shows how risk can be reduced, contained, and sometimes brought down toward zero. Even the most jaded options sophisticates will find new ideas in this book.

The author has also accomplished what few people can claim—he has invented a new options strategy! Actually two: one for equity LEAPS and its twin for Index LEAPS. Each of these strategies is a systematic method of investing that should appeal to the most conservative among us. The second of these is my personal favorite. But I think that every reader will find one or more strategies in the book that seem expressly tailored for him or her. The author has interesting insights into the myriad factors that drive various investors' thinking; strategies are devised to appeal to every viewpoint, desire, and need.

The author avoids the trap of misguided all-pervasive optimism. Readers are warned off certain types of transactions. In an incisive analysis the author leads the reader through the possibilities of stock, options, and LEAPS, showing how to match instruments to expectations.

The book is highlighted with pellucid insights, imaginatively articulated. In one case the author turns to the thinking of a professional matchmaker to solve the problem of strike selection. Strategies are devised and described with intelligence and erudition. Yes, erudition. How many option books have you read that start with a biblical story and have quotes from Shakespeare, Lewis Carroll, St. Paul, and Damon Runyon?

I'm an old hand in this business, but I gained fresh insights from this book. I also thoroughly enjoyed reading it—and I predict you will too.

Alger B. Chapman, Chairman
Chicago Board Options Exchange

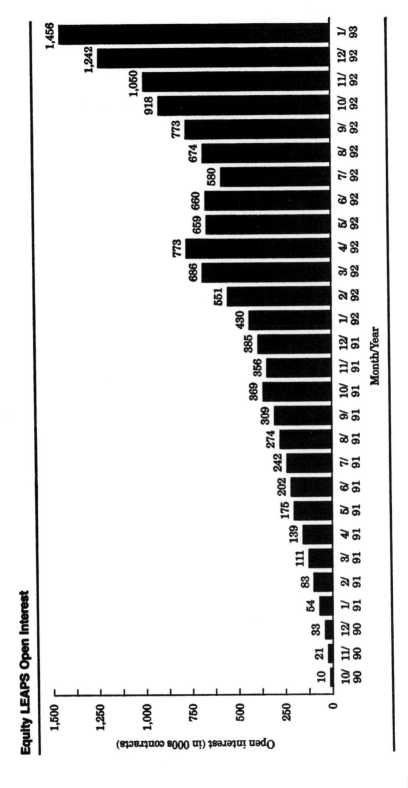

Equity LEAPS Open Interest

ACKNOWLEDGMENTS

To Michael Hart and George Sommerfeld,
each of whom read portions of the manuscript
and made very helpful suggestions,
and to Robert M. Greenberger of Cowen & Co.,
who almost coauthored the tax chapter.

CONTENTS

INTRODUCTORY MATERIAL

1 Introduction to LEAPS, 3
2 The Big Secret of Options and LEAPS, 8
3 A Brief History of LEAPS and Options, 11
4 What LEAPS Are and How They Work, 14
5 Why Use LEAPS?, 18
6 LEAPS Basics, 23
7 LEAPS Are Different—and Better!, 33
8 You Can Beat the Experts with LEAPS!, 38
9 Margin for LEAPS, 41

THE BASIC LEAPS STRATEGIES

BULLISH STRATEGIES

10 Buying LEAPS Calls, 46
11 LEAPS Covered Call Writing, 54
12 Writing LEAPS Puts, 63
13 Writing LEAPS Covered Straddles, 72
14 Writing LEAPS Covered Combinations, 80
15 Protective LEAPS Puts, 86
16 LEAPS Married Puts, 92
17 Bull Spreads with LEAPS Calls, 99
18 Bull Spreads with LEAPS Puts, 108

BEARISH STRATEGIES

19 Buying LEAPS Puts, 116
20 Writing Uncovered LEAPS Calls, 125
21 Bear Spreads with LEAPS Puts, 130
22 Bear Spreads with LEAPS Calls, 134

NEUTRAL STRATEGIES

23 Writing Uncovered LEAPS Straddles, 138
24 Writing Uncovered LEAPS Combinations, 142
25 Buying LEAPS Straddles or Combinations, 148

ADVANCED LEAPS STRATEGIES

26 Synthetic Stock with LEAPS, 159
27 Synthetic Short with LEAPS, 164
28 Ratio Writing with LEAPS, 166
29 Ratio Spreading with LEAPS, 174
30 Averaging Down with LEAPS, 178
31 Dollar-Cost Averaging with LEAPS, 183
32 LEAPS Fences, 188

STRATEGIES UNIQUE TO LEAPS

33 LEAPS Surrogate Therapy (DIM LEAPS Calls as Stock Substitute), 195
34 LEAPS Replacement Therapy, 198
35 Time is of the Essence (Long LEAPS/Write Shorter-Term), 203
36 LEAPS Affirmative Action (Sell Half Position, Write LEAPS Straddles), 209
37 Reduced-Risk Equity Trading with LEAPS, 212
38 Index LEAPS, 219

FOLLOWING UP ON STRATEGIES

39 LEAPS Enhancement, 235
40 LEAPS Repair, 251

OTHER LEAPS TOPICS

41 LEAPS and Program Trading, 263
42 LEAPS and Taxes, 266
43 Practical Aspects of LEAPS, 274
44 The Best Strategy with LEAPS, 284
45 Discipline and the LEAPS Work Sheet, 288
46 A LEAPS Summary, 298

APPENDIX: LEAPS LISTS, 303
INDEX, 317

INTRODUCTORY
MATERIAL

CHAPTER 1
INTRODUCTION TO LEAPS

. . . the introduction of a new order of things.

Cellophane, Aspirin, and Vaseline.

We are starting with neither an inventory nor a (bizarre) recipe. These, like LEAPS, are brand names that became generic nouns. Introduced by the Chicago Board Options Exchange (CBOE) on October 5, 1990, **LEAPS** have mushroomed in growth. The acronym stands for **L**ong-term **E**quity **A**ntici**Pa**tion Securities. It is not a well-constructed acronym, but the term itself has firmly taken root.

The CBOE has given free (actually they charged $1) franchised use to the other options exchanges, and the word has become established in the financial marketplace. LEAPS started on 14 stocks. There are now longer-term options on 127 stocks, trading on five exchanges.

LEAPS should really be printed something like "LEAPS™," but we trust its appearance here in this form will suffice for the rest of the book.

Is that all there is to the mysterious name? LEAPS are options, but with a longer life? The answer has to be both yes and no, but there is no ambivalence here. Although LEAPS are, technically, longer-term options, this assentive answer is a long way from the whole truth. The longer span makes them behave, for the better part of their life, in a strikingly different manner from shorter-term options. In particular, the bane of options trading—the possibility of up to 100 percent loss of options capital—is not at all the same for LEAPS. Rather, it is not the same if you know what to do. And that is what this book is about.

There are other dissimilarities. The premiums (prices) for LEAPS have two remarkable differences from the lesser-lived options. For LEAPS Writing (selling) strategies, the larger dollar premiums make the strategic analysis completely unlike the usual. And the cheaper cost (per unit of time) also stands conventional studies on their heads.

What's in this Book

This book is written in a structured form, but with an informal style. It is divided into seven sections: Introductory material, a retrospective view, discussions of basics, a division by attitudinal outlook—bullish, bearish, and neutral. After that, some more advanced strategies and strategies unique to LEAPS are presented. Then, follow-ups for all strategies—both enhancement and repair. Last, some special topics, including practicalities and a summation.

We recognize that readers will come to this book with varying degrees of knowledge. To keep things orderly, the first time any term appears in the text, it will be in **boldface** type and accompanied by a definition. That definition might be expressed rigorously or informally, but it will be there. It might precede rather than follow the new term. The cognoscenti among us might want to skip over these elementary expositions, but we want to warn those experienced skimmers that our thesis is that LEAPS are not just long-dated options. This basic distinction has an immediate corollary: much higher dollar premiums. Those two aspects are sufficient to change much of the conventional wisdom on options.

Each chapter will open with an apposite quotation for your delectation. Each strategy chapter opens with an outline giving a capsule description:

STRATEGY
OUTLOOK
ADVANTAGES
DRAWBACKS
DEGREE OF RISK

and ends with a

SUMMARY.

Between the opening and the closing there will be a brief description of the strategy. This will focus on how that strategy is implemented with the better-known non-LEAPS options. Incidentally, for these options, we will employ several synonymous terms: ordinary, usual, regular, conventional, shorter-term, and shorter-lived. We will even say, simply: "options." All will refer to *listed* equity or index options that are not LEAPS.

Then we'll study the strategy in a LEAPS environment. In addition to the philosophy and practice of the strategy, there will be many *EXAMPLES* to elucidate the analyses. While these will all be drawn from real data, the stock names and symbols, will, in general, be changed to the ubiquitous "last word in stocks": XYZ Corp. and its permutations. In all of these examples, we'll not consider commissions and other transaction costs. This is not to exaggerate the worth of the techniques, but just to keep things as simple as possible. In the same way, options and LEAPS will be considered at any time to have but a single price. Again, this is not to ignore the reality of bid/offer spreads, but to simplify the explanatory process. Both commissions and quotes will be discussed in Chapter 43, which takes up the practical aspects of LEAPS.

There may also be *a gentle note to the reader.* There is an intention here besides being cute. At times, unavoidably, the text must reach some degree of complexity. The notes offer a breathing space and reassurance against being overwhelmed.

Cast of Characters

There will also be a character who will appear in these pages from time to time. He has many names: Mr. Skeptic, Mr. Mischief, etc. His function is to provoke us. He represents the negative viewpoint on options (and LEAPS) that is so prevalent in the marketplace, but we will make good use of him. Some of his objections deserve a reply; our responses will be positive and informative.

What's Not in This Book

Complicated mathematical or statistical formulae. Exaggerated claims. Impenetrable, didactic prose. Full-page complex work sheets promising ravishing returns.

What to Expect from This Book

A down-to-earth exposition of what various LEAPS strategies are, and how to use them. That will include, unlike many texts, discouraging comments on some techniques.

The Book's Viewpoint

LEAPS are not for everybody. But they can be used—for profit and protection—by a wide range of investors and traders. Almost all the standard option strategies can be translated into LEAPS territory. Some become much better from this translation. Further, some LEAPS techniques cannot be done with ordinary options.

The Special Work Sheet

There is only one work sheet in this book. It is, in our opinion, more important than all the others combined, and it is not in any other book.

A Final Gender Note

The text will frequently say "you" or "they" in referring to participants in the marketplace. It is both impossible and undesirable to avoid singular references in this context. The form used for that will be "s/he." The author recognizes the clumsiness of this form, but nobody has yet found a better one. This usage is more than an acknowledgment of women. While they constitute more than half the human race, they represent a minority in the stock, options, and LEAPS markets. The usual explanation for that is that they are unwilling to take much risk. Good for them!

In that case, they (along with men) should be delighted to learn about LEAPS.

SUMMARY

This book will explain how LEAPS have a risk component different from options, and how they can increase capital, limit losses, and protect profits, positions, and portfolios. That certainly sounds good, but what about the name LEAPS itself? Never mind the clumsy phrase underlying the acronym. The label, like Vaseline, has stuck. Remember, nobody goes into a drugstore and asks for a jar of medicated, white petroleum jelly!

CHAPTER 2
THE BIG SECRET OF OPTIONS AND LEAPS

The human species is composed of two distinct races: the men who borrow and the men who lend.

The big secret is that all options can be regarded as a form of borrowing money. When you buy a Call that controls 100 shares of stock, you usually pay a sum of money that is a comparatively small fraction of the underlying stock's price. How does it happen that you can do this? Somebody is lending you the money even though you might not realize that that process is in effect.

Suppose you came to me—your kind old Uncle Harry—with the following sad story:

"Oh, Uncle Harry, my aunt (on the other side of my family) just passed away. I'm going to inherit $10,000 from her, but I won't get it for six months. Just now, I've discovered a stock selling at $100 a share that I'm positive will go much higher. If I had the $10,000 today I could buy 100 shares and make a good profit later. Without the money I don't know what to do."

Uncle Harry might reply: "Well, I can buy the stock for you now, if you pledge to buy it back from me later. When the six months is up, you'll pay me the $100 a share that I paid for it."

This is a nice friendly arrangement between relatives. What about the economic realities? First, the uncle must be compensated for the two commissions (one to buy, one to sell) he incurs. Second, he must be repaid the interest he is giving up (presumably the $10,000 is in a CD or another similarly low-risk instrument). This amount might be reduced by any dividends that the stock will pay during the six months, and, even among relatives, the "pledge" should be a contractual one.

This arrangement is almost a Call on the stock. Because of the pledge—the guarantee that the stock will be bought—it's what is known as a **Future.** If we remove the guarantee, it becomes a **Call.**

Specifically, a future is the obligation to buy and the Call is the right, but not the obligation, to buy. That's quite a change; it exposes Uncle Harry to a vastly different set of risks. During the six months, that stock could fluctuate a great deal.

If, at the end of that period, it is under $100, nobody would want to buy it at 100 and Uncle Harry is set for a loss. If the stock moves the other way, he might be missing out on a great profit potential. As structured, this loan has two risks—dollar loss and opportunity loss. In fairness (one could pun and say "in equity"), Uncle Harry should be paid additional money for assuming these two risks. How much should this payment be? Subjectively, it would vary with how much the lender shared the optimistic view of the borrower. More objectively, it is a function of how much the stock price might vary and swing back and forth, over the next six months. Can we measure this expectation? Mathematicians have a concept that does just that: It is called the *standard deviation.* In the marketplace we label it the stock's *volatility.*

A gentle note to the reader:
   We have just seen, very smoothly, the determining factors of an option's price. They are: the cost of the underlying stock, the length of time until expiration, the risk-free interest rate, the stock's dividend, and the stock's volatility.

We kept it simple by pricing the stock at exactly $100. In the real world, stocks don't sell at round numbers. The contract to buy the stock at 100—the Call—might be initiated when the stock was trading at 98½ or 101¾. This would add another determinant to the evaluation: the difference between the stock's market price and the contractual price. This latter is the **Striking Price** or more briefly the **Strike.** It is also known as the **Exercise Price.** The first name comes from the agreement: The terms of the loan are struck. The last name is because the Call owner may, or may not, decide to exercise his or her right to acquire the stock.

There are two other influences on a Call's price. One is psychological. In our avuncular anecdote we referred to the lender sharing the optimism of the borrower. This is a major point. What is happening here is that the stock is, in effect, the collateral for a loan. The lender must like the stock or it won't be deemed *safe* collateral. The more s/he likes it, up to a point, the more willing s/he would be to enter into the contract. That point (again, to pun, we might call it the point of no return), has to do with what we labeled the opportunity loss. If the expectation was for the stock to skyrocket, s/he might prefer to own it outright. We will say more about this in Chapter 11 on covered Call writing. The last determinant is not usually included in the textbooks. It is, very simply, the law of supply and demand. Options and LEAPS are listed, SEC-regulated securities that are traded on exchanges. As buyers and sellers compete in the marketplace, there will be temporary imbalances of demand and supply for specific options or LEAPS, which will drive their prices up or down.

Does this mean you have to study the intricacies of interest rates or memorize tables? Certainly not. You should be aware of interest rates as a prime determinant for options and LEAPS. We will discuss this, and the other factors, at greater length in chapters on individual strategies.

SUMMARY

LEAPS and conventional options have quantifiable determinants. Among these are interest rates and the volatility of the underlying stock. LEAPS (and shorter-term options) are regulated, listed securities that are traded on national exchanges.

CHAPTER 3
A BRIEF HISTORY OF LEAPS
AND OPTIONS

Those who do not remember the past are condemned to repeat it.

And Abraham begot Isaac and Isaac begot Jacob and Jacob. . . . *Stop!* No, you are not in the wrong book. This story will turn out to be incredibly relevant.

And Jacob went to Laban the Syrian whose daughter Rachel he found comely. And Jacob asked Laban for Rachel's hand in marriage. And Laban said this could be if Jacob worked for him for seven years. And Jacob worked for Laban for seven years. And, at the end of the seven years, Laban gave Jacob another daughter, Leah, who was not so comely as Rachel.

Here we have the first option! Some will dispute this. Purists will say it was a future and not an option. Even more rigorous ones will label it a forward contract. We'll stay with it as an option. There are other historical instances of options. Many are more fiscally oriented. Aristotle tells of Thales "giving deposits" (we would say, buying Calls) for all the olive presses before the olive harvest. Afterward he cashed in at a great profit.

In Holland in the 1620s, the famous tulip bulb craze swept away all logic. People traded options, futures, and forwards on the bulbs. The madness culminated in houses being mortgaged for a contract on a single bulb. This dementia is historically noteworthy. It preceded the first organized stock exchanges (in Germany) by about a century.

Later, in Great Britain, futures trading flowered (but not on tulips). Two of its aspects—the backwardation and the contango—evolved to more recognizable forms of options as we now know them. In the United States, options flourished under the financier Russell Sage. Although many of his apparent options dealings were merely a front for usurious loans, he did structure strategies that are common today. Speculative buyers in Britain and America as well as around the world then began to trade with those who wanted to protect themselves against such adversities as crop failures.

The Securities Exchange Act of 1934 created the Securities and Exchange Commission (SEC) and gave it the power to regulate options trading, but the business did not really grow until the end of World War II. Then members of the Put and Call Brokers and Dealers Association traded (as intermediaries) between member firms of the New York Stock Exchange (NYSE). They used physical certificates for options, but there was no secondary market. That is, if you bought 10 Calls—five in the morning and five in the afternoon—you would probably have two different striking prices. If you bought more the next day, you would have a different expiration date. At that time strikes were not uniform, and expiration dates were one, two, three, or six months. The last was really six months and 10 days. All of them were carefully measured on the calendar. But this meant that if your Call became profitable, there was no ready way to sell it out. First of all, nobody knew about it. Second, even if people did know, few would want to pay very much over the intrinsic value (the difference between market price and strike price). They could negotiate for a new Call (with a strike closer to the market) for far fewer dollars. Put + Call brokers would take orders for the resale of profitable options and even advertised such *specials* as they were known. All of this seems so inefficient now. Today we have fixed expirations, standard strikes, and exchanges making a continuous secondary market in options.

Then, on April 26, 1973, the financial world changed forever. On that date the Chicago Board Options Exchange (CBOE) started trading *listed* options contracts. Only Calls were traded in the beginning—and that was on only 16 stocks. But later the options markets expanded considerably. More exchanges, more options stocks, and the addition of Puts were all a part of this development. In 1983, the CBOE introduced OEX, originally the CBOE 100, and then the Standard & Poor's (S&P) 100. This was the first vehicle for index options trading. Soon others followed with variants, including the CBOE's listing of options on SPX— the S&P 500—for many years a market benchmark. Narrow-based or industry indexes, like the Gold/Silver Index were added. Some products were started but did not survive the rigors of the marketplace. These included the NYSE-Beta Index, the PSE Technology Index, the ASE International Index, the PHLX Gaming Index, and GNMA ("Ginnie Mae") options on the CBOE.

One new product, however, did have staying power. In November 1987 the CBOE started trading SPL options. These were options whose underlying was the S&P 500, but with a major difference. The "L" in SPL stood for "Long." They had a two-year life, and are still being traded. Obviously, although they were not so named, these were the first listed LEAPS.

On October 5, 1990 LEAPS trading started and has never looked back. The number of stocks with LEAPS has grown to 127. Open interest—the number of contracts outstanding—has exploded and now covers over 100 million shares. More index LEAPS have been created. All five options exchanges now trade LEAPS, although the NYSE does not use that name; it refers to its "longer-dated options." Well, "a rose by any other name would smell as sweet," and LEAPS with other names can still be used to make profits and/or provide protection.

Although some may think that the biblical example of Jacob and Rachel is not applicable, we beg to differ. First, like tulip trading, Jacob's experience was an early archetype of a disappointment from options. These two occurrences were primitive contributors to the bad repute options acquired. But we must observe that although speculation was a part of these early endeavors, so was hedging. We have a final comment that has never been made before on Jacob's trade. Without any quibbles on exactly what kind of transaction it was, the significance for us is that it was seven years long. This was the first trading in LEAPS! The first LEAPS trade wasn't all bad. There was a happy ending to the story: Jacob married Rachel after all!

SUMMARY

Our good book will tell you how to avoid disappointments with LEAPS—how to use them for income and insurance, for profit and protection. And you won't have to wait seven years, either.

CHAPTER 4
WHAT LEAPS ARE AND HOW THEY WORK

The material always comes before the work.

We have told you how LEAPS originated. And we have revealed the secret behind options and LEAPS. Now we want to go into some detail about how LEAPS work and what you can do with them.

We will start with a Question and Answer format. All the information in this chapter is limited to LEAPS on stocks. Index LEAPS have a full chapter of their own.

QUESTIONS AND ANSWERS ABOUT LEAPS

Where do LEAPS trade?
Currently, on the Chicago Board Options Exchange (CBOE), the American Stock Exchange (ASE), the Philadelphia Stock Exchange (PHLX), the Pacific Stock Exchange (PSE), and the New York Stock Exchange (NYSE). Sometimes single symbols are used to refer to these exchanges. They are, respectively, C, A, X, P, and N.

When do LEAPS trade?
Generally, from 9:30 A.M. to 4:10 P.M., Eastern Time (on all the exchanges).

Who creates the LEAPS?
The Options Clearing Corporation (OCC) is the issuer and guarantor of all LEAPS.

What's the unit of trading for LEAPS?
If you mean the contracts, you can buy one little LEAPS Call or Put if you want to do so. If you mean the stock underlying

the contract, the unit is usually 100 shares. The exceptions come about because of splits like 3 for 2 in the stock.

How are LEAPS quoted?

Just like other options. In points and fractions of a point. One point represents $100. A premium quote of 3⅜ is $337.50. The minimum change in a premium under 3 is ¹⁄₁₆ and above 3 is ⅛.

When do LEAPS expire?

The Saturday after the third Friday of the expiration month. The last trading day is the business day preceding that Saturday. For further details, see Chapter 43, the practicalities chapter.

When is Payment due for LEAPS?

The next business day. That is the theory. In practice, most firms will allow you the same five business days that they do for stock payment.

When can LEAPS be exercised?

Any time after purchase and up to the last trading day.

If LEAPS are exercised/assigned, when is stock/payment due?

Exercises settle with stock to be delivered (and paid for) on the fifth business day after exercise. Note the wording—*after exercise,* not after the notice of exercise. We don't mean to be mysterious here. You will usually receive an assignment notice before the opening of the market, but the exercise that generated it took place the previous day. That's when the clock starts.

Is there a Limit for LEAPS on a stock?

Yes, it's labeled the **Position Limit.** It gets combined with the limit on that stock's options. The limit varies (3,000; 5,500; or 8,000 contracts) with the stock. There are some technical complexities; even the lowest limit—3,000—represents 300,000 shares of stock. If you need to know about exceeding that, the author would love to hear from you.

What are the commissions on LEAPS?

Who's your broker? What's the firm? More details will be found in Chapter 43.

What's the Margin for LEAPS?

There's an entire chapter devoted to that question, (see Chapter 9).

How are LEAPS taxed?

There's a chapter for that topic, too. (see Chapter 42).

What stocks have LEAPS?

See the Appendix.

Where are LEAPS quotes found?

If you mean intraday, you'll find them on your broker's desktop quotation terminal. If you mean later, try *Barron's*, and check this point in Chapter 43.

What are the LEAPS's symbols?

See the Appendix.

If you buy a LEAPS Call and the stock goes way up, do you have to exercise it?

No. You can sell it out any time until the closing on the last trading day.

What can be done with LEAPS?

Amazing things. Read the strategy chapters. You will even find miracles there. We kid you not.

Aren't LEAPS just a fancy name for options?

Why should anybody get involved with LEAPS?

No. They are a lot more than that. Get involved to make and/ or keep money. Read the rest of the book to be convinced on both points.

The last double question and answer is somewhat facetious. We just mean it to serve as a bridge away from that format. We believe that, while LEAPS are not for all, they can benefit many. As for LEAPS being fancified options, the big drawback of options is the inexorable force of time working against you. With LEAPS, time is on your side.

"Wait, wait!" screeches Mr. Nudnik, I have some questions you didn't answer.

Maybe it's in the book. If not, try one of the following exchange hotlines:

C—1-800-OPTIONS (1–800–678–4667)

A—1-800-THEAMEX (1–800–843–2639)

X—1-800-THEPHLX (1–800–843–7459)

N—1-800-NYANYSE (1–800–692–6973)
P—1-800-TALKPSE (1–800–825–5773)

SUMMARY

LEAPS are somewhat like options in how and where they trade. However, they not only do not have the major temporal liability of options, they also have time on their side. Time is a very powerful force, and if you do get involved with LEAPS, we will wish on your behalf: "May the Force be with you!"

CHAPTER 5
WHY USE LEAPS?

The multitude is always in the wrong.

Before we can answer the chapter title's question, we must pose a subordinate question: Why use options? Watch out—here comes Mr. Bigot, our unbidden spokesman: "Yeah, I know. It's a crapshoot. You might triple your money, but mostly you'll lose it all."

We can decry the prejudice; unfortunately it is quite widespread. It is usually neither phrased so succinctly nor so roughly, but the ideas are the same. We will embark on a personal reminiscence. When your author first entered the options world, he resolved to learn everything he could on the subject. This entailed a visit to Room 315 (the Main Reference Room) of the New York Public Library. Nowadays that immense room is filled with computer terminals, but then its walls were lined, literally floor to ceiling, with card catalogs. It was hard to find a card for "Options," but finally the search produced one: Options—See Puts & Calls. The search there was more protracted and finally an ancient and yellowing card produced the answer: Puts & Calls—See Speculation(!).

We are happy to report that there are over 100 titles now listed there, and none are so pejoratively linked. Let's be honest. Options certainly can be used for speculation. So can other securities. You can speculate with stocks, bonds, warrants, rights, and even Treasury securities. But none of these are so firmly coupled in many minds, with speculation—if not gambling—as options. Possibly some of the events in the history chapter (Chapter 3) can account for this.

What we want to make clear is that there are other uses for options. You can gamble, you can speculate, you can do what we label intelligent speculation, and you can even "scalp." Beyond these, you can trade and you can invest with options. And there is one more thing: You can protect with options. You can protect, hedge, even insure with options.

Mr. Bigot was heavy-handed or at least heavy-tongued. He did, unknowingly, give us the case *for* options. Yes, you might lose it all. But if you're sensible, that "all" would be a small and limited dollar amount that you could afford to lose. And if successful, you could profit from leverage and make a multiple of your invested funds.

We confess to telling a little lie. To keep the dialog going, we mentioned "the case for options" in the previous paragraph. It is not. It is at most the case for Calls. It is even less than that. It is the case for buying Calls. The misidentifying of *buying Calls* with *options* is responsible for a lot of the negative aura carried by these securities.

All right, we think we've made our point. Now what about LEAPS? "Go with the flow." "The trend is your friend." "Don't fight the tape." And so forth. But what about "The herd is always wrong"? All these aphorisms do have the ring of truth in them. But the last one certainly seems to contradict the others. Nevertheless, all of them are true. How can this be? The resolution comes from realizing that the conforming statements apply to shorter-term trading. The contradicting one applies with equal force to longer-term investing.

Example

When the "nifty fifty" fervor was in force, incredible statements were made. For our younger readers, this was the view that one should buy only growth stocks and hold onto them. The 50 stocks in this category with the highest growth rates got that wonderful appellation. Others struggled to gain improved identity and added words like *computer, technology,* and *synergistic* to their corporate titles. Near the end of this fad, "Minnie Pearl's Chicken Houses" changed its name to "Responsive Environments." Yes, it was a fad. But it did not pay to fight it. These stocks rose as if there were no tomorrow, and the culminating wisdom was that these were *one-decision stocks.* That supreme enlightenment proclaimed that not only should you buy these stocks, you should never sell them! Not too long after this analytic gem, the stocks started reversing and fell from favor. They also fell in price and did so for several years. Many lost 50 percent to 80 percent of their value.

This is our rationale for using LEAPS. If you have a view on the (mis)fortunes of a company over a one-year to three-year time frame, you can implement that view with LEAPS.

Example

For quite a few years, the research departments of many NYSE firms sung the praises of International Business Machines (IBM). If you envisioned the shift away from mainframes and the consequences of that, you would not have wanted to own IBM for the long term. Actually you could have owned the stock and done many different things with options to protect, hedge, or enhance that position. You will find details in the different strategy chapters, but the right place to be was on the other side. Some shorted the shares of IBM and profited by it. The chapter on buying LEAPS Puts (Chapter 19) shows why there was a much better alternative. You could have bought IBM LEAPS Puts and reaped profits beyond the dreams of avarice— well beyond our dreams anyway.

Example

On July 9, 1992 you could have bought the IBM Jan 1994 85-strike LEAPS Put for 5. That was a contract giving you the right (but not the obligation) to sell 100 shares (per Put) of IBM at 85 any time until the third Friday of January 1994. "5" means each Put would have cost you $500. The stock was then 97½. On December 24, 1992 the stock was at 52¾ and you could have sold out the LEAPS Put for 33½. And may all your Christmases be that merry!

> *A gentle note to the reader:*
> *We do not intend to suggest that all LEAPS trades will be anywhere near this profitable. It is shown here as a dramatic but true example.*

We are constrained to comment that the typical example of trading in this book has been designed to be an 18-month LEAPS option that can sometimes give great leveraged results after only six months. The example above proves that "life imitates art." Note that the example we showed was for a downtrend. LEAPS work in the other direction as well.

Example
On June 22, 1992 you could have bought the Compaq Computer Jan 1994 25-strike LEAPS Call for 5¼. Compaq was then trading @ 24. We look again at prices on Christmas Eve, and find the stock @ 47¾ and the LEAPS Call @ 25.

It is easy to go back in time and, with hindsight, find examples to support a theory. We avow to the reader that we have not done that here. Our thesis is that many people were able to figure out the comparative expectations for IBM and its competitors, but few of them were willing or able to utilize LEAPS to pecuniarily practice what they preached.

The beauty of options and LEAPS is that you can use them for either a positive or a negative expectation. In some chapters we will show how you can even profit from foreseeing majorly neutral outcomes. Not only can you actualize your viewpoints with LEAPS; you can also do so with many methods. If you flip back to the table of contents, you will find listed nine different bullish strategy chapters. The same variation of opportunities exists for bearish predictions and for neutral outlooks. There is even a technique with LEAPS that tells you what to do when you don't know what to do! See Chapter 36 on Affirmative Action.

And now, the best of all. Each and every one of these strategies can be implemented in a conservative, moderate, or aggressive manner. The matching of risk aversion to strategy selection will be covered in almost every one of the strategy chapters.

SUMMARY

LEAPS, like options, can be utilized in a very wide strategic spectrum. Within each strategy, the implementation can be for a stance that corresponds to your degree of risk aversion. This matching, combined with a longer time period, make LEAPS an added attractive tool in the investment arsenal. In the past, many could have profited hugely with LEAPS. They did not because of fear, ignorance, or arrogance. It is well to remember:

> For of all sad words of tongue or pen,
>   The saddest are these: "It might have been!"

The sensible use of LEAPS can make it *be,* for you.

CHAPTER 6
LEAPS BASICS

What do you read, my lord?

Words, words, words.

In order to understand how LEAPS differ from ordinary options and what their advantages are, we must first have a working knowledge of the latter. We must also acquaint the reader with the jargon of the trade.

Options are listed, regulated securities that trade on national exchanges. You can buy and sell them just as you would more familiar securities, that is, stocks. There are some different risks in trading or investing with options.

We have already had a glimpse of the material we need to cover in Chapter 2, which outlined the determinants of a Call's price in a narrative form. Here we will document them, but try not to get too complex. To recapitulate:

The Call, trading on an exchange, will have its price vary depending on:

1. The price of the underlying stock
2. The length of time until expiration
3. The difference between the striking price and the market price
4. The dividend on the stock
5. The volatility of the stock
6. The prevailing "risk-free" interest rate
7. The forces of supply and demand.

Some of these are obvious upon reflection but we will give illustrations for all of them.

1. *Price.* A Call on a $60 stock will cost more than one on a $30 issue. Will it be exactly twice as much? It would be

if that were the only factor, but we know that there are others.

2. *Time.* A Call that lasts for a year will be more costly than one for only three months. If all the other factors were held constant, would the longer be four times as much as the shorter?

Absolutely not. There is a famous equation—the "Black-Scholes formula"—which generates the value of an option when all the other variables are known (numbers 4 and 7 above are not included).

Theoretical option price $= pN(d_1) - se^{-rt}N(d_2)$

$$\text{where } d_1 = \frac{\ln\left(\frac{p}{s}\right) + \left(r + \frac{v^2}{2}\right)t}{v\sqrt{t}}$$

$$d_2 = d_2 - v\sqrt{t}$$

A gentle note to the (perhaps frightened) reader: Relax. We are not going into higher mathematics. There won't be anything here you can't follow.

Notice in the equation the SQR T. This stands for the square root of time. That simply means that if the length of time (measured in years and fractions of a year) is given, its square root should be used in the calculations. In our example above—comparing a one-year Call with a three-month Call—one option's time to expiration is four times the other. The equation tells us that (other elements being constant) the first will be *two* times the cost of the second. (Two is the square root of four; that is, two is the number that when multiplied by itself gives four).

This seems contradictory to our intuitive sense. We promised we would not go into higher mathematics, but neither do we want you to just accept this concept on pure faith. Consider the following situation:

You are at the center of a street that extends indefinitely in both directions. You will take a number of one-unit steps. Each such step will be either to the left or to the right of where you are after the previous step. The direction—left or right—will be determined randomly (by a coin toss or a random-number generator). After, say, 10 steps, the odds are that you will not be exactly at the point where you started. And after 100 steps, the probability is that you will be farther away from your starting point than you were after 10 steps. But you are not likely to be 10 times as far away. Congratulations! You have just stepped through the famous "random walk theory."

3. *Price/strike difference.* If you buy a 50-strike Call on a stock selling at 50, you will pay more than you would for the same Call with the stock selling at 48. Would it be two points ($200) more? No. To understand this concept, we introduce you to *delta,* one of many Greek letters used in option analytics. Some of these Greek-letter analyses are highly erudite. We'll deal only with delta and keep it simple.

Delta, which is the fourth letter of the Greek alphabet, measures the expected move in a Call for the first one-point move in the stock. Deltas are a lot like baseball batting averages: They are quoted as integers but are actually percentages. A 300 batting average is really .300 or 30 percent. A 50 delta similarly means 50 percent— that is, a Call with a delta of 50 would be expected to rise (or fall) one-half point if the stock rose (or fell) one point. Even the very best of baseball players does not bat 1,000; a good player might get, very briefly, a 100 percent result at bat. In the same way, Calls do not have 100 deltas, but rather deltas of 100 percent or 1.00. A Call with a delta near 1 could be expected to move almost dollar-for-dollar as the stock rose or fell.

We have never been able to persuade the world to revise the baseball usage, and we will accept the option terminology as well. That is, in this book, we will talk about deltas of 50, 100, etc. Deltas do not remain constant. As the stock moves, they will also change. They are applicable for small, near-term movements only. Another Greek letter is used to measure the change in delta: *gamma.* We are not going to pursue theory that far.

Why do we want you to know about delta? Because it will give you a rough idea of what you can expect when you buy an option. Incidentally, we do mean option. We formatted our discourse in terms of Calls, but all that has been said applies equally to Puts as well. For Put deltas, we point out the obvious: Puts have *negative* deltas.

Example

XYZ @ 40

XYZ 2-month 40-strike Call @ 2   delta   50
XYZ 2-month 40-strike Put @ 1½   delta −50

XYZ rises to 42 the next day. The Call moves from 2 to 3; its 1 point rise is 50 percent of the stock's move.

The Put falls from 1½ to ½; its 1 point fall is −50 percent of the stock's move.

If the stock had fallen 2 points, the Call would have declined 1 point, and the Put would have increased by that amount.

We said we would not explicate gamma. What we will do is to tell you how to (roughly) approximate it. For stock moves beyond a point or so (but not extremely large), just add 10 percent to the delta.

Example

XYZ @ 40

XYZ 2-month 40-strike Call @ 2   delta   50
XYZ 2-month 40-strike Put @ 1½   delta −50

In a week XYZ moves to 46. You can calculate the Call's expected new price as 5 (an increase of 3—half the stock's move). To make new calculations, assume a new value of 55 (50 + 10 percent) for the delta.

If the stock, in the above example, moved up 6, where would the Put move? To 1½ less 3? A value less than zero? Certainly not. It would not even move all the way to zero. That's because of some of the other determinants. The time left to expiration and the supply/demand force would link to assure some value for options like these.

4. *Dividend*. The dividend on the stock. Technically, we should say the *expected* dividend. This factor has both implicit and explicit effects. For the latter, let's look at this example:

Example
XYZ @ 40
XYZ 2-month 40-strike Call @ 2   delta   50
XYZ 2-month 40-strike Put @ 1½   delta −50

XYZ will sell ex (without the right to receive it) its 25 cent per share dividend the next day. If XYZ is unchanged the next day, where will the two options be? We are not going to answer the question in that form because it is a false-to-fact hypothesis. If all else were constant, the stock would obviously reopen the next day at 39¾. Very long-term studies (with nothing to do with options) have empirically confirmed this theoretical view. If the next day the stock did sell @ 40, the Call would probably trade @ 1⅞. Why? Because it is intrinsically less valuable now. Before, it had the right to acquire the stock @ 40 and, if exercised, would have entitled you to that dividend. Now it still allows the stock acquisition, but not the dividend. Then why didn't it fall by ¼? Because its delta was 50. We can now infer the general result of dividends: the higher (and the closer) the dividend, the lower the expected Call value, and, of course, the higher evaluation for the Put. Before you have delirious dreams of buying Puts just before a high-yield stock goes ex dividend, relax. You may have just acquired this knowledge but others know about it also. This factor is smoothly built into options pricing. That's the explicit impact we referred to. What's the other? A high-dividend stock tends to have other characteristics as well. Specifically, it tends to fluctuate less as it is being bought primarily for its yield, not its potential price appreciation. In a word, it is less volatile. That brings us to the next, and perhaps most important, factor.

5. *Volatility.* Volatility is the technical name for the measurement of fluctuation. Volatility, like delta, is expressed in a way that leaves off the implied percentage number. A number like 25 really means 25 percent. The 25 percent means that, most of the time, the stock's price will vary by 25 percent over a year. To get a volatility estimate for a longer or shorter period, you would multiply the annual volatility number by the square root of the

time ratios involved. You do not have to be concerned with understanding this measurement. What you do want to know is whether the stock you are considering is very volatile, of average volatility, or fairly stable. We will teach you a trick. Look up the stock in the newspaper tables. To the left of the stock's name you will find a 52-week range for it. Take the difference between the high and low, double it, and divide that by the sum of the high and low. You can round the numbers if you want to make the calculation mentally.

Example
XYZ @ 44   52-week range: high-65⅝; low-43¾.
Difference (with rounding) 66 − 44 = 22.   Doubled = 44.
Sum 66 + 44 = 110.   Division 44/110 = .40 = 40 percent = 40 volatility.

While this is only a crude approximation of volatility derivation, it will do for our purposes. Those who want more can ask their broker for assistance. Also, see the practical aspects of LEAPS in Chapter 43. Forty is a slightly high volatility, but not at all atypical for an option stock. The current approximate average volatility for stocks underlying LEAPS is 31.

What do you know, now that you have this number? Again, as a crude approximation, you can calculate the expected range for this stock. Multiply the volatility (as a percentage) by the stock price. Then add that to the stock's current price. Finally, subtract it from the current price. The result will be the projected range.

Example
XYZ @ 44   Volatility 40
40 percent 44 = 17.6   44 + 17.6 = 61.6.
44 − 17.6 = 26.8
The projected range for the stock is 61⅝ to 26⅞.

We must remind the reader that two assumptions support this projection. One, that our approximate derivation for volatility was a reasonable one. Two, that this figure will be relevant for an entire year. Since neither of these suppositions is entirely correct, proceed with caution. Don't persuade yourself that you know where the stock will be. It's only a guideline.

6. *Risk-free rate.* Almost all interest rates are tied together. When the discount rate goes up, so does your mortgage rate. When the prime rate goes down, so does the rate for a new car loan. And as the rate on short-term Treasury securities varies, so will option premiums. That effect is sometimes hard to see because of the other factors impinging on prices, but it is surely there. We don't think you need overly concern yourself with this aspect except for one very basic thought. When it comes to evaluating the merits of a strategy, you should reflect on what your money would bring if invested elsewhere.

7. *Supply/demand.* One way to view this is to go back to the discussion on dividend impact. There we spoke about a $2 Call moving to 1⅞. In practice, this Call might be quoted 1⅞ to 2⅛. If the first trade that morning in that Call was a market order to buy, it would be filled at 2⅛. We just finished saying that the Call would be at 1⅞ and here we have it up, not down at all. That's because the highly practical supply/demand influence superseded the other theoretical impingements. Clearly, this type of effect is not limited to dividends. At any time, a preponderance of orders (buy or sell) in an option will impact its price. In fact, it may influence the prices of *all* the options—Puts as well as Calls—on that stock. This is a fact of life that occurs in all securities (and commodities) markets. Prices will readjust, and we should view positively, not negatively, this phenomenon. That's because it can provide you with an opportunity. For example, see the chapter on LEAPS and program trading (Chapter 41).

OK, we're finished with the determinants. Is there anything else? Yes, we want to define some technical terms that will be used frequently in this book. We have previously defined a few in passing; now we will be more precise.

At the money. This means simply that the strike and the market price are quite close. More precisely, there is *no* strike closer to the stock's price.

In the money. Calls are in the money when the strike is below the market. Puts are in the money when the strike is above the market.

Out of the money. The exact opposite of the above.

Examples

XYZ @ 40

1. XYZ 30 Call	—**Deep in the money**	**DIM**
2. XYZ 30 Put	—**Far out of the money**	**FOM**
3. XYZ 35 Call	—In the money	**ITM**
4. XYZ 35 Put	—Out of the money	**OTM**
5. XYZ 40 Call	—At the money	**ATM**
6. XYZ 40 Put	—At the money	ATM
7. XYZ 45 Call	—Out of the money	OTM
8. XYZ 45 Put	—In the money	ITM
9. XYZ 50 Call	—Far out of the money	FOM
10. XYZ 50 Put	—Deep in the money	DIM

Notice that we used the examples to define two additional characterizations. We also introduced the standard acronyms that will be used in this book. FOM has an alternate symbol: DOOM. This stands for deep out of the money. This is not our choice, although it may be used to predict the fate of those who use it.

Intrinsic value and *time value.* In example 3 above, if XYZ 35 Call were trading at 6¼ (with XYZ @ 40), the Call's intrinsic value would be 5 (40 − 35) and its time value would be 1¼ (6¼ − 5). In examples 5, 7, and 9 above, any price would be all time value and zero intrinsic value.

Premium. The option's price. In example 3 above, 6¼ is the premium.

Exercise. If you own a Call and want to own the stock, you exercise the Call. Similarly, you exercise an owned Put if you want to sell the stock.

Assignment. This is one of the most misused words relating to options. *Exercise* is what an owner does. *Assignment* is what a writer receives when someone else exercises an option.

Theoretical value or *fair value*. This is the estimate from a mathematical model of the worth of an option. The estimate may be for the current price or projected forward in time. The numbers derived in this way are no better than the assumptions used. Or, as the computer people themselves say, GIGO (garbage in, garbage out). See Chapter 8 on beating the experts.

Volatility. Didn't we already define this term? Yes, we did, but there is more than one type of volatility, and we did not identify all of them. The types are historic, forecast, individual, and implied.

Historic volatility. That's the correct name for what was defined above (5 in the determinants list). It can be derived from the stock's prices over different ranges of time, using a weighted or an unweighted average. The industry standard here is a six-month period.

Forecast volatility. That can be an outright assumption that the expected volatility for a given time beyond the present (say, the lifetime of a LEAPS Call) will be what it is now. Alternately, a prediction may be made as to what it will be.

Individual volatility. The "individual" referred to is not a person, but a single option. Here the Black-Scholes equation (or other models) is turned around. That is, the actual price of the particular option is input along with all the other variables except for the volatility. Then the equation is solved for the volatility factor. Phrased another way, this tells us what the stock's volatility would have to be to produce the option's actual market price.

Implied volatility. The same process—solving the equation backward—is used. Rather than a single option, *all* the options on a given underlying are taken. Some analysts eliminate, or underweight, far-out (in time or price) options before making this calculation. Again by rephrasing, this tells us what volatility for the stock would give us the "best fit" for the market prices of all (or most) of its options.

We can summarize the different volatilities by a comparison to weather reports. If you are told what the weather has been on this day in the past, that corresponds to historic volatility. If the Weather Bureau gives you its prediction for the day's weather, that is like forecast volatility. But, if after hearing a sunny prediction you look out the window and see a preponderance of umbrellas, that's implied volatility!

SUMMARY

The LEAPS vocabulary is not very difficult. It does use some words in a narrow meaning peculiar to the investment industry. Those terms that we have not defined in this chapter will be clarified as they arise later on.

CHAPTER 7
LEAPS ARE DIFFERENT— AND BETTER!

I can call Spirits from the vasty deep.

Why so can I, or any other man.

But do they come when you call them?

Now that you have read about (or skipped over) option basics, we are ready to tackle LEAPS. Here we need to consider both practical and theoretical aspects.

Practical

LEAPS have a limited, (i.e., lower number) of strikes and expiration months. For the ordinary options there is a wealth of choices. There are four different months from which to choose. For strikes, every month starts with one ITM, one ATM, and one OTM. As the stock price fluctuates, whenever it reaches the highest or lowest existing strike, a new one (either up or down) will be created. By way of contrast, LEAPS have only a limited choice of months—currently, January in one of two different years. For strikes, in theory, there will be the same choice of ITM, ATM and OTM, but there are differences here. The ITM and the OTM strikes are designed to be, at their creation, about 20 percent to 25 percent away from the market price. Stock prices do move about though, and as they do, LEAPS may get to be quite DIM or fairly FOM. There may be more of a delay in creating new strikes, and there will be no automatic new month, created every month. In brief, in both the lay and the technical senses, LEAPS have fewer options.

Theoretical

Many people, in selecting which option to buy, will look at its theoretical value. This may or may not be a desirable approach for equity options. For LEAPS, several problems prevail. We have already seen in Chapter 6 the determinants that go into an option's price. Some of these are factual, and others are predictive in nature.

Example

The stock's price as well as the difference between market price and strike are examples of factual data. The stock's expected dividend and its projected volatility are instances of predictive data. The dividend is one of the predictive facets. For now, we will just note that fact. There will be more on this topic in the next chapter.

The underlying stock's volatility is both essential and very difficult to predict. If it is difficult to predict for even, say, one month, it might be said to be next to impossible when dealing with periods as long as three years. Think about it. Take any stock (other than extremely stable ones such as utilities) that you are familiar with, and mentally review its price performance over the previous three years. Those for whom this process is arduous may look up annual ranges in, say, *Standard & Poor's Stock Guide*. It is worth knowing that the *New York Times* on Mondays has a list of 50 active stocks (usually, almost all have LEAPS) showing their five-year ranges.

Almost inevitably this procedure is bound to produce surprises. "I didn't realize it had been that high (or gone that low)," you might say. It is not so easy to predict the future. Or rather, as our opening quote shows, it is easy to predict; it is hard to be accurate!

If it is hard to forecast price ranges, it is much more difficult to forecast how a stock will get to those ranges. What does that mean? It means that just because you know a stock's range (for any period—days through years), it does not mean that you know how the stock fluctuated during that interval.

FIGURE 7.1
Year's Performance of XYZ and ZYX

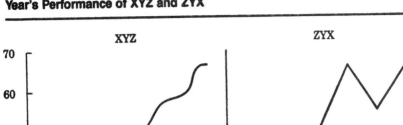

Examples

XYZ rises slowly from its January 2 starting price of 30. It moves slowly but steadily upward, occasionally pausing to consolidate. Continuing this placid pattern all year, it ends on December 31 at 66. Its year range is 66–30. ZYX also starts the year at 30. It moves quite quickly up to 40, where rumors boost the stock rapidly to 50. Then a real story of great import emerges and the stock skyrockets to 66. The story is proved false and the stock plummets to 55. Near the end of the year, another story appears and the stock escalates again, closing the year at 66. Its year range is 66–30. Both stocks have the same starting and finishing points and the same range. But the second is unmistakably more volatile than the first (see Figure 7.1).

If predicting volatility over long periods is so hard and thus estimating "fair value" so difficult, does that mean we shouldn't trade LEAPS? No, not at all. What it does imply is that this is the incorrect approach. In the author's view it was always the wrong way. It had tremendous appeal in the early days of listed options trading. Then buying undervalued Calls and writing overvalued ones produced profits of great magnitude. Now everybody has the same, or similar, computer capability. If a Call (or Put) is overvalued or undervalued, it is because a significant plurality of players know something you don't. Or they think they do. The latter, from the practical point, is just as important. If you want to "bet against the house," we wish you luck because you will need it. This may be the wrong quote. "Don't fight the tape" is more relevant. That said, what should you do? Our answer is to look for the best fit; there we can get inspiration from a surprising source: "Matchmaker, matchmaker, look through your book / and make me a perfect match."

Luscious lyrics, poor philosophy. A professional matchmaker knows better. S/he knows that looking for "Mr. Right" will be a long and losing proposition. It is much better to search for "Mr. (or Ms.) Best Fit." What does that mean for options? It means that you must match expiration and strike respectively to your stock expectations and to your attitude toward risk. For conventional options, that meant picking a month far enough out in time to avoid expiration before the desired triumph occurs. Then you need to select a strike that will fit the degree of risk aversion. With LEAPS, the problem of time is self-solved. For the strike, you still need the best fit. We will give you specific illustrations of just how to do this in the first strategy chapter (Chapter 10).

Finally, you have to match the LEAPS strategy itself to your attitudes about stock and risk. The first cut here is obviously into bullish, bearish, and neutral. But for each stance, there is a lot more than one technique available. This will come as a surprise to those who equate all of options trading and investment to Call buying. Yes, we said "investment." We will see that there are many involvements with LEAPS that deserve this description, rather than trading. We will also see that each and every strategy can be implemented in a conservative, moderate, or aggressive manner. The beauty of LEAPS participation is that it will not only allow you to take a longer-term stance but that it will also largely insulate you from the short-run perturbations of the market. In the years since the almost unbelievable downmove of October 1987, monthly, weekly, and even daily whipsaws in the market have become commonplace. LEAPS liberate you from that and allow you to be "away from the fray."

We cannot write a chapter extolling LEAPS's differences without going into one technical aspect. *Time decay* is the name given to the wasting away of an option's value with the passage of time.

We have spoken about an option expiring before a desired watershed event occurs. That's the all-or-nothing problem. But time decay causes ordinary options to become *wasting assets*. That's what the standard textbooks say. We prefer to compare them to a greengrocer's inventory: If they are not sold in time, they will rot away! LEAPS do not behave like that. More to the point, they do not behave like that until they get into the same temporal range as ordinary options. We will elucidate on this aspect of LEAPS in many chapters. For now, we just comment that for the typical LEAPS commitment (18 months), you will have about a year with a larger window of opportunity in this respect.

A gentle note to the reader:
We have been lauding LEAPS. That, of course, is the purpose of this book. But we do not think that ordinary options are terrible. They have less time to work, but they certainly do have their uses, and these beneficial uses are many and varied. There are so many good aspects of options that a book could be written about them. Indeed, many people have, and maybe someday we will too.

SUMMARY

LEAPS do not share the major drawback of conventional options. Their long life has many beneficial consequences. A good working knowledge of LEAPS allows conservative and moderate stances as well as the better-known aggressive type. LEAPS can also allow more peace of mind in turbulent times in the market.

CHAPTER 8
YOU CAN BEAT THE EXPERTS WITH LEAPS!

An expert is someone who knows more and more about less and less.

Whenever you see a claim like the title of this chapter, it is usually a good idea to keep your wallet closed. Someone may want to sell you a bridge in Brooklyn or a beautiful beach in Utah. If so, why are we championing such a cause? The reason is that LEAPS are really fundamentally different from conventional options.

Let's keep in mind, however, that the methods for calculating theoretical value for options has been carried over into the LEAPS arena without any changes. And those analytic analyses contain huge doses of uncertainty. LEAPS have a very long time in which what starts out as a small divergence can magnify into a giant discrepancy. This does not apply uniformly. Some may not have a terrible impact. One such example is the predicted dividend for the underlying stock. While the prediction (usually close to the status quo) may turn out to be erroneous, not too much damage may be done. But, and it's a very big but, the same is not true of two of the most important parameters. These are the risk-free rate and the stock's volatility. Interest rates have varied beyond the imagination of sophisticated traders. To take just one example, Treasury bonds have varied more in a week than they used to do in a year! This example is actually a double one; it speaks to unexpected changes in both interest rates and volatility.

The risk-free rate variation ranges across the entire scope of the LEAPS field. It can result in gross miscalculations for LEAPS's expected valuations.

Example
XYZ @ 40
XYZ Jan (1½ year out) 40-strike LEAPS Call

1. Presumed interest rate 3½ percent   LEAPS Call theoretical value 6
2. Presumed interest rate 4½ percent   LEAPS Call theoretical value 7

Note that the one percentage point differential in the projected risk-free interest rate changes the LEAPS Call's theoretical value by almost 17 percent. As important as this factor is, it is dwarfed by the other one. If the expected volatility is wrong, the resultant error can be enormous.

Example

XYZ @ 40
XYZ 1992 (monthly basis) Historic volatility range: 59–30.
XYZ   last month   Historic volatility: 37.
XYZ   Implied volatility: 48.
XYZ Jan (1½ year out) 45-strike LEAPS Call

1. With forecast volatility 37—LEAPS Call theoretical value 6¼.
2. With forecast volatility 48—LEAPS Call theoretical value 8½.

Note that two different volatility estimates—both comfortably within the annual range—lead to valuations 36 percent apart! So if your view is that interest rates are going to change radically, you can select an interest-sensitive stock with LEAPS. This can bring you a two-way profit (assuming, of course, that you are correct). The first will come from the type of stock selected; the second, from the wrong prediction. Care must be taken here that the two forces are working in the same direction.

Similarly, if you expect a very big move in a stock, you can back your view with a LEAPS Call (or Put). The predicted volatility used implies a future range for the stock. If you are right and the range will be much greater because of a major move (either up or down), you will have bought a bargain. Appropriately traded, this bargain can produce profits. In Chapter 25 on buying LEAPS combinations, we will tell you how to make money if you expect a very large move, even if you are unsure of which direction.

"Now just a minute," says Mr. Scoffer. "These LEAPS are being traded by professionals. That includes the market makers and specialists on the floor and the pros upstairs. They're not so dumb. Isn't it the height of presumption to think you can beat them?"

No, it's not. They are bright, not dumb, and they know what they're doing. But what they're doing is not what you want to do. They, in general, are not concerned with the longer-term view. They are trying to exploit shorter-term (sometimes extremely short) anomalies. For what they do, their models are very good. But, to repeat, it's not what you want to do. You are willing to risk your dollars on a view of the underlying for the longer period. If your view prevails, it can produce profits to reward you.

Suppose you are wrong? This has been known to happen. One of the great advantage of options is the limited-risk aspect. Assuming you have not committed the size error (see Chapter 10 on buying LEAPS Calls), you will lose a comparatively small amount, compared to a direct stock investment. With LEAPS, this is even more of an advantage. If you buy a shorter-term Call, you might lose money even if you were right. This can happen if the Call expires before your prediction materializes. Obviously, that won't happen with LEAPS because of the long-range expiration. There is another benefit here. Even if you are totally wrong, you will have two things going for you with LEAPS. First, the time erosion will not weigh so heavily against you. Second, you have more of an ability to repair your position (see Chapter 40 on LEAPS repair).

SUMMARY

The bottom line is this: LEAPS allow you to pit yourself against the experts. You'll have a leveraged reward if you are right and a limited loss if you are wrong. We think that's a pretty good deal.

CHAPTER 9
MARGIN FOR LEAPS

Minimum margin is a sign of minimum intelligence.

Before we start, a gentle note to the (possibly) frightened reader: Please read on. We are not advocating buying LEAPS on margin. In fact, that would be illegal. We want to introduce you to the col-lateral requirements for certain positions. We emphasize that word because, except for stock purchases on margin, these positions do not generate a debit balance and there is no margin interest to pay.

It is desirable to know what these collateral requirements are in order to be able to compare different LEAPS strategies. This would include positions within a given strategy and compari-sons across different LEAPS techniques. We'll show these requirements with the understanding between author and reader that they are the initial requirements, the *current* ones; they are the exchange's *minima;* many firms can, and do, ask for more. Despite what we just said, we will display something a little dif-ferent. Because there are changes and because firms are so var-ied in their rules, we are going to use a basic requirement in this book, of 25 percent on uncovered options (and LEAPS) positions.

Single Positions

Long
Buy stock   Cash account—Pay in full.
                             Margin account—borrow 50 percent.

Buy LEAPS Call   Must be paid for in full.
  or LEAPS Put

Short
Short stock   Leave proceeds and add 50 percent.

Write LEAPS Call
  or LEAPS Put
	Leave premium; post 25 percent of
	  stock price less OTM amount with
	  a minimum of 10 percent of stock.

Multiple Positions

Without stock

Spreads	*All spreads must go in a margin
	  account.* The long leg must expire
	  with or after the written leg; either
	  pay any debit or post as collateral
	  the strike difference less any credit.

Pseudo-spreads	If written leg expires after long leg,
	  pay in full for long and margin
	  written as uncovered.

Written LEAPS Call
  and LEAPS Put
	Leave both premiums. Add the
	  greater of the two requirements for
	  the single positions.

With stock

Long stock,
  LEAPS Call
  written
	No additional requirement for LEAPS
	  Call written.

Alternative Methods

Some positions can be margined in more than one way. You are entitled to select the lower collateral calculation.

SUMMARY

Margin requirements are set in a hierarchy of the Federal Reserve Board, the exchanges, and brokerage firms. While these are rigorously stated requirements, we have attempted to frame them informally. For simplicity and consistency, we will use 25 percent as the basic collateral needed for uncovered equity and index options and LEAPS. Knowledge of collateral requirements for varying positions allows intelligent comparisons of LEAPS strategies.

THE BASIC LEAPS STRATEGIES

Bullish Strategies

CHAPTER 10
BUYING LEAPS CALLS

Caveat emptor   (Let the buyer beware)

STRATEGY	Buying LEAPS Calls
OUTLOOK	Bullish to very bullish
ADVANTAGES	Leverage to high leverage; limited dollar risk
DRAWBACKS	High percentage at risk
DEGREE OF RISK	High, but can be reduced

Our opening quotation really says a lot. Far too much money has been lost in the strategy we will view first. **Buying Calls** is a very simple strategy. Unfortunately it has proved more seductive than profitable to many. How does it work? How should it work? The mechanics are surprisingly simple. Over 1,000 stocks have listed options trading on five different options exchanges. If the stock you are interested in is one of these, you've passed the first hurdle. Next, you have a choice of expiration months. These would be the nearest two months plus two additional ones. (Yes, two. We know the newspapers print only three in total). After you have the stock and the month, you can choose a striking price.

Examples
(set on Monday, January 2)

	Stock	Price	Month	Strike	Premium
1.	XYZ	78	Jan	80	3½
2.	XZY	39	Apr	45	1¾
3.	YZX	59	Apr	60	4½

Let's follow these Call examples through several scenarios:

1. On January 20 ("Expiration Friday") the stock is at 79¾, the option expires, and you lose all your money. Near the end of February XYZ sells at 84.

2. From the day of purchase through expiration, XZY never reaches 45 and you lose all your money.

3. YZX trades in a narrow range with a slight upward bias and reaches its high—63—on the last day. You don't lose all your money this time, but you don't make a profit either. You will get back $300 (63 − 60) of your $450 investment. Better than the first two examples, but still pretty poor.

We hope the reader is beginning to see that making money through buying Calls is not so easy.

A gentle note to the reader:
Don't be disturbed by this devil's advocate negative exposition. It is necessary to understand the pitfalls before you commit capital. We're going to show you how you can make money buying Calls that are LEAPS.

Examples

Stock	Price	Month	Strike	Premium
4. YXZ	80	Mar	80	5
5. YXZ	80	Mar	85	2½

4. On the third Friday in March, YXZ trades at 88. Hurrah, you finally have a profit! Your Call—bought for $500—is now worth $800.

5. Same stock, same price move, but with the 85 strike. Here your Call went from $250 to $300.

These last two examples show the essential difference between ATM and OTM Call buying. In the first, we see the power of leverage. On a 10 percent upmove in the stock, the Call rose 60%! The second example also showed leverage—a 20 percent Call rise. But that got you only a $50 profit.

We have already met informally some of the cast of characters promised in the Introduction. Now let's hear the gospel from an all-too-frequent critic, Mr. Greedy: "Hey, you didn't buy enough in example #5. With the same money you spent in example #4, you could have bought twice as many of the OTM." *Stop! Stop! Stop!* Close your ears to the siren's song. This way lies bankruptcy! Is that an overreaction? No, it is not. We will expound further on this topic later in this chapter. For now, let's just say that people who have done what Mr. Greedy espoused are the ones who have contributed (their dollars as well as their experiences) to the tales you hear about losing all your money in options.

We have now looked somewhat at the strategy of buying calls. Is there anything special to say about **Buying LEAPS Calls?** The answer is an unqualified assertive positive.

On the mundane level for LEAPS, the usual question of which month is transformed into which year. There has been quite a bit of variation in LEAPS's expirations, but the matter seems to have settled down to two different years trading at any one time with expirations in January for each. As time passes the nearer expiration will change from LEAPS to conventional when the time left is six to eight months. (It will be six, seven, or eight depending on which of the three cycles the conventional options trade.) When that transformation does occur, a new year will be introduced. Thus we currently have a system with a range of a minimum of eight months and a maximum of two years and eight months, and at all times the two LEAPS extant will be one year apart. We do not have a specific recommendation as to which of these is the best for each strategy. In some cases the longer one is better, and in others the shorter. In most cases the decision will be ruled by your own predictions, expectations, and aversions. For most of our discussions, unless otherwise noted, we will make the tacit assumption that we are talking about a LEAPS's life of approximately one and one-half years.

Then we have strike selection. Here, even for those who are quite risk-averse, the OTM (but not too far out) LEAPS Call can be attractive. That is because the usual problem—the stock doesn't have enough time to move up to a profitable level—doesn't obtain with LEAPS. Still this strike should be selected only if it fits with the thesis of matching strike selection to stock expectation.

This concept is nothing to be casual about. Before you commit your capital to a LEAPS Call position, you should have a quite clear idea about where the stock is going. If you have a vague idea that "it's a great company and the stock is going up," we don't think you should be in the LEAPS marketplace. If you are looking to "scalp" a few points—that is, make a fast in-and-out foray—you clearly shouldn't be doing that with LEAPS. These are longer-term options and not meant for that type of trading. If you expect the stock to have a fairly good rise (more than 10 percent), you should ask yourself when you expect that to happen. If the answer here is "quickly," you probably should buy either the stock or a conventional Call. If your response is that it might take some time, then you can LEAP into this new market. For a modest move, an ITM or ATM LEAPS Call is probably best for you. It is when you are looking for a larger move that we can suggest viewing the OTM choices.

The above analysis is an ordinary one and is given in many books on options. We think that the strategy of buying LEAPS Calls has a divergence from the conventional. That essential distinction is that you need not fear moderately OTM LEAPS. For conventional options trading, it has been said that the most popular option strategy is buying OTM Calls and watching them expire. Obviously, we don't want you to do that. But if you are proficient with predictive powers or your analytic abilities are able, you certainly can take advantage of the extra leverage possible here. And you can do it without the usual risk attendant on such a procedure. That is because the method often fails with options even when the stock rises. It fails because there is not enough time for the stock to rise sufficiently to produce profitability. And you may even need what we will label "extra profitability" to make up for losses when the stock selection was wrong.

The bottom line is that you should both consider your expectation and look at the LEAPS panoply with a risk-oriented viewpoint. But within that framework our assessment is that OTM LEAPS Calls can be appropriate selections.

Examples (set on July 15 of this year)

Stock	Price	LEAPS Call	Strike	Premium
XYZ	38	Jan (1½ year out)	30	10¾
XYZ	38	Jan (1½ year out)	45	6½
XYZ	38	Jan (1½ year out)	55	2½

In these examples we would opt for (deliberate pun) the OTM 45 strike. The ITM and the FOM have their uses as well and we will take them up in other chapters. Here we just emphasize the moderately out-of-the-money (should we label it MOM?) LEAPS Call as our basic choice for this technique.

There is another area where we must issue a very stern warning. Size—the number of LEAPS Calls to be bought—must be severely restricted. The only suitable selection, in our opinion, is the number of options corresponding to the number of round lots (hundreds of shares) that you would have been comfortable buying.

Examples

You would ordinarily consider buying 500 shares of a $38 stock on which you had a very strong bullish outlook. Don't buy more than five LEAPS Calls. Your colleague is even more bullish than you and s/he has more money. S/he would usually buy 1,000 shares in such a situation. S/he should be self-limited to a maximum of 10 LEAPS Calls.

There is a reason why we are so adamantly opposed to increasing the number of LEAPS bought. One of the two great advantages of LEAPS (or conventional) Call buying is leverage. The other, however, is limited-dollar downside risk. Let's look at what could happen if you decided to increase your exposure in the last illustration.

Examples
Stock position   LEAPS position
Buy 1,000 @ 38 = $38,000   Buy 60 Jan 45
                                        LEAPS Calls @ 6½ = $39,000

Now suppose you are wrong and the chosen stock declines instead of advancing. You now will find yourself in the unenviable position of having *all* your capital at risk. When we say all, we don't mean all that you chose to place into a LEAPS venture. We mean the much larger amount that would have been used for buying the stock. If you leverage yourself to the hilt, you will have thrown away the benison of keeping losses limited while having multiple profit potential.

All our remarks on this subject have been in the context of this first strategy: buying LEAPS Calls. But they should be taken more generally. As we proceed through this book and deal with many different types of strategies, keep in mind this proscription on inappropriate size. OK, if we sensibly limit the dollar investment, what should we do with the excess money? That is, we can regard the difference between the LEAPS investment and the cost for a corresponding number of shares as "excess."

Example

Stock position	LEAPS position	Excess
500 @ 38 = $19,000	5 Jan 45 LEAPS Calls @ 6½ = $3,250	$15,750

What might be done with this money? Of course, anything you want. You could buy other stocks, purchase bonds, buy Treasury securities, etc. There is another LEAPS possibility. You could use the lower dollar investment to diversify instead of trying for further leverage. That is, you could buy LEAPS Calls on another stock in the same industry group. If you were unable to decide whether to buy one of two equities that were equally meritorious—for example, XYZ or ZYX—you could, with LEAPS, take a long position in both!

Example

Stock positions	LEAPS positions	
500 XYZ @ 38 = $19,000	5 XYZ Jan 45 LEAPS Calls @ 6½	= $3,250
500 ZYX @ 50 = $25,000	5 ZYX Jan 60 LEAPS Calls @ 9	= $4,500
Totals	$44,000	$7,750

You could do this with more than two stocks and, in many cases, not spend more than you had originally planned to allot for one stock.

Examples

500 ZYX @ 50=	$25,000	5 XYZ January 45 LEAPS Calls @ 6½	= $3,250

	5 ZYX January 60 LEAPS Calls @ 9	= 4,500
	5 XZY January 70 LEAPS Calls @ 11	= 5,500
	5 YXZ January 50 LEAPS Calls @ 8¼	=4,125
	5 YZX January 90 LEAPS Calls @ 13	= 6,500
Totals	$25,000	$23,875

While extending from one stock to several in the same sector can overcome the risk of "right church, wrong pew," it still does carry some risk. Beware of overly "hot" groups. Stock prices in these areas can discount not only the future but an afterlife as well. One way to avoid that problem is to use LEAPS Calls to diversify outside of one sector. You could buy LEAPS Calls on three or four different stocks in *different* industry groups that you had analyzed for profitable moves. You could consider that you were using LEAPS Calls to create your own minimutual fund. And just think of the superior management that "fund" would have!

There are two cautionary observations to be made here. First, remember that you want to limit your dollar exposure. Don't get carried away. No matter how good a package you assemble, you want to keep the total dollar expenditure under control. As a rule-of-thumb, nobody, except highly professional options traders, should have more than 10 to 15 percent of their investment capital in LEAPS (or any other option positions). Even that is on the high side. Start out with a 5–10 percent ceiling.

The second warning is about overall market direction. While the use of LEAPS will insulate you somewhat from many short-term and intermediate market moves, you must keep alert to this factor. It will not help you to pick the best LEAPS Calls on the best three stocks if the market moves strongly downward and takes them along with it. We will have more to say on this subject in the chapter on Index LEAPS (Chapter 38). For now remember this risk as you ponder your LEAPS investments.

We have looked at expiration, strike, leverage, size, diversification, and market overview. While these parameters are cogent to safety, they are peripheral to the question of financial enrichment. Peripheral is too strong a word. Let's say "secondary." How can you make money buying LEAPS Calls? Easy, if you bear in mind our advice above, both positive and negative. Easy? Yes, it is easy, but there is only one catch. You have to pick the right stock! How do you do that? The same way you would ordinarily if LEAPS were not involved. You could use fundamental research, technical analysis, cycle theory, relative strength searches, management review, a combination of these, or any other method. As long as you are both comfortable and experienced with the procedure, you can make a progression from stock selection to LEAPS choice. The only departure from you habitual ratiocination is that you must make a more detailed probing than usual in the temporal perspective. At the risk of being repetitive, we say that after selecting the stock (or stocks), you must match strike and expiration to your expected target for the stock.

A gentle note to the reader:
Don't be disturbed by the length and breadth of this chapter. It will be one of the longest in this book. Its span was large and broad because we had to introduce, and then generalize, several comprehensive concepts.

A few loose ends need to be tied up. There is one more purchase possibility we have not explored. That is DIM LEAPS Calls, which we will discuss separately in Chapter 33 on LEAPS surrogate therapy. Finally, we will deal with follow-up action—enhancement and repair—in separate sections.

SUMMARY

Call buying, while sometimes risky, need not be pure speculation. And with LEAPS, that becomes even more true. The two advantages—upside leverage and limited downside dollar risk—are intensified with LEAPS. Buying moderately OTM Calls can be very rewarding if practiced sensibly.

CHAPTER 11
LEAPS COVERED CALL WRITING

I cover all.

STRATEGY	Covered Call Writing with LEAPS
OUTLOOK	Mildly bullish
ADVANTAGES	Downside cushion; cost reduction; good return
DRAWBACKS	Limited upside
DEGREE OF RISK	Comparable to stock ownership

What is covered writing? First, the question is wrong. It should be: "What is **Covered Call Writing?**" OK, but what is that? The word *writing* means selling. It does not mean selling out something you own; it refers, in this case, to selling a Call option. The word *covered* means that you have bought the stock and thus have it to deliver if the Call is assigned to your account.

Example
Starting from a zero position, you buy 500 XYZ and write (sell) 5 XYZ Calls.

That is how it works, but what is the motivation that would make somebody do it? Although that question deserves a conceptual answer, we will get to it by an indirect route; we will look at the profit potential.

Example
Buy 500 XYZ @ 40
Write 5 XYZ six-month 40-strike Calls @ 4

Our hypothesis is that the stock is above 40 at the end of the six months and the Call is assigned. That means you sell the stock at 40 (recovering your original investment) and keep the $2,000 ($400 × 5) option premium. You will thus make (per a unit of 100 shares/1 call) $400 on $4,000. Nice? No, nicer! You will actually make $400 on an investment of only $3,600. That's because $3,600 is all you needed to deposit in your account to pay for the stock. The other $400 was there from writing the call. Four hundred on 3,600 is a *period return* of 11.1 percent; if you could replicate that performance in the ensuing six months, you would have an *annualized return* of 22.2 percent.

Before we continue, let's explain why we "annualize" the return. It's not to inflate the rate. If you were offered two different automobile loans from two different banks, you would want to compare them. If there were no other significant differences, but one bank quoted its rate over a four-year period and the other over five years, you could evaluate them by placing each on an "annualized" basis.

When we do this with LEAPS or option investments, we make an assumption, that is, that the type of trade can in fact be repeated as many times as necessary to produce a yearly rate. Thus, if we wrote a covered Call for only three months, the annualizing has the effect of implying that we could do it another three times that year. This assumption is not always valid. In the early 1980s interest rates rose to over 20 percent and covered Call writing returns were magnified, but not repeatable for long.

We make three observations:

1. Very short time periods produce an exaggerated annual rate. In fact, it is illegal to annualize returns of under 60 days.

2. We have multiplied the period return to get the annual one. For example, our six-month writing return was doubled to get the annual rate. If we calculated a three-month return we would have to quadruple it to get the yearly rate. For LEAPS, we would have to *divide* (or multiply by a number less than 1) to show the annual rate, for example, an 18 percent return for a year-and-a-half is a 12 percent annual return.

3. As we said in the previous chapter, these comments are made in the context of covered Call writing but should be taken more generally. They apply to all the strategies.

Now let's go back to our specific strategy. What's the risk you would take in exchange for this nice reward? There are two separate and indeed very different risks that a covered Call writer takes. First and foremost, there is the risk that the stock will go down. In our example, if the stock were held to expiration and was then selling at, say 30, there would be a *loss*. Stock bought at 40 and selling at 30 results in a $1,000 loss for each hundred shares. In this case, however, the loss would be somewhat ameliorated by the Call premium of $400. That would reduce the loss to only $600. But it would still be a *loss*. Thus we see the first risk as very similar to the risk of a far better-known strategy: owning stock.

The second risk can be seen if we again posit holding the stock until expiration, but this time assume that it is then trading at 70. How much money would be lost in that case? None. You would have to fulfil the terms of the contract—that is, deliver stock out at the agreed strike of 40. You would profit by the amount of the Call premium—$400, but that would be all the profit. Someone who had bought the stock and had not sold a Call would have a greater profit: $3,000. This second risk then, is one of opportunity, not of dollars. In each of the two risks, the option premium can be regarded as a payment for assuming that risk. In the down case, it would "cushion" the loss. On the upside, it would give you some profit to make up for missing a larger one.

Now we see the conceptual answer: This strategy should be used by someone who believes the stock will go up, not down, over the life of the Call. S/he also believes that the rise will not be a highly substantial one. In brief, someone who could be labeled "mildly bullish." It also has to be someone who has an attitude toward risk very different from the one implicit in the profile of the Call buyer. There is no question here of either tripling one's money or of losing anywhere near 100 percent of invested capital. The risk can be likened to a banker's risk. You—the covered Call writer—are lending money, and the underlying stock is your collateral for the loan.

Now we can look at **LEAPS Covered Call Writing.** The first thing to say here is that there is an important improvement. Even without egregious examples such as the one cited previously from the early 1980s, projections from period to annual return are not always realizable. With LEAPS covered Call writing you nail down that return. You still require the stock not to decline. But if it doesn't, you will have actualized that sometimes elusive annual return.

Now compare the rates of return. In general, the shorter the time period, the greater the rate. However, that rate is obtained at the expense of a lower absolute dollar amount. That amount can be either a profit or a downside protection. Depending on which is more important to you, you can find covered Call writing opportunities with LEAPS.

Example
Buy XYZ @ 40.
Write XYZ Jan (1½ year out) 40 LEAPS Call @ 8.
The potential profit is $8/32 = 25\% = 16.7$ percent annually. The "cushion" (amount the stock could drop without loss) is $8/40$ or 20 percent.

There is another aspect to consider here. We have talked about buying stock simultaneously with the writing of the Calls. In the jargon of the trade, that's often named a **buy-write.** There is another form of covered Call writing: owning the stock and seeking either a cushion hedge for it, incremental income from it beyond the dividend yield, or both.

Example
You bought XYZ @ 32 and it is now @ 40. The writing of the LEAPS Call in the above example will net you an additional eight points profit if the stock rises and protect you down to your cost basis if the stock falls.

We must note that for someone long the stock, a covered Call write could be appealing for two separate reasons. S/he might be worried about a decline. Or the concern could be about setting up an exit point for the stock. LEAPS fill both bills very nicely. The usual problem with a Call write, rather than a

Put purchase, to protect a long position is the size of the premium received. While it is a money inflow, it might not be sufficient protection if the stock broke. But with LEAPS there are high dollar premiums, and this speaks to the heart of the problem.

As for the "exit point," we all know what a problem that can be. Some do attempt to solve it by writing Calls. Often, depending on the vagaries of the market (not to mention Murphy's Law), the stock does go higher than desired. We think LEAPS can provide the solution.

At this point, we ask the reader to remember the distinction we made in Chapter 10 on Call buying. We pointed out that for conventional options OTM Calls were usually both a more aggressive stance and a more dangerous one. With LEAPS, that was not necessarily true. The same principle applies with covered Call writing with LEAPS. By selecting an OTM (but not too far out) strike, you get a good deal in two respects. First, because LEAPS last so long, the dollar premium (in absolute terms) is a high amount. This gives you a good cushion for the long stock. Second, because the stock has a good length of time in which to appreciate, you could get not only the Call premium but the difference between market price and strike as well.

Example
Buy XYZ @ 38. Write Jan (1½ year out) 50 LEAPS Call @ 4.

If the stock ends @ 38 (without a previous assignment), you will be ahead $400. If the stock rises above 50 and you are assigned, you will make the $400 plus another $1,200 (50 sale minus 38 cost). There can be a refinement to this technique. If you are long, say 2,000 shares of stock, and are beginning to think about getting out, consider writing OTM LEAPS Calls on *part* of the position.

Example
You bought 2,000 XYZ @ 32. When it reaches 40, you write 5 of the 40-strike calls @ 8. If the stock rises more, you can repeat the process.

Example
When the stock reaches 45, you write 10 of the 50-strike @ 4. Note that we wrote more the second time. That was to reflect a more firmly held view about the stock's "topping." Finally, we could conclude the procedure.

Example
With the previous LEAPS Calls assigned and the stock @ 55, you write five of the 60-strike @ 5. Let's suppose that on this final time the stock did not rise. Instead, it fell. That would not be enough to take a closing action. What would have to change, besides the stock price, is your attitude toward the stock. If you thought the fall was temporary, you could hold on. You could also feel secure while you did this because of all the LEAPS premiums you took in. Continuing in this mode, let's suppose further that the stock recovered somewhat, but that then you did change your mind. While there are a plethora of possible actions here, we will here consider only one. (The others will be dealt with in Chapter 40 on LEAPS repair.) *Get out.* Sell out the remaining stock and, of course, buy back the written LEAPS Calls.

Example
When the stock (looking bad on its chart) breaks 50, you decide to sell out. You sell 500 @ 49⅜ and buy back the five written LEAPS Calls @ 2½. In the above analysis, we branched off at the first choice. Let's go back to that point and examine the alternative. That would be that you wanted out then and there. OK, do it. Buy back the LEAPS Calls and sell out the stock, just as we did in the first example.

Example
When the stock hits 35½, you sell all 2,000 shares and repurchase the five written LEAPS Calls @ 5. In the last example, we saw a reversal of your expectations for the stock. This can happen. What is important is that you realize that you are no more wedded to the LEAPS position than you are to the stock. Nor should the presence of the LEAPS component influence your analysis of the stock's price movements.

What you have done in the above two examples is to add a LEAPS involvement to a standard stock strategy called *scaling out*. Instead of selling out all at once, you pick your spots and feed out the stock at successively higher prices. This is a well-known and often practiced method, but it is used mostly by larger holders. Thanks to LEAPS, a smaller trader can also participate. But with LEAPS, you are doing more than just participating. You are outperforming! If you had just sold your stock as indicated in the examples, you would have gotten out at some pretty good prices. But with the sales from LEAPS (and one buyback), you got far better prices.

Example
Original Cost 32.
First sale—500 @ 48 (40 strike realized at assignment plus 8 premium).
Second sale—1,000 @ 54 (50 strike realized at assignment plus 4 premium).
Third sale—500 @ 51⅞ (49⅜ stock sale plus premium of 2½ [5 sale less 2½ repurchase]).

Recapitulation
Bought 2,000 @ 32

Sold	500 @ 48	=	$ 24,000.00
Sold	1,000 @ 54	=	$ 54,000.00
Sold	500 @ 51⅞	=	$ 25,937.50
Total	2,000 shares		$103,937.50
Original cost			$ 64,000.00
Profit			$ 39,937.50
Average effective sale price			51.97

Now let's see what would have happened without any LEAPS Call writes. We make the arbitrary assumption that stock sales would have been made at the price points when sales from LEAPS were made.

Recapitulation
Bought 2,000 @ 32

Sold	500 @ 40	=	$20,000
Sold	1,000 @ 50	=	$50,000
Sold	500 @ 55	=	$27,500
Total	2,000 shares		$97,500
Original cost			$64,000
Profit			$33,500
Average sale price			48¾

Thus the LEAPS trades produced an average sale price more than three points higher per share; they also generated $6,437.50 additional profit. Lest you think that we loaded the dice for our comparison, we will point out that without LEAPS the third sale was made @ 55. In the LEAPS scenario, the stock was held after it turned down and then sold at 49⅜. The fact that the stock was held illustrates a LEAPS advantage over and above the extra profit. That is that the LEAPS Call writes in our depiction allowed the stock owner to hold on while the stock increased. Later the last LEAPS write forestalled a sellout that could have been a panic-provoked error.

In sum, LEAPS covered Call writing—against all or part of a long stock position—provides protection on the downside and profits from upmoves. There is even a refinement to the scaling out strategy, but we will save it for Chapter 39 on LEAPS Enhancement.

Before we finish the subject, we want to make a formal *warning*. Some of the percentage returns we saw in our examples were attractive, and in real life you might find even higher ones. Don't let this sway you. These are not returns; they are only projections of returns. Those projections will be met only if the stock does not decline. Those projected returns would not be so high if there were not high risk accompanying them. Remember the rule: "How much profit is enough?" LEAPS covered writing is a fine strategy. It is even finer if you employ it only on stocks with which you are comfortable. To wrap up the subject of covered Call writing, this type of trading can be done in either a cash account or a margin account. If you buy the stock on margin, you have to do what you usually do, that is, pay interest on any debit balance. Your out-of-pocket cost will, however, be lowered because of the LEAPS premium.

Example

Buy 500 @ 40 in Cash Account—Cost	$20,000
Write five 40-strike calls @ 4—Credit	$ 2,000
Out-of-pocket cost	$18,000

Buy 500 @ 40 in margin account—Cost	$20,000
Borrow one-half from brokerage	$10,000
Credit from five calls written @ 4	$ 2,000
Out-of-pocket cost	$ 8,000

Buy 500 @ 40 in margin account—Cost	$20,000
Borrow one-half from brokerage	$10,000
Credit from LEAPS Calls written @ 8	$ 4,000
Out-of-pocket cost	$ 6,000

In general, even though you will have to reduce any profit by the amount of margin interest paid, you will obtain a higher return on margin. Do not make the simplistic error of thinking that the return will be doubled. And don't even think of doing this type of trade on margin unless that is what you would usually do when LEAPS were not involved.

SUMMARY

Covered Call writing has been established as a sound and sensible approach for what we might call the "banking mentality." Using LEAPS allows both a higher potential return and a larger downside cushion without an undue additional risk. As with Call buying, LEAPS covered Call writing with OTM strikes, sensibly handled, offer additional profits.

CHAPTER 12
WRITING LEAPS PUTS

True ease in writing comes from Art, not Chance.

STRATEGY	Writing LEAPS Puts
OUTLOOK	Bullish to very bullish
ADVANTAGES	Low capital needed
DRAWBACKS	Needs close monitoring
DEGREE OF RISK	Moderate

First, let's discuss the name of the strategy. *Writing* means selling, but not selling something already owned. Please refer back to Chapter 11 on covered Call writing for a full description. Second, let's correct a widespread misconception: LEAPS are not Calls, that is, the LEAPS label applies to Puts as well as Calls. That said, what stance is **Writing Puts?** Is it bullish, bearish, neutral, or something else? That's easy to answer if we examine possible outcomes.

Example
XYZ @ 40
Write (sell) a 40-strike Put

At expiration, the stock is above 40. You keep the Put premium. At expiration, the stock is below 40. The Put will be assigned and you will buy the stock @ 40. That will happen no matter how far below 40 the stock is. (Assuming you did not repurchase the Put before the assignment; once you were assigned, it was too late.) Presumably you will not be averse to the Put assignment, which results in your buying the stock. You might even make money later from this occurrence. It's when that doesn't happen that you make the profit without any further waiting.

OK, we want the stock to go up. Just as in the strategy of covered Call writing, we don't want the stock to go down because we will lose money. And we don't want the stock to rise greatly because we will lose an opportunity to make a greater profit. Just as in covered Call writing, we are compensated for these two very different types of risk by the option premium.

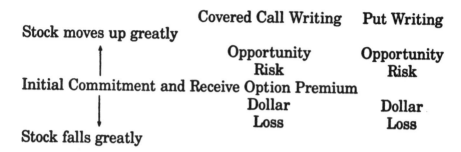

	Covered Call Writing	Put Writing
Stock moves up greatly ↑		
	Opportunity	Opportunity
	Risk	Risk
Initial Commitment and Receive Option Premium		
	Dollar	Dollar
↓	Loss	Loss
Stock falls greatly		

The point we are trying to make may begin to occur to the reader. Uncovered equity Put writing is very similar to covered Call writing. They have the same risk/reward profile. But Put writing might be deemed a superior strategy. That is because the reward/payoff is greater. Consider the two in tandem:

Example

Buy 500 XYZ @ 40   Write 5 XYZ 40 Calls @ 4
    Capital $18,000
No stock position   Write 5 XYZ 40 Puts @ 3
    Capital $ 5,000

The first example can be checked in Chapter 11 on covered Calls. The second is described in Chapter 9 on margin.

We must interrupt our strategy explication to note some very practical points:

1. We have used, in our examples, close to the minimum margin requirement. Many brokerage firms will ask for more—in some cases, a lot more. We continue with our assumption for explanatory purposes.

2. In addition to margin requirements, many firms have a problem with the strategy. They mistakenly lump together two extremely different techniques—writing uncovered Calls and writing uncovered Puts—as *selling naked options*. This is both wrong and offensive. The risk

for the first is comparable to a short sale of stock, and for the second it is comparable to stock ownership.

3. Some investors are frightened by the concept of *margin*. The requirement here is better described as a need for collateral. If you elect to write Puts in a quantity commensurate with stock purchases, you are not leveraging yourself. That is, if you would buy 500 shares of a stock, you could write five Puts. Further, unlike stock margin, there would be no debit balance incurred and you would pay no margin interest.

4. While the profile and the results may be similar in both strategies, there is an important psychological distinction. Covered Call writing includes stock ownership. That is something that almost all investors are familiar and comfortable with. Uncovered equity/LEAPS Put writing does not (initially) include stock ownership. Therefore, it becomes incumbent on the Put writer (and/or the broker) to monitor the position. You must be aware of the possibility of assignment and ready to alter or close the position. If you weren't planning on buying the stock, you might be in for a rude shock.

Now let's look at some cases of **Writing LEAPS Puts.**

Example
XYZ @ 40
Write XYZ Jan (1½ year out) 40 LEAPS Puts @ 6

We will devote some space to analyzing this position and its implications. It is the direct counterpart to the first LEAPS example in the covered Call chapter. Initial collateral requirement—25 percent of $4,000 = $1,000. Technically the requirement is the above plus the Put premium. So what we have given is really the out-of-pocket capital needed. We note that the requirement specifies both the *current* stock price and option premium. As the stock price changes, so will the requisite collateral capital.

If there is no assignment by expiration, your profit will be the $600. That is $600/_{1,000}$ or a fantastic period return of 60 percent. The annual return here is 40 percent. This annual return for the corresponding covered Call was 16.7 percent. This is one reason why we like this technique.

What about the downside? If you are assigned, your effective purchase price will be 34 (40 strike less six premium). That's 15 percent down from the current market price and pretty close to the $32/20 percent down point in the covered Call example.

Despite our strategic preference, we must emphasize the comment in point #4 above: Covered Call writing starts with long stock; Put writing may end with it. As one wag once phrased it: "When you write Calls, you buy the stock now; when you write Puts, you buy the stock later."

"Many a true word is said in jest." We may laugh at the phraseology, but we must be cognizant of its implications. We say, unequivocally, *never* write a Put (options or LEAPS) on a stock that you are not comfortable owning. Further, the written Put position must be constantly monitored for both price fluctuations and to assure that your expectations for the stock are unchanged.

Next, the usual questions. Which expiration and which strike should you select? And the usual answer: Match your expectations and your risk attitude to these variables. In the two previous chapters we emphasized OTM options as being superior choices in the LEAPS domain. Is that true of writing LEAPS Puts as well? Yes, but with a twist. With ordinary options there is the usual trade-off between attitude and dollars. That is, you can be conservative but expect to make less money. For Put writing, that translates into a structural similarity to the other strategies studied so far. As the mathematicians say: "Similar, but not congruent." That is, the ATM Put write is, as always, the moderate choice. After that, there is a role reversal. The ITM Put write is aggressive; the OTM, conservative.

Examples
XYZ @ 40
OTM—XYZ Jan (1½ year out)   35 LEAPS Put @ 3
ATM—XYZ Jan (1½ year out)   40 LEAPS Put @ 6
ITM —XYZ Jan (1½ year out)   45 LEAPS Put @ 9

The initial collateral requirements for these three are, respectively, $500, $1,000, and $1,000 (the premiums must be left in each case). As we have seen before, the trade-off is between how much money you might make and the probability of making it. The two selections of ATM and ITM are certainly suitable to those with the combination of greater bullishness and greater risk taking (especially the ITM). We suggest writing an OTM LEAPS Put that should give at least a reasonable return and subject you to an acceptable level of risk as far as the stock's potential purchase price is concerned.

If you have identified the appropriate degree of risk you want to assume, but are dissatisfied with the available returns, there is another possibility. That is writing covered straddles, which we will examine in the next chapter. At this point, we issue a warning. It is the same warning we gave in the covered Calls chapter: do *not* write solely for return. Write a LEAPS Put only if it gives you a satisfactory return and if the stock is one you want to buy.

There is another way of looking at Put writing, LEAPS or otherwise. That is to regard the potential acquisition price as primary and the return as secondary. You might, for instance, be enamored with the idea of owning ZYX at $60. If that were the paramount issue for you, you could write the January 1995 65-strike LEAPS Put for at least five. Whatever the return might be, your risk (and your desire) would be stock ownership at the calculated 60 level.

We have stressed that Put writing often leads to stock ownership. We did compare the collateral differences between Put writing and Call writing. Now let's compare the collateral requirement for the Put and the margin or cash needed for outright stock purchase. We will find a large difference.

Example
XYZ @ 40
XYZ Jan (1½ year out) 40 LEAPS Put @ 6
Initial Stock Cost—Cash $4,000   Margin $2,000
LEAPS Initial Collateral—$1,000

What can we do with the excess money? We did the same investigation in Chapter 10 on buying Calls. There we cautioned against overleverage and recommended diversification instead. We believe exactly the same viewpoint is applicable here. We can use the additional funds to write more Puts, but on different stocks. We can do this either within a favored industry or diversify across sectors.

Example

The dollar amounts are the collateral needed and the parenthetic numbers are the stocks' market prices.

Stock position	LEAPS written position
500 XYZ @ 50 = $25,000	5 XYZ (50) Jan 45 LEAPS Puts @ 6½ = $ 3,750 5 ZYX (71) Jan 60 LEAPS Puts @ 6 = $ 3,550 5 XZY (69) Jan 70 LEAPS Puts @ 11 = $ 8,625 5 YZX (98) Jan 90 LEAPS Puts @ 10 = $ 8,250
Totals $25,000	$24,175

We saw this method in Chapter 10 on Buying Calls. In each case we are utilizing the lower cost of LEAPS (versus stocks) for safety through diversification, rather than for leverage. Bully for us!

We have taken in almost $17,000 in premiums which we must leave in the account. If there are no assignments at all, we would never end up buying any of the stocks. Not to weep. Instead of buying one stock for a $25,000 cost, we have an almost equal sum committed for collateral against the possibility of buying four different stocks. We would be provided with a very nice return in exchange for committing capital to buy these stocks. Don't lose sight of what's meant here. If the stocks all went down below their strikes (and you never repurchased any Puts), you would have to buy all the stocks, albeit at lower prices.

Stock	Strike	Premium	Effective Cost	$Cost—500
XYZ	45	6½	38½	$19,250
ZYX	60	6	54	27,000

XZY	70	11	59	29,500
YZX	90	10	80	40,000
				$115,750

That's quite a hunk of change. It certainly is considerably less than the $144,000 it would have cost to simply buy the package of stocks outright originally. The savings came from the LEAPS Puts premiums combined with the fact that all but one were written OTM. You did save over $28,000, but is it what you wanted to do? This is a concrete illustration of the absolute necessity of monitoring the position. Again we say that the monitoring must be for both stock prices and to check on your own expectations. If you are satisfied with this possible result, then we know you have a good deal here. The stocks-up scenario brought a great return; the stocks-down result brought you bargain acquisitions.

We iterate our view that this technique is similar to, but superior to, covered Call writing. When the stocks went up, you got a higher return. When they went down, you ended owning them at lower prices. Naturally, we do not mean to imply that all the stocks will necessarily move in the same direction. This would be especially true if you had used our system of diversification across, rather than within, sectors. This would diminish the probability of your being caught in an industry-specific downdraft.

Finally (we're back to discussing excess money), we can simply buy other securities. That might include Treasury issues, where the interest payments would provide additional income and another band of safety.

Example
Buy XYZ @ 40
or
Write XYZ Jan (1½ year out) 40 LEAPS Put @ 6
Initial Stock Cost—Cash $4,000   Margin $2,000
Post either $3,400 (cash) *or* $1,400 (margin)
Excess (cash cost less LEAPS collateral) $3,000
Buy ZYX @ 30 *or* buy $3,000 worth of Treasury securities.

There is a still more conservative way to write LEAPS Puts. That is to calculate the amount of money that might be needed to buy the stock if the Puts were assigned. This calculation could be done on either a cash or margin basis. In fact, it should be done just as you would usually choose to pay for stock purchases. There is a difference: the LEAPS Put premium received. You can subtract that to calculate the amount of money you must post.

Example
XYZ @ 40
Write XYZ Jan (1½ year out) 40 LEAPS Put @ 6
Initial stock cost—cash $4,000   Margin $2,000
Post either $3,400 *or* $1,400 (margin)

Now your ultraconservative instincts are satisfied. If something unforeseen occurs and the stock declines badly, you know you will be able to pay for it. There is nothing wrong with this method of writing Puts—LEAPS or standard—but it is probably too conservative for many. It goes to show that LEAPS trading can be done by conservative investors, not just wild speculators.

While this method satisfied financial conservatism, it is not enough to do only that. You (or your faithful broker) must still monitor the position. It would be the height (or maybe the depth) of fiscal foolhardiness to say: "OK, I've got the money there, I don't have to worry about the position." The monitoring should appeal to these people just because it is itself a very conservative way to deal with your investments. If you don't like the way the stock is behaving and you change your opinion on the stock, take action. Just as you would sell out the stock, do the equivalent: buy back the LEAPS Puts. If your outlook would have been to sell out half the stock, do so. Buy back half the LEAPS Puts. Finally, we are not suggesting that you place stagnant dollars in your account. To collateralize the obligation in full, you could use the borrowing power of fully-paid-for stock. Or you could buy Treasury securities and use them for the collateral. (Most firms will lend you approximately 90–95 percent on them).

SUMMARY

Writing Puts has been an underutilized strategy. It is similar in nature and risk to covered Call writing but offers higher returns. It was (mistakenly) thrown into disrepute in the wake of the 1987 cataclysm. Despite that, with LEAPS it is an appropriate strategy for many who understand its risks. It can even be done by very conservative investors. Writing Puts with LEAPS on stocks deemed attractive combines a good return with an acceptable risk.

CHAPTER 13
WRITING LEAPS
COVERED STRADDLES

Anything will do so long as he straddles.

STRATEGY	Writing Covered LEAPS Straddles
OUTLOOK	Very bullish
ADVANTAGES	Combines covered Call writing with Put writing; Collect two premiums
DRAWBACKS	Needs monitoring; may be too great a commitment
DEGREE OF RISK	More intense than stock

We have looked at writing covered Calls and examined writing uncovered Puts. Now we will view the two together—writing covered straddles. What is a covered straddle? You can't have a stock position that covers you on a written Call and a written Put at the same time. It's all a matter of nomenclature and we will adhere to the industry jargon: **Writing Covered Straddles** means being long stock and writing both a Put and a Call on the same underlying. To be more precise, the Put and Call that are written are not only on the same underlying stock but also share the same expiration date and striking price.

Example
Buy XYZ @ 40
Write XYZ 6-month 40-strike Call
Write XYZ 6-month 40-strike Put

What is the motivation for such a trade and what are its benefits? By now you should know that we must also ask: What are the risks involved? Let's look back at the examples in the chapters on covered Call writing (Chapter 11) and uncovered Put writing (Chapter 12). If we combine them we get:

Example
Buy XYZ @ 40
Write XYZ 6-month 40-strike Call @ 4
Write XYZ 6-month 40-strike Put @ 3

The benefits here can be summed up this way: If the stock goes up, you will be called away and you will collect not only the Call premium but the Put premium as well. If the stock goes down, you will be assigned on the Put, but your cost basis for the stock thus acquired will be reduced. It will be lessened by not only the Put premium but by the Call's as well.

Example
Buy XYZ @ 40
Write XYZ 6-month 40-strike Call @ 4
Write XYZ 6-month 40-strike Put @ 3

1. At expiration XYZ is @ 50, the Call is assigned, you sell the stock and make $700.
2. At expiration XYZ is @ 35, the Put is assigned, you buy the stock, and your cost basis for the new stock is 33 (40 strike less total premium 7).

Basically this technique allows a reasonable chance to collect two premiums instead of one, while benefitting from either of the two substrategies. There is, of course, another possibility. The stock might go up first and then down. Or it might go down first and then up. In either case both options might be assigned. What would happen then?

Example
Buy XYZ @ 40
Write XYZ 6-month 40-strike Call @ 4
Write XYZ 6-month 40-strike Put @ 3

1. Three months after strategic inception, XYZ is @ 50, the Call is assigned and you sell the stock. XYZ then declines until, near expiration, it is @ 38, the Put is assigned, and you buy the stock. You finish with a long stock position near its original price and you are ahead $700 in cash.

2. Three months after the straddle initiation, XYZ has declined to 35, the Put is assigned, and you buy the stock. It then consolidates and subsequently rises until, at expiration, it is at 41½. The Call is assigned, and you sell out the stock. You wind up with long stock above its original price and ahead the same $700.

These results, however, would depend on doing nothing after the first assignment. Doing nothing is seldom a good way to proceed in the marketplace. If either option is assigned, you should take action. The obvious course would be to buy back the other option.

Example
Buy XYZ @ 40
Write XYZ 6-month 40-strike Call @ 4
Write XYZ 6-month 40-strike Put @ 3

1. Three months after inception, XYZ is @ 50, the Call is assigned, and you sell the stock. The Put has declined to ½ and you buy it back (a closing transaction). You have now made only 6½, but you are out of all three elements of the position (long stock, written Call, written Put) after only three months.
2. Three months after the straddle initiation, XYZ has declined to 35, the Put is assigned, and you buy the stock. You now own 200 shares at an average price of 36½ (first lot @ 40; second lot @ 33 (40 less 7).) You still have a written Call outstanding (now @ 1).

You can do several things. You could close the entire position by selling 200 shares and buying back the single Call. You could sell 100 shares and keep the rest of the position, which would have become a straight covered Call. You could write a second Call to keep the posture of covered Call, but on 200 shares. As always, which action you should take will depend on how you view the stock at that point. We note that the stock presumably came close (@ 35) to a point where you should have been reconsidering your outlook.

There is another alternative besides doing nothing and total or partial closure: **Rolling.** Rolling means to buy back a written option and to write another in its place.

Example
Buy 500 XYZ @ 40
Write 5 XYZ 6-month 40-strike Calls @ 4

After three months, XYZ has risen to 44 and the Call is at 7. You could buy back the Call and write a 45-strike that had another six months until expiration. It might be selling for 5½. You would lose 1½ points in this transaction, but you would now be in position to be called away five points higher.

We have mentioned rolling for introductory purposes only. Because it is a general concept and is applicable to many maneuvers, we will save our exposition of it for Chapters 39 and 40 on enhancement and repair.

The strategy of covered straddle writing is for only those who are strongly bullish. But for them, there is a convenient way to view the method and to implement it. Consider how much stock you might be thinking of buying. Do only half that amount and then write the covered straddles.

Example
When that great security XYZ is @ 40, you are contemplating buying 1,000 shares. Here's the alternative:

Buy 500 XYZ @ 40
Write 5 XYZ 6-month 40-strike Calls @ 4
Write 5 XYZ 6-month 40-strike Puts @ 3

Before we, so to speak, jump into LEAPS, we must look at the margin or collateral requirement for covered straddles. It is, obviously, the requirement for the covered Call write and the requirement for the uncovered Put write. We saw these separately in their respective chapters. Now we will combine them.

Example
You buy XYZ @ 40 on margin; you must post $2,000.
You write XYZ 40-strike Call; the long stock is sufficient collateral.
You write XYZ 40-strike Put; you need another $1,000.

That's the initial requirement when you buy the stock on margin. If you buy the stock for cash, it's so easy we won't even need an example. The loan value of the stock (50 percent) satisfies the Put margin (25 percent). That's an oversimplification, but the bottom line is that you won't need additional funds for the initial margin requirement.

Now what about covered straddles using LEAPS? This is a very natural transition. You will get much higher premiums (in absolute dollar amounts) than from equity options. When you get two of them, you have a good range of protection. The protection we speak of is for the two different types of risks we looked at earlier: dollar loss on the downside and opportunity risk on the upside.

Example (set on July 15 of this year)
Long XYZ @ 40
Written XYZ (1½ year out) 40 LEAPS Call @ 8
Written XYZ (1½ year out) 40 LEAPS Put @ 6

If the stock is called away you gain $1,400. If more stock is put to you, your effective acquisition cost will be 26 (40 strike less 14 total premium). Incidentally, that $1,400 represents a very nice return. If you bought the stock for cash, it comes to $1400/5000$ or 28 percent for a period return, which is 18.7 percent annualized.

We viewed covered Call writing twice—first, starting from a zero position. Then we looked at writing Calls against stock already owned. We can do the same with covered straddles. Suppose you own a stock and are well satisfied with its performance. You might feel that you would sell out some of your position on a moderate price increase, but would like to add to it on a decline. Talk about "a marriage made in heaven"! The covered straddle is ideal for your expectations, and even more so with LEAPS.

Example
You bought XYZ @ 32 and it is now 40
Write XYZ (Jan 1½ year out) 40 LEAPS Call @ 8
Write XYZ (Jan 1½ year out) 40 LEAPS Put @ 6

If the stock rises and you are called, you have a bonanza. You sell @ 54 (40 plus combined premiums of 14) for a total profit of $2,200. Actually, you should settle for less than that. If things work out this well, you should not hesitate about closing the LEAPS Put position. If the stock falls and you are put, you will get your desired second lot of stock. It will cost you only 26 (40 less combined 14). You now own stock with an average price of 33 (1 lot @ 40; 1 lot @ 26).

We used a cute phrase above: "a marriage made in heaven." That doesn't mean we think writing covered straddles with (or without) LEAPS is always wonderful. We said that because there was a perfect fit between the technique and the expectations. You should not do covered straddles unless you are extremely bullish on the stock. What is the degree of bullishness needed for this strategy? That's easy. It's the amount you need to want to buy the stock now and be willing to buy more later if it goes down. Notice that LEAPS make this a better technique because the second buy would be at a significantly lower level. Also recommended is the method described above: Buy one-half the desired amount of stock at first; write the LEAPS straddle. You will either end up with the amount originally wanted, or you will miss that, but obtain a good return.

The LEAPS Money Generator

This is a form of systematic covered writing using straddles, Calls, and Puts (see Figure 13.1). Before we describe it, we repeat our comment about the need for a very bullish outlook on the underlying stock. With that condition satisfied, we can take an almost mechanical approach. Start off by writing LEAPS Puts on the selected stock. If the stock rises, the premium becomes your profit. In fact, if the stock rises with rapidity, you could buy back the LEAPS Puts, make less of a profit, but be ready for a new trade. If the stock falls and you do not change you attitude (by closing the LEAPS Put position), when you are assigned you will own the desired stock at a lower level. At this point you write covered LEAPS straddles. If the stock now rises and you receive a Call assignment, you will be out of the stock and ahead by three premiums—originally 1 LEAPS Put, and later 1 Call and 1 Put from the LEAPS straddle write. Should the stock fall again, you will probably be assigned on the Put. This will leave you with a double position in the stock. Now

FIGURE 13.1
The LEAPS Money Generator

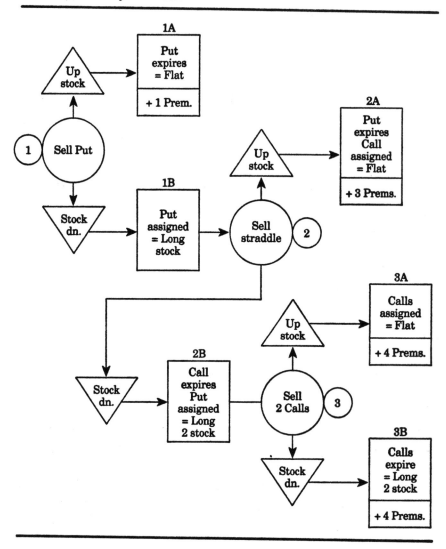

write as many Calls as you are long stock (or one less, as you still have one outstanding). Alternatively, you could buy back that single and write the full complement. Now on a stock rise you will be called away and have collected four premiums. Finally, if the stock falls once again, your position would be best described as "long and wrong." But the resultant unrealized loss will not be attributable to LEAPS. Its cause was your selection of a stock that thrice declined when you predicted upward moves. Even in this worst case, your stock cost would have been reduced by four LEAPS premiums.

SUMMARY

For the knowledgeable and sophisticated investor, covered straddle writing can be a highly rewarding strategy. In fact, historical studies have shown it to be one of the best strategies over complete market cycles. There have not yet been academic studies on how using LEAPS in this strategy affects the outcome. However, it is intuitively obvious that taking in larger amounts of money makes this a safer as well as a more rewarding strategy with LEAPS.

CHAPTER 14
WRITING LEAPS COVERED COMBINATIONS

A combination and a form indeed.

STRATEGY	Writing Covered LEAPS Combinations
OUTLOOK	Very bullish
ADVANTAGES	Combines covered Call writing with Put writing; collect two premiums
DRAWBACKS	Complex; needs monitoring; Double Commitment
DEGREE OF RISK	More intense than stock

We have just looked at writing covered straddles and defined that technique as long stock, written Call, written Put, with Put and Call at the same strike and with the same expiration. Now we can broaden our approach by considering what would happen if we wrote a Put and a Call on the same stock with different strikes (but retained the same expiration). That would be a **Covered Combination.**

Example
Buy XYZ @ 40
Write XYZ 6-month 45-strike Call
Write XYZ 6-month 35-strike Put

Before we start our strategy discussion, a few words about nomenclature. Many of the names for options-trading techniques have been borrowed from the commodities world. Their name for what we are labeling *combination* is **strangle.** We find that term ugly, and mention it here only to be informative. You might find articles elsewhere on the subject under that heading. We will stay with our name.

This method can be summarized very quickly. When compared to the covered straddle write, on the upside you will make more money if the Call is assigned because you will get not only the Call premium but the distance between the stock cost and the Call strike as well.

Example
Buy XYZ @ 40
Write XYZ 6-month 45-strike Call @ 2
Write XYZ 6-month 35-strike Put @ 1

At expiration XYZ is @ 50, the Call is assigned, you sell the stock and make $800. The $800 consists of $300 in premiums and $500 from the difference between stock cost (40) and stock sale (45). Similarly, if the stock were put to you, you would acquire the additional stock (beyond the original purchase) at a still lower price. It would be reduced by not only the two premiums but the fact that the Put strike was lower.

Example
Buy XYZ @ 40
Write XYZ 6-month 45-strike Call @ 2
Write XYZ 6-month 35-strike Put @ 1

At expiration XYZ is @ 34, the Put is assigned, you buy the stock, and your cost basis for the new stock is 32 (35 strike less total premium 3).

Once again, LEAPS enhance an existing strategy. With conventional options, there are two schools of thought on covered straddles versus covered combinations. Some opt for (pun intended) the covered straddle: "Get the dollars." For others the covered combination write is deemed better because you stand a higher chance of collecting both premiums without any assignment. However, you would usually have to settle for somewhat low premiums on both sides. With LEAPS, even though either or both of the strikes might be far away from the market price, a fairly large dollar premium is not unusual.

Example (set on July 15 of the year)
XYZ @ 80
XYZ Jan (1½ year out) 90 LEAPS Call @ 8
XYZ Jan (1½ year out) 70 LEAPS Put @ 5

When we spoke about "profit" above, we were referring to the dollar amount that you might end up with. Profit is also measured in percentages. We have calculated "returns" before; this one will be just a little more complex. We must look carefully at two aspects of collateral requirements: the out-of-the-money amount and the minimum percentage. See Chapter 9 on margin.

Example
XYZ @ 80
XYZ Jan (1½ year out) 70 LEAPS Put @ 5
Initial requirement—$2,000 less $1,000 (OTM amount) and
　　　　　leave premium.

XYZ @ 80
XYZ Jan (1½ year out) 65 LEAPS Put @ 3
Initial requirement—$2,000 less $1,500 (OTM amount)
　　　　　= $500 = NO GOOD. Becomes minimum
　　　　　of $800 (10 percent market value) and
　　　　　leave premium.

If you did the trade above, go back one example:
Buying XYZ @ 80
and writing
XYZ Jan (1½ year out) 90 LEAPS Call @ 8
XYZ Jan (1½ year out) 70 LEAPS Put @ 5,
you would have to post $8,000 for the stock and no more for the Put *or* $4,000 for the stock and $1,000 for the Put (cash and margin respectively). If the stock ended between the 70 and 90 strikes—without any previous assignments—you would make $1,300. (You might have an unrealized profit or loss on the stock position.) In the first case that would be a period return of 16.3 percent and an annual return of 10.8 percent. In the second case, with an assumed 5 percent margin interest rate you would have to deduct $300 and net $1,000 on $5,000 or 20 percent for the period and 13.3 percent on a yearly basis. These percentages

are lower than the ones we showed in the previous chapter. But there we had the assumption of Call assignment. If that happens here, you would make—on a cash basis—$1,300 plus an additional $1,000 (90 sale minus 80 cost). Not bad!

The bottom line is that we have here a strategy that has, as usual, both risks and rewards. As always, the two must be traded off against each other. We have not yet found a method that produces lots of profits with little risk! Because of this risk we have a suggested guideline: Do it on only one side. That is, buy the stock and write the OTM Call and the ATM Put. Or write the ATM Call and the OTM Put. This way, you will be taking in a higher premium on one side. You will still be adhering to the concept of selling the stock higher (the covered Call leg) or buying more stock at a lower level (the writing Put part).

Example
XYZ @ 80
XYZ Jan (1½ year out) 90 LEAPS Call @ 8
XYZ Jan (1½ year out) 80 LEAPS Call @ 13
XYZ Jan (1½ year out) 80 LEAPS Put @ 10
XYZ Jan (1½ year out) 70 LEAPS Put @ 5

Which side should be ATM and which OTM? That's an easy one to answer. Just ask yourself: "Am I more concerned with giving up some additional profit from a stock rise of greater than expected?" "Or am I more worried about the price at which I might have to buy more stock if it declines by more than I had anticipated?" This self-analysis should evoke the desired solution. Whichever way it is done, we think this substrategy provides a sensible compromise between risk and reward.

Examples
XYZ stock 45

	Both OTM		*Put ATM*		*Call ATM*	
Jan 50 Call	4¾	Jan 50 Call	4¾	Jan 45 Call	6¾
Jan 40 Put	3¾	Jan 45 Put	5¾	Jan 40 Put	3¾
Total premium	8½		10½		10½

Effective sale price if assigned	58½	60½	55½
Effective cost basis if assigned	31½	34½	29½

We are about to say some extravagant things about this technique and our recommended substrategy. Before we do, it is incumbent upon us to note a practical point. There may not be any ATM strike. If so, just find the closest one you can.

These examples (drawn from real data) are instructive. If you paid cash for the stock, that would cover the collateral for the Put in all three cases. By doing one LEAPS option ATM you brought in more money. By tailoring the strikes to fit your particular combination (pun very deliberate) of fear and greed you were able to obtain the desired results.

These three choices could serve as examples *par excellence* of our basic theses. First, choose the LEAPS strategy that corresponds to your basic expectation on the stock *and* your attitude toward risk. (Note that there is a lot more to bullish strategies than just Call buying.) Then fine-tune within the chosen technique to accomplish the optimal mix between risk and reward.

Whether you use this particular variation or others in either LEAPS covered straddle writing or LEAPS covered combination writing, you will find that you have achieved an objective that investors are always struggling to accomplish. You will have bought low and/or sold high! Some of that is due to the nature of the technique, and some to the fact that you are doing it with LEAPS.

A Final Note

The LEAPS money generator described in the previous chapter can be used here as well. In fact, its structure is identical to the previous one, except for the second step, which would be a combination rather than a straddle.

SUMMARY

Covered combination writing, like its cousin covered straddle writing, is a complex strategy suitable for those who are quite bullish and sophisticated. Using the strategy with LEAPS overcomes some of its conventional defects and, with a little tinkering, can lead to a good balance between safety and profit.

CHAPTER 15
PROTECTIVE LEAPS PUTS

They say the first instinct is to protect oneself.

STRATEGY	LEAPS Protective Puts
OUTLOOK	Bullish, but nervous
ADVANTAGES	Guarantees profit; assures sound sleep
DRAWBACKS	Less than maximum possible profit
DEGREE OF RISK	Extraordinarily small

What is a protective Put? For the answer, let's look at Larry Luck who bought a stock at 30 and three months later finds it at 60 (we should all be so lucky). Larry knows there are many things he can do with options to enhance/protect his position. We will look at only one here: the **Protective Put.**

Larry buys a 60-strike Put for $400 and relaxes, comfortable in the knowledge that no matter how far the stock might retreat, he has locked in a guaranteed price of 56—a 26-point profit—during the life of the Put. We said: "a guaranteed price of 56" above. In fact, we should have said: "a guaranteed price of at *least* 56." If the stock rises substantially after the Put purchase, an even greater profit can ensue.

Examples
At expiration the stock is @ 52⅝. Larry exercises the Put, selling the stock @ 60. His profit is 60 sale less 30 stock cost less 4 Put cost or 26. Alternatively, at expiration the stock is 65⅞. The Put has gone to zero. Larry sells the stock and makes 31⅞ (65⅞ less 30 less 4).

A gentle note to the reader:
We must make a comment here. Note the phrase above: "The Put has gone to zero." How often have you heard critics of options declaim about "losing all the money in options"? Well, here's a case

where that happened and the option's owner is delighted! Obviously, our comment is not restricted to this one strategy.

That is the basic idea, and there are many enhancements and variations. Some involve other options, like buying the Put and selling a Call (See Chapter 32 on LEAPS fences). But here we will view only the protective Put. Larry has a choice over which protective Put to buy. There is the usual trade-off between less dollar cost and greater protection. If we choose a lower strike, it costs less but gives a lower "out" price, that is, less overall profit if the stock goes down.

Examples
Stock cost 30
Stock price 60

55-strike Put @ 2	Out price 53	Minimum profit 23
60-strike Put @ 4	Out price 56	Minimum profit 26
65-strike Put @ 7	Out price 58	Minimum profit 28

As we keep on saying, the choice of option is a function of the interplay within yourself between fear and greed. Specifically, you want to look at the amount of accumulated profit, your fears about the stock's decline, and your worry about missing out on further profits. There is also a trade-off in time. The longer the life of the Put, the longer the position can be protected, but the more that protection will cost. Perhaps it will cost so much that it will cut significantly into the accumulated profits.

Example
2-month 60-strike Put @ 3
3-month 60-strike Put @ 4
6-month 60-strike Put @ 6
8-month 60-strike Put @ 7½

At this point Mr. Skeptic (we've warned you about him) shows up and says something like: "Who the hell needs these crazy options? I can do the same things without them. You bought stock at 30 and now its 60; sell out the damned stock and be glad you did it. You don't need to spend any more money on those stupid @#*@% options!"

Wow! What can we say? Well, we can say, first of all, that selling out stock to nail down a profit is often a very good idea. However, it's also often a very bad idea. If you sold Microsoft after it had first doubled, you would have missed out on a great success story (and a lot of money). Wal-Mart has had an even more spectacular success story. If you bought just 100 shares when it first went public, you would now—nine 2/for/1 splits later—have 51,200 shares!

Of course, not all stocks sport records like these. The problem is that not all of us are as smart as Mr. Skeptic. We don't know which of our good stocks will turn out to be the great ones over time. Nor do we know whether the downturn that the stock, the industry, or the overall market, is in, will take our stock all the way down or if it's just "an intermediate correction." In brief, there is much uncertainty in the market and the world. Some may make money in the face of this uncertainty by stubbornly championing "buy and hold." But the marketplace is littered with the corpses of those who always "knew better" and hung on waiting for the rebound they "knew" must come. The protective Put solves (at a cost) those problems. It is especially good for the stock whose owner fervently feels "it will come back."

Indeed, it may come back and even go substantially higher. For this outlook our favorite protective Put is the ITM. Here the bulk of the profit is guaranteed and sleep is assured. We do not advocate a very DIM Put, but merely one that is ITM.

Once we focus on the ITM Put, we see the familiar pricing. The further months out at the same strike (if they exist) do not cost substantially more than the nearer ones. Aha! Yes, enter the LEAPS ITM Put! Here you can buy protection cheaply (low time value premium over the intrinsic value) and for a very long time.

Table
XYZ @ 60

2-month	65-strike Put	@ 6
3-month	65-strike Put	@ 6¼
6-month	65-strike Put	@ 7
8-month	65-strike Put	@ 7½
18-month	65-strike LEAPS Put	@ 9¾

This is tailor-made for the view described above. That is, someone who really believes that the stock will weather any downleg and come back with a vengeance over time. If it does, s/he can make more money. Once the stock goes above the Put strike, more money can be gained.

Example

We saw that process in the very first (non-LEAPS) illustration. The general concept is easily grasped. If the stock ends above the Put strike, the stock will be sold at the market rather than through exercise, which would generate only the strike.

Our exposition is interrupted by the arrival of Mr. Smart Alec. "You can't fool me," he shouts. "You talk about an impending downleg, but I know the stock is already in a downmove. Otherwise there wouldn't even be such an ITM Put!"

Well, as has been said before, "A little learning is a dangerous thing." Mr. Smart Alec might be right with ordinary options, but he is way off base with LEAPS. The former have the next higher strike created when the highest existing one is touched. For the latter a new strike is also created, but it is designed to be about 20 to 25 percent OTM. That is, it will be that percentage *above* the stock price. That will lead to OTM Calls, but ITM Puts.

Example

XYZ has a 52-week range of 58 to 28. It has a 60-strike trading for both options and LEAPS. When it reaches 60, the 65 conventional and the 75 LEAPS (in each case, both Puts and Calls) are brought into being.

Suppose that the owner is dead wrong and the stock does not come back, let alone rise still further. We say, "So what." Others would be sorry, but s/he has no problem. S/he did tie up money for a time (and had the hidden cost of giving up risk-free return on a portion of capital), but there was well-nigh perfect protection—upside potential and no sleepless nights.

Here comes Mr. Smart Alec's cousin, Mr. Wiseacre, and he's about to spout a mouthful! "Hey, lay off with that option stuff. You're just trying to get more commissions. You don't need options to lock in a profit. Just pick your point and put in a stop-loss order. That's all there is to it!"

Mr. Wiseacre isn't very wise, and he's all wet. He has the name wrong; it should be a *stop order,* and there's a lot more to it than that. A stop order is an order placed below the market price of the stock (for a long position) and left on the specialist's book. If the stock reaches the price specified in the order (10 percent down is frequently used), the stop order becomes an order to sell the stock at the market (at the then prevailing best bid).

Example
With XYZ @ 60, an order is entered that reads: GTC (Good Till Canceled) Sell 100 XYZ @ 54 STOP [54 is 10 percent below 60].

As XYZ fluctuates, nothing happens unless and until it sells at 54. The order then is changed to: Sell 100 XYZ @ market. Well, what's wrong with that? It would give you an "out" price of 54, which is of the same magnitude as 53, 56, and 58 in our first non-LEAPS example. There's a lot wrong with it. First, if you ever do sell the stock higher up, you should surely remember to cancel the stop order or you may be in for a very unpleasant shock. Second, there is no guarantee of your getting 54 (or any other number you specified). The order became a *market* order and might be filled at 53¾, 53½, or even less. That's not just a quibble. If the stock broke sharply to reach 54, there might be a lack of bids below that level. It is no exaggeration to say that orders like that have been filled at *substantially* lower prices at times of market turmoil.

Next, there might be more than your stop order at 54. That could result in a large supply of stock suddenly offered for sale at the market. Further, the stock might reach 54 and stop trading because of bad news. We don't want to frighten you, but we have seen many such cases as a trading halt at 54 and a reopening at 49!

Less frightening, but also disturbing is another possibility. The stock, under selling pressure, is ground down to just above 54. Then somebody sells 100 shares at that price and touches off your stop order. You are sold out @ 53⅞ and the stock then turns and rises for the next two weeks, finally reaching 60 again. There are even the (possibly) paranoid theorists who think that such occurrences are not purely random events.

Why have we gone on at such length and with such fervor in response to Mr. Wiseacre? Because he's as wrong as can be. When you purchase a protective Put, *you* control the price at which the stock will be sold. And *you* control when it will be sold. Neither random events nor Machiavellian conspirators can do anything to you. Once again, the option critics not only don't know what they're talking about; they have it 180 degrees backwards.

We must mention that the LEAPS protective Put, especially the ITM variety, is not for all. Some will feel better with an outright stock sale, but there are other LEAPS choices. Those who prefer getting dollars to paying them, could write a LEAPS Call. Those who want the Put protection, but don't like the price, could build a "fence." Those who don't want to abandon upside potential but want most of their capital freed, could try "replacement therapy." Really sophisticated traders could employ Affirmative Action. All of these LEAPS strategies are covered in detail in other chapters. What is notable and wonderful is that there are LEAPS techniques to match the expectations and fears of different types of investors. This applies not only at the onset of a stock position, but afterward as well.

Taxes

If you own stock and buy a Put (LEAPS or otherwise), there will probably be a tax impingement. We will deal with this in the separate chapter on taxes (Chapter 42).

SUMMARY

The protective Put strategy gives the lie to those who think of options as merely speculation, if not gambling. It allows an investor to buy "insurance" for his appreciated stock. It also allows retaining what might be a stellar performer while sleeping comfortably. ITM LEAPS Puts are the least expensive way of doing this.

CHAPTER 16
LEAPS MARRIED PUTS

It is better to marry than to burn.

STRATEGY   LEAPS Married Puts
OUTLOOK   Bullish, but wary
ADVANTAGES   Limits loss; assures sound sleep
DRAWBACKS   Increases break-even point
DEGREE OF RISK   Very small

The married Put is a strategic maneuver that takes its name from an old Internal Revenue Service ruling. At that time someone who had owned stock for less than the requisite time interval to acquire long-term status, and purchased a Put, had tax consequences. The IRS said that the position was not at risk, and their ruling stopped the holding period on the stock.

Example
Linda Luck buys stock at 30 and 5 months later finds it at 60. She did this when the long-term holding period was defined as over six months. If she could hold on for another month and a day, she would pay less in taxes on the profit. But the profit might not be so great because the stock might decline during that time. What to do? Linda, a smart woman, buys a two-month Put to tide her over the interval. Enter the tax meanies who say that her holding period has stopped, dead in its tracks, and will not resume until the Put is gone. There was an exception to this ruling: If you bought both stock and Put on the same day and identified them as "married" to each other, there would be no interruption to the holding period.

Example
When Linda bought her stock at 30, she bought a seven-month Put on it at the same time. She had the legend "versus XYZ

stock bought at 30 on Jan 13." placed on her stock confirmation. "To be delivered on exercise of Put bought Jan 13" was also marked on the stock confirmation. When the Put expired, she sold the stock at 55⅝.

Caveat

This chapter is designed to show you the profit potential and the protection afforded by LEAPS married Puts, but all trades like these can have considerable impingement from tax laws. We are not tax experts. These laws and rulings change as do judicial interpretations of them. Further, they will impact different people in different ways and even the same person in different ways at different times and with different positions. Nobody should enter into any such trading without individual, competent tax advice. For most people now, a long-term holding status is not that important. Still, the married Put does have a great value even if all tax consequences are removed. The double holding of stock and Put on that stock means a guaranteed maximum risk. No matter how far the stock might fall, there is a limit to losses.

Example
ZYX bought @ 60
ZYX 6-month 60-strike Put bought @ 5 (same day and identified)

Even if we envision the unimaginable—the stock falls to *zero!* —there would be no loss beyond the $500. So long as the Put was still in existence, the stock could be sold @ 60. Thus the maximum possible loss would be 5 points or 7.7 percent of invested dollars.

What about **LEAPS Married Puts?** The positive aspect here is that you can buy a very long-life Put and thus limit stock losses for a great deal of time. Also, when buying conventional Puts, there can be a problem when they expire. Sometimes protection during that time period is all that is desired, but at other times more may be needed. That would imply purchasing a new Put or "rolling" the old Put into a new one. That means more commissions, raising the cost of protection. With LEAPS, one purchase is usually all that is needed, but there is a negative to the transaction. When you buy a married Put, the dollar cost must be made up to attain profits on the stock position.

Example

ZYX bought @ 60

ZYX 6-month 60-strike bought @ 5 (same day and identified)

If you held on until the Put expired and then sold the stock @ 64, you would lose money overall. Your total investment was 65 (stock 60 + Put 5).

The cost of the LEAPS Put, while very low in percentage terms per time unit, can still be a comparatively large dollar amount. There are several answers to this problem.

The technique may work best with very volatile stocks. That is because they are the most risky on the downside. Further, especially with LEAPS, they can move enormously up as well as down. Thus the married Put can work out well on either side.

Example

Buy Consolidated Computerized BioTech Systems (CCBTS) @ 60

Buy 18-month CCBTS 60 LEAPS Put @ 9 (with ID)

1. Three months after the double purchase, Amalgamated SuperComputerized HyperBioTech (ASCHB) wins a patent suit against CCBTS. The latter plummets to 20. Stock owners lose two-thirds of their money overnight and vow never to do it again. You lose 9 points or 13 percent. That's nothing to write home about, but the people who didn't buy the LEAPS Put aren't writing anywhere.

2. It goes the other way. CCBTS wins the infringed patent suit versus ASCHB and the former skyrockets to 90. Jubilant stockholders cash in and make 50 percent profit. Not you. You also sell out @ 90 and check the LEAPS Put quote. It's down to 2. You sell it out there. You lost 7 on the LEAPS Put, made 30 on the stock, netting 23. (The possible tax consequences of trades like these are ana-

lyzed in Chapter 42 on taxes.) Your percentage profit is "only" 33.3 ($^{23}/_{69}$), but you are quite content with it when you think of possibility #1.

A gentle note to the discerning reader:
You may have by now noticed that we always say "the LEAPS Put." There is a reason for this and our next scenario will show it.

3. As above, CCBTS beats ASCHB, you sell out @ 90, but you realize that the LEAPS Put still has 14 months to go. It's 30 points OTM now, but a lot might happen in 14 months, especially with a stock like this. You mentally write it all off and calculate your profit as only 21 points. CCBTS drifts downward over the next year, reaching the low 70s. Then Conglomeratized HyperComputerized Magnified BioTech (CHCMB) announces a revolutionary new discovery rendering all similar methods totally obsolete. CCBTS collapses to 40 and you cash in your LEAPS Put for 22 (20 points intrinsic value plus the 2 points time value the hungry buyers are anxious to pay). You decide to write home and tell everybody about LEAPS, especially married Puts.

These examples are not mere fabrications. They are exaggerations made to prove a point. They come from real data, and they show the twin virtues of the married Put. You can be protected from the outset against a terrible loss, and you are not barred from further profits despite the cost of the LEAPS Puts.

Even without an excessively volatile stock, the time of LEAPS life can allow a great appreciation for the stock, thus allowing a satisfactory profit after allowing for the LEAPS Put's cost.

Example
Buy Prosaic Patterns @ 60
Buy 18-month Prosaic Patterns 60 LEAPS Put @ 7 (with ID)

The stock just creeps slowly upward. It never makes any spectacular moves, and it frequently consolidates the gains it has made. Still a year and a half later, it is @ 87 where you sell it. The LEAPS Puts has gone to zero (another "worthless" option!) and you net 20 points. No fireworks as in the previous examples. Just a sweet little profit you were able to make without ever worrying about a large loss.

Further, you may decide after a while that you no longer want the protection of the LEAPS Put. You could sell it out, retain the stock, either alone or with some other strategy, e.g., covered Call writing (check Chapter 42 on taxes for implications). If you do sell out the LEAPS Put, you will find another LEAPS advantage. There has been less lost than would have been the case if the Put were a conventional one. This comparison can be complex. It depends on how much time has passed, how much time is left, and what the stock has done. Still the general principle does hold.

Example

Buy Prosaic Patterns @ 60
Buy 18-month Prosaic Patterns 60 LEAPS Put @ 7 (with ID)

Six months after you take on this double position, their respective prices are 72 and 5. You decide that the "insurance" part is no longer necessary and you sell out the LEAPS Put. It has lost ⅖ or 28 percent of its cost, but to you the significant description of the change is: $200 loss (with $1,200 unrealized stock profit). Are you being brave or foolhardy in doing this? We don't know. It's a decision you make, based upon your analysis of the situation. It is certainly not one we would always rule out. We comment that you might now want to hedge in a different way, say, by writing an OTM LEAPS Call. There are many other possible alternatives. We want to focus not on an alternative strategy, but on a trading technique.

That is to be aware of the desirability of avoiding all-or-none thinking. If you were long 1,000 shares and 10 Puts, and the stock appreciated greatly in a relatively short time, you might consider selling out *part* of the Put position. After that, if and when the stock attained some predetermined level, you could discard more of the Puts. If the stock failed to perform as expected, you would still own some LEAPS Puts that would rise while the stock fell.

The dividend paid by the stock can be an important factor here. Let us revert to the conventional Put and examine the impact of a high dividend.

Example
ZYX bought @ 60
ZYX 6-month 60-strike Put bought @ 5 (with ID)

ZYX pays $5.00 per share in annual dividends (current dividend yield 8.3 percent). If it goes ex dividend twice during the six months (a normal occurrence), you will be entitled to collect $2.50 per share. In dollars, that means that you paid $500 for the Put, but got $250 in dividends. Thus we see that in extreme cases the dividend can be said to pay for the Put.

Example
ZXY bought @ 40
ZXY 6-month 40-strike Put bought @ 3 (with ID)

ZXY pays $4.00 in annual dividends (current dividend yield 10.0 percent). With a combination of luck and careful timing, you buy ZXY just before it goes ex dividend. You have seen that you will collect *three* dividends during the six-month period (not usual, but it does happen). The total of these—$300—is equal to the Put's cost. In this example we see that if we change our viewpoint from "yield is good" to "protection is better" we can get a position with zero risk! If we have titled our technique *married Puts,* we might label this variation: *better to marry rich!* Actually, the risk is not really zero: The dividend might be cut or even omitted. Even then, the married Put keeps the risk substantially lower than would have been the case without it.

Example
Same example as above with the same timing. After one dividend, the company finds itself in a cash squeeze and eliminates the dividend. Disappointed stockholders sell in droves, sending the price down to 29. Others (who bought the stock at about the same time you did) lose $1,000 per 100 shares, You lose only $200 ($300 Put cost less one $100 dividend).

Now let's return to LEAPS. Of the 127 LEAPS currently trading, all but 22 pay some dividend, and 42 of them yield 3 percent or more.

SUMMARY

The married Put is simply the protective Put acquired initially with the stock rather than afterward. This technique enables investors to take positions they might otherwise find too risky. The lower cost per time unit of LEAPS is an added positive. There are complicated variations (which could have tax implications) on keeping one, the other, or both, through the life of the LEAPS Put. If you are interested in LEAPS married Puts, we urge you to read Chapter 42 on taxes before spending any money. LEAPS married Puts limit losses, but allow profits in both directions.

CHAPTER 17
BULL SPREADS WITH LEAPS CALLS

Masters, spread yourselves.

STRATEGY	Bullish LEAPS Call Spreads
OUTLOOK	Moderately bullish
ADVANTAGES	Cost reduction; limited dollar risk
DRAWBACKS	Limited profit
DEGREE OF RISK	Moderate

First, we define **spread.** A spread consists of buying and writing equal amounts of the same type (Puts or Calls) of options on the same underlying with (in general) the same expiration.

Examples
Buy   5 3-month 30-strike XYZ Calls
Write   5 3-month 40-strike XYZ Calls
                          or
Buy   10 4-month 95-strike ZYX Calls
Write 10 4-month 85-strike ZYX Calls

The first spread, and one of those most frequently used, is the **Bull Call Spread.** It is also known as the **bullish Call spread.** In addition to the definition, it has one other distinguishing characteristic. The strike on the buy side is lower than the strike on the sell side.

Examples
The first example above is a bull Call spread; the second is not. What is the purpose/motivation for doing a bull Call spread? First of all, it reduces costs. Because you are writing a Call as well as buying one, your outlay is reduced.

Example

Buy   5 3-month 60-strike XYZ Calls @ 4   Total $2,000
Write 5 3-month 65-strike XYZ Calls @ 2   Total $1,000
Net investment cost $1,000

If you had just bought the Call, you would have spent twice as much as the spread cost. This has the effect of reducing the risk as well.

Example

Buy   5 3-month 60-strike XYZ Calls @ 4   Total $2,000
Write 5 3-month 65-strike XYZ Calls @ 2   Total $1,000
Net investment cost $1,000

If the stock ends under 60 (without any previous exercises or assignments) you will lose all of the $1,000. If you had done just the buy side, you would have lost twice as much. We can generalize the process we just saw to calculate the theoretical break-even (B/E) point (at expiration) for a bull Call spread. It is simply the net debit added to the lower strike.

Example

Buy   5 3-month 60-strike XYZ Calls @ 4
Write 5 3-month 65-strike XYZ Calls @ 2

The net debit on this spread is 2 (4 spent less 2 received). Break-even point is 60 strike plus 2 debit = 62. As a check, look at the expiration stock price of 62. The written Calls will not be assigned (nobody would demand stock from you @ 65 if it's selling @ 62). You sell out your long Calls for 2 (their intrinsic value) and recover your debit, thus breaking even. We also can calculate the maximum profit than can accrue in this type of spread. It is the separation between the strikes (upper minus lower) less the initial cost.

Example

Buy   5 3-month 60-strike XYZ Calls @ 4
Write 5 3-month 65-strike XYZ Calls @ 2
Strike separation (65–60) is 5. Cost is 2. Maximum profit = 3.

It is important to note that the spread can never be worth more than this. Pick a price for the stock well above the upper strike. Say, for example, 36 points higher. You will be assigned on the upper strike, and you will exercise at the lower strike, thus realizing the strike differential (separation).

Example
Buy   5 3-month 30-strike XYZ Calls
Write 5 3-month 40-strike XYZ Calls

If the stock ends at 76, someone will demand stock from you @ 40 (that is, you will be assigned on this written Call). You in turn, will demand stock from somebody at 30 (you exercise your long Call).

Note that if the price were 48 points higher (or any other number), exactly the same thing would happen. This limited profit is one of the essential differences between buying Calls and bullish Call spreads. Now for the good news. All that has to happen for you to realize that maximum at expiration is for the stock to end up at the upper strike or higher. Notice that we calculated the maximum money that can come out of the spread. The maximum profit would be that amount less the original debit incurred in buying the spread.

A bullish Call spread then falls into the category of lowered costs and lower maximum profit potential, as compared with an outright Call purchase. Bullish Call spreads have a great similarity to covered Call writing. You could think of the long Call component of the spread with its lower strike price as similar to the long stock in the covered Call. Indeed, if that long Call is a DIM, it takes on almost all of the attributes of the long stock (except for any dividends from the stock during the option's life).

Example
Buy   500 XYZ @ 40
Write   5 XYZ 3-month 45-strike Calls
                    or
Buy   5 3-month 30-strike XYZ Calls
Write   5 3-month 45-strike XYZ Calls

Despite the great similarity, the spread's cost is substantially lower.

Example

In the previous example the stock is at 40; 500 shares would cost $20,000. The 30-strike Calls might cost 13; 5 Calls would cost $6,500. There is a little more to say on this aspect. The lowered cost of the bull Call spread (as opposed to the similar covered Call writing stance) gave you more leverage, but leverage always cuts two ways. People who buy stock on margin have more leverage on the upside, but they also lose more money on the downside. The same is true here. If the stock declines instead of rising, you will lose more money with the spread than with the covered Call write. That's even true with the DIM Call. It comes about because of the time value component.

Example

Buy   500 XYZ @ 40
Write   5 XYZ 3-month 45-strike Calls
or
Buy   5 3-month 30-strike XYZ Calls
Write   5 3-month 45-strike XYZ Calls

If the stock ends @ 35, you will lose 5 points per hundred long shares. In the spread, you would probably lose 8 points per long call. The Call would sell for only its intrinsic value at expiration, and you paid a three-point time value when you bought it. We didn't consider the money inflow from the written Call in either case because it was the same for both situations. The moral is to look for an even deeper ITM Call, so that it will have less time value. Here we are again in a trade-off: paying more money to avoid more risk. But it would still be less money than the Call write (not to mention an outright stock purchase).

We just explored the dual nature of leverage. It is something to be very careful with. At the risk of being repetitive, we must now make our usual warning about size. Just because the bullish Call spread mimics the covered Call write, but at a fraction of the initial cost, does *not* mean that you should multiply the number of spreads you will do. Limit the number of spreads to correspond to the number of Calls in the covered write. And again, we repeat our suggestion that the "excess money" can be used to buy other securities or to do more spreads diversifying within or across stock sectors. No example is needed here. The technique is exactly as we described it in the buying Calls and covered Call writing chapters (Chapters 10 and 11, respectively).

Whether you are doing a small, or a large number of spreads, the usual comments about risk attitudes are applicable. That is, one can approach the strategy with a viewpoint that is aggressive, moderate, or conservative. Like its covered Call cousin, the bull spread is conservative when the lower strike is in the money. That corresponds to writing an ITM Call against stock. Similarly, using OTM Calls is more aggressive in both strategies. These remarks apply, however, more to conventional Calls than to LEAPS. Just as we saw that writing an OTM LEAPS Call against stock would make sense because of the long time involved, the same is true of bull Call spreads.

Example
With XYZ @ 40
Buy   5 LEAPS 40-strike XYZ Calls
Write 5 LEAPS 50-strike XYZ Calls

There are three other ways to use bull Call spreads with LEAPS. The first is to buy a DIM Call and write a FOM Call. The DIM Call corresponds to long stock.

Example
With XYZ @ 40
Buy   5 LEAPS 30-strike XYZ Calls
Write 5 LEAPS 50-strike XYZ Calls

The second strategy is to extend the concept of *much time to appreciate*. Here we have two different possibilities. We can buy an ITM and write an OTM, but select strikes that are fairly far apart.

Example
With XYZ @ 40
Buy   5 LEAPS 35-strike XYZ Calls
Write 5 LEAPS 60-strike XYZ Calls

Doing this with options that had a shorter lifetime would usually deserve the appellation *foolhardy*. Here it is aggressive but not foolish. Because of the fact that we bought an ITM and got a respectable dollar premium on the OTM, we have a reasonable chance at a hefty appreciation on a lower-risk, lower dollar investment. Our second choice would be to both buy and write OTM calls.

Example
With XYZ @ 40
Buy   5 LEAPS 45-strike XYZ Calls
Write 5 LEAPS 60-strike XYZ Calls

This last example is much more aggressive than the previous ones, but produces much higher leverage because of the still lower funds committed.

> *A gentle note to the reader:*
> *The current rule, according to the exchanges and the Federal Reserve Board is that all spreads must go in a margin account. Don't panic. This would not mean that you are buying on margin. It would not mean that you are borrowing funds, that you have a debit balance, or that you will pay margin interest. Just be sure you have a margin account for this purpose.*

We must now make explicit what has been tacit. The cost of the bullish Call spread—no matter whether one or both components are OTM, ATM, or ITM—is simply the difference in premiums (excluding commissions). This highlights the attractiveness of the strategy. If you pay 10 and might get back 20, its limited dollar return becomes much more engaging when viewed as a percentage return. This leads to a rule-of-thumb. If you choose to buy a bull Call spread with an OTM component, you should not spend more than half the strike differential as net payment for the spread.

Example
With XYZ @ 40
Buy   5 LEAPS 30-strike XYZ Calls
Write 5 LEAPS 50-strike XYZ Calls

Whether or not you should do this type of spread is your decision to make. All we say here is that we don't think you should pay more than 10 points (one-half of 50 less 30) for it. In most of our strategy exegeses we look at results at expiration. Here we also want to look at the possibility of closing out the spread prior to expiration. There are several reasons why you might want to do this. First, the stock might have reached a point well above the upper strike. If this happens the spread will not necessarily have achieved its maximum potential.

Example
With   XYZ @ 105 and 12 months to go
Long   LEAPS 80-strike XYZ Calls @ 30
Written LEAPS 100-strike XYZ Calls @ 17
Spread value   13

Whatever you paid for this spread, you might be somewhat disappointed. You gauged the stock's move very well and you presumably have a profit, but the naive view is that, with the stock above the upper strike, the spread should be worth more. Is this a prototypical example? Just how much can we expect the spread to discount its whole potential after the stock rises to a suitable level? Unfortunately there is no single answer to this question. But there is a general rule: The higher the stock price, the closer the spread will sell to maximum.

Example
With   XYZ @ 115 and 6 months to go
Long   LEAPS 80-strike XYZ Calls @ 36
Written LEAPS 100-strike XYZ Calls @ 19
Spread value   17

But this is not the only determinant. The length of time remaining until expiration and the level of interest rates prevailing will both exert strong pressures on the premiums. This is easy to see if we just consider how things would look to a buyer of your spread. S/he would run the risk of a decline in price. And the longer the time left, the greater this risk would be. Also, the higher the level of interest rates, the more s/he would be ceding by holding the spread rather than investing the money at the risk-free rate.

This leads to a problem. For any given set of circumstances—amount in the money, time remaining, and interest rate levels—should you hold on to the end or cash in then and there? In almost all of our explications, we have preferred the conceptual overview to the complicated mathematical analysis. In this case we have to ask you to do some of both. You still have to base your decision on your expectation for the stock. But even if you think the stock will stay up, you also have to decide whether it will be worth it for you to stay with the position.

Example

The last example will do here. With six months to go, you could realize all but 3 points of the spread's maximum 20 point potential. Should you cash in here or hang on for the whole ride?

We hope you know the answer because we don't. Actually, we should say, "We hope you can decide what the answer is." You may be able to intuit it, but most would prefer at least a little analysis. We are not being flip when we deny knowledge here; we don't know how valuable either time or money are to you at this point. It is easy to find arguments for each side. But we do not know where interest rates are or what alternate investments are available. But since you will know all these things, it shouldn't be too difficult to decipher. Our emphasis is on the possibility. Too many have made the tacit assumption of retention as automatic.

This leads us to the second reason for closing a LEAPS bull Call spread position before expiration. Even if the stock has not gone above the upper strike, you might want to do that. That would be the case if you felt strongly that you had a better use for the dollars supporting the position. No, we are not suggesting short-term trading with LEAPS—bull spreads or otherwise. But we live with flux; the world changes as do stock prices, interest rates, and investment opportunities. There is nothing wrong with changing your mind as to where and how you want your investment dollars deployed. If after careful study you think this a desirable course of action, we say: Go for it!

So far, we have looked at favorable stock price movements. Yes, a stock you pick for a rise can instead decline. That's not the end of the world, especially if you are using LEAPS. With conventional options, this could decimate your investment. Just as we indicated above, you can change your mind. If the stock takes a sufficient fall, maybe you should close the position. How much is sufficient? That's a very easy question, but only you know the answer. As always, it depends on how you view the stock. What would you have done if you had bought the stock outright instead of using LEAPS? Would you have sold it when it got to the level you are now considering? If so, there is no doubt about what to do with the spread. Close it at once. But, says the troublemaker, you will lose money doing that. Of course you will, just as you would have lost money on the stock investment and subsequent sale when it violated one of your guidelines.

There is more to say on this subject, but we will say it at length in Chapter 40 on LEAPS repair. For now we want you to remember that LEAPS are securities traded on exchanges, and that you are no more wedded to a LEAPS bull Call spread (or any other LEAPS investment) than you would be to the stock involved.

SUMMARY

Bull Call spreads reduce cost and limit profit. That limitation can still represent a high percentage return, but you must take care on leverage and even more so on size. Using bullish Call spreads with LEAPS offers many attractive opportunities and fits some investors' specific outlooks very nicely.

CHAPTER 18
BULL SPREADS WITH LEAPS PUTS

Put money in thy purse.

STRATEGY	Bullish LEAPS Put Spreads
OUTLOOK	Moderately bullish
ADVANTAGES	Get money; limited dollar risk
DRAWBACKS	Limited profit
DEGREE OF RISK	Moderate

We have just looked at bullish spreads using Calls. Can we do them with Puts? And there's a better question: Why would we want to do them with Puts? There is no doubt that some find **Bull Put Spreads** (also known as **Bullish**) preferable to their Call cousins. That is because the former can be done for a net credit while the latter incur a debit. Before we look at examples that illustrate this point, we must mention a common misconception. In the bull Call spread, we are long the lower strike and write the higher. It is the same way for the bull Put spread. No, that is not a misprint. Let's go to specifics.

Examples
Buy   5 YZX 3-month 50-strike Calls @ 9
Write 5 YZX 3-month 60-strike Calls @ 3
or
Buy   5 YZX 3-month 50-strike Puts @ 2
Write 5 YZX 3-month 60-strike Puts @ 6

Let's mentally move the stock, first way up and then way down, for each position.

1. Stock ends @ 66. As we saw in the previous chapter, the Call spread becomes worth its maximum value. For the

Put spread, both elements will become worthless. You will get to keep the 4 points generated at inception (bought for 2, sold for 6).

2. Stock ends @ 44. Here both legs of the Call spread go to zero, and you lose all. With the Put spread, you are assigned at 60 (you have to buy the stock there), and you exercise your 50 Put. (You make somebody else buy it there.) You still keep the aforementioned 4, but you *lose* the strike differential this time. Overall, you have a loss.

In brief, for each spread when the stock moved up (enough), you earned a profit. When it went down (enough), you suffered a loss.

A gentle note to the reader:
In the second example, in the Call spread, both options went to zero. "You lost it all, the options expired worthless," shout the options decryers. But they are strangely silent when it comes to the Put spread in the first example. There, as we just saw, the maximum profit is produced when "both elements become worthless." This is another example of delight, not displeasure at such occurrences.

Now that we have got that straight, let's look at the credit/debit difference.

Examples
Buy   5 YZX 3-month 50-strike Calls @ 9
Write 5 YZX 3-month 60-strike Calls @ 3
or
Buy   5 YZX 3-month 50-strike Puts @ 2
Write 5 YZX 3-month 60-strike Puts @ 6

What is the basic difference between these two types of spreads? In each the maximum profit occurs when the stock is above the upper strike at expiration. The Call spread becomes worth the strike differential. For the Put spread, both sides become worthless and you keep the original credit.

Now we see why some prefer the Put spread. It is because of the credit generated. The risk/reward profiles seem similar, but you start off getting money in one case and paying it in the other. Sounds good, but we think that it's not usually such a good idea. When you do the Call spread, you are buying a Call with a comparatively low time value and writing one with more. In fact, if you buy a DIM Call, the time value may be only a nominal amount. And if the written leg is an OTM Call, all of its premium will be composed of time value. For the Put spread, exactly the opposite is true. You are buying more time value and writing less. If we go back to the exposition at the beginning of the book, we see that we can express this thought in terms of borrowing money. You are borrowing more and lending less with the Put spread. You are also lending more and borrowing less with the Call version.

While starting with a credit instead of a debit may be beguiling, it is not so simple. As we know all too well, you don't get something for nothing. Nevertheless, this technique might fit for some. It may appeal to them as an abstract principle or it may be attractive because they could use the credit. That brings us to the familiar questions. Which expiration and which strikes? As always, the strategy can take a form that is conservative, moderate, or aggressive. For the bullish Put spread, those viewpoints would usually correspond to: both sides ITM, one side ITM and one side OTM, and both sides OTM, respectively.

When we looked at these spreads using Calls, the cost was simple: Pay the difference between the two premiums. It is not so simple here. The rule for Bullish spreads with Puts is: Post as collateral the strike differential less the credit received (see Chapter 9 on margin).

Example
Buy   5 YZX 3-month 50-strike Puts @ 2
Write 5 YZX 3-month 60-strike Puts @ 6
The differential is 10 (60–50). You must post that amount per spread, but the 4 points you received on each (6–2) can go toward it. While that posting is the *initial* requirement, it must be maintained through the life of the spread.

We already know the maximum profit that can come from this technique. It is the credit received when the spread was done. In order to realize that maximum, the stock must end above the upper strike. In the same way as with the Call spread, it will not matter how far above. If it is any number of points above the upper strike, neither the long Put nor the written Put will be exercised. You will keep the entire credit originally received. The return on that possible maximum is simply that credit divided by the initial collateral requirement.

Example
Buy   5 YZX 3-month 50-strike Puts @ 2
Write 5 YZX 3-month 60-strike Puts @ 6
Collateral (out-of-pocket) per spread $600 (10-[6–2])
Maximum profit return 400/600 = 66.7 percent

What will happen if the stock goes the other way? Will all the money be lost? Not necessarily. We have to inspect two different cases.

Examples
First, the stock ends below 60, but at or above 50. Here you will be assigned (buy the stock @ 60) and sell it out. The result will depend on just what price you get when you do sell the stock. The lower the price, the greater the loss. Second, the stock ends below 50. You will be assigned, as above, but you will also exercise your long Put (selling the stock @ 50). Thus it does not matter in this strategy how far below 50 the stock falls; your loss is limited to the strike differential (you buy at 60 and sell at 50, losing 10).

Even if the stock does end under the lower strike, all might not be lost. You start the trade with a credit. This leads us to the derivation for the maximum loss. If the stock ends under the lower strike, both Puts will come into play. In a manner analogous to the Call spread, it will not matter how far below. This loss will be reduced by the original credit. So the maximum possible loss is the strike differential, less the credit received—the same as the posted initial collateral requirement.

Example

The stock ends at 47. You lose 10 points, but you started with a credit of 4, so your net loss is only 6. Where does all this fit with LEAPS? As we have seen for all the previous strategies, the essential LEAPS difference—long life—operates here as well. If you are right in stock selection, this gives the stock more time to move up and away from the strikes. Let's look at some possibilities:

XYZ @ 55. No stock position. All the LEAPS Puts are 1½ years out.

Buy the 40 Put @ 2. Write the 50 Put @ 5. Credit 3. Both OTM

or

Buy the 50 Put @ 5. Write the 60 Put @ 11. Credit 6. 1 OTM, 1 ITM

or

Buy the 60 Put @ 11. Write the 70 Put @ 19. Credit 8. Both ITM.

These examples exhibit the usual trade-offs. The highest credit (and the lowest collateral) come with both sides ITM. But this is also the highest risk, for the stock has to move up much more for you to avoid a loss and then to make a profit and finally to make the maximum profit. In the last example, you would need a 27 percent move (at expiration) to realize the maximum. If you are the aggressive type and very sure, this might be for you.

These results occur when the position is held until expiration. What about closure before that? We already have these answers. They are exactly the same as in the previous discussion on Call spreads. If you change your mind, you can close the position. You could change because you thought the stock had gone about as far as it was going to go or because something happened that made you completely reverse your outlook on the stock. These changes and closings could lead to either a profit or a loss. While we hope it would be a profit, we want to emphasize that any losses would come, not from LEAPS, but because you started out with a longer-term positive stock opinion and then reversed that view.

SUMMARY

Bull LEAPS spreads using Puts are less desirable in our view than the same strategy using Calls. For those whose view and/or needs suggest a credit spread rather than a debit one, this technique would be attractive. The LEAPS involvement adds to the benefits and allows the strategy to be practiced in any mode—conservative, moderate, or aggressive.

Bearish Strategies

CHAPTER 19
BUYING LEAPS PUTS

A Put, in time, makes money.

STRATEGY   Buying LEAPS Puts
OUTLOOK   Bearish to very bearish
ADVANTAGES   Leverage to high leverage; limited
                        dollar risk
DRAWBACKS   High percentage at risk
DEGREE OF RISK   High, but can be reduced

Figuring out the concept of **Buying LEAPS Puts** should be easy, you think. We have analyzed Call buying and so all we need to do is reverse everything. Right? Wrong! While Puts are the reverse of Calls—the right to sell stock rather than to buy it—there's a lot more to consider. First, there is an external difference: Stocks behave differently falling than they do rising. We'll say more about that in this chapter, but for now let's look at an internal difference.

Let's suppose that we constructed a perfect hedge in which we were short stock and long a Call with a delta of 100 against it. A *perfect hedge* means that the long and short gains and losses should offset each other. Delta has been described and explained in Chapter 6 on LEAPS basics. Now let's carry our supposition a step further and create a second perfect hedge in which we were long stock and long a Put that also moved point for point with the stock (but in the opposite direction). Assuming all other considerations—commissions, etc. were eliminated—would the two situations be symmetrical? Absolutely not. In the first case we would have a credit balance, and in the second a debit. That is, we could collect interest in the first case, but have to pay it out in the second. This is an oversimplified and partial description of the intrinsic difference between Puts and Calls.

In other words, interest—earned or paid—is at the heart of Put and Call price determinations. Check back in Chapter 2 on the big secret of LEAPS and options. Now that we are aware of this extremely important factor, let's see what else there is to say about buying Puts. At the start, we will note that people buy Puts for more than one reason. Obviously, some if not most are looking for downside leverage. This would be the inverse of the Call buyer. Ordinarily the Put buyer expects the stock to decline. S/he thinks that decline will be sufficient to profit from a Put purchase.

Examples (set on Monday, January 2)

Stock	Price	Month	Strike	Put cost
XYZ	82	Jan	80	3
XZY	51	Apr	45	1¼
YZX	61	Apr	60	3¾

Let's follow these examples through several scenarios.

1. On January 20 (Expiration Friday) the stock is at 80¼, the option expires, and you lose all your money. Near the end of February, XYZ sells at 77.
2. From the day of purchase through expiration, XZY never reaches 45 and you lose all your money.
3. YZX trades in a narrow range with a slight downward bias and reaches its low—58—on the last day. You don't lose all your money this time, but you don't make a profit either. You will get back $200 of your $375 investment. That is better than the first two examples, but still pretty poor.

We have constructed partial analogies to the Call buying examples in that chapter. The moral is the same for both. It's not such a simple thing to make money buying options, but it's not an impossibility either. And there are certain advantages with LEAPS. We could say with these examples under our belt that a Put purchaser is like a short seller: S/he expects the stock price to have a good (and profitable) downmove.

A gentle note to the (possibly) frightened reader:
Please read on. All we have said is that the outlook for these two (short seller and Put buyer) is the same. The Put buyer does not take the same type of risk as the short seller.

In fact, the Put buyer is much better off than the short seller. We will expound on some of the reasons.

Short Sales	Puts
Borrowing Stock	**No Borrowed Stock**
A short sale is, of course, a sale of stock. Since it is stock that is not owned, it must be borrowed. This act of borrowing could take some time to accomplish. During this time interval the stock might move lower before the sale could be executed	There is no need to borrow any stock in order to buy any Put.
Uptick	**No Uptick**
A short sale must be done on an "uptick" (a higher price than the last *different sale*). This could also take some time. In a severely falling market this wait could cause considerable price erosion before an execution.	A Put may be bought without waiting for an uptick.
Initial Margin	**No Initial Margin**
In addition to the sale proceeds, the seller must deposit 50 percent of the value of the sold securities.	You simply pay in full for the purchased Put.

Margin Calls

As the stock rises, a short seller may have to post additional funds to satisfy a maintenance margin requirement.

No Margin Call

The Put buyer can never get a margin call. The Put buyer will never have to pay any additional funds.

Dividends Owed

The short seller owes out all dividends—cash or stock—that occur during the short sale's life.

No Dividends Owed

The Put buyer will not owe out dividends. In fact, when the stock sells ex dividend it will decline, thereby enhancing the Put's value.

Discomfort

As the stock rises, discomfort over the situation may impel the short seller to cover the position.

Discomfort

A stock rise might cause discomfort and could impel selling out the Put to limit losses.

Panic

If the stock rises greatly and/or rapidly, not discomfort, but panic could ensue. This could compel the short seller to close the position, creating a loss.

No Panic

No matter how much the stock rises, the maximum possible loss is known in advance. Hence discomfort will not evolve to panic.

Return of Stock

The stock lender may ask for the stock back. This could lead to covering at a large loss.

No Stock Return

There is no stock lender involved.

Deals

The stock might become involved in a deal, real or rumored. Either way, a lender is certain to insist on the return of the stock. Now the forced cover could be at a much higher price.

Unlimited Risk

The short seller faces an unlimited risk. If right, there is profit; if wrong, there is no limit whatsoever on losses. This could become a fearsome situation.

Deals

A deal involvement, real or rumored, could cause a higher stock price. This would lead to a lower Put price but, for the reasons given above, no panic.

Limited Risk

There is a finite and well-defined risk. The Put is the right but not the obligation to sell the stock at the Put's strike. The cost of the Put is the maximum possible loss no matter how high the stock rises. This could represent up to 100 percent of the original dollar cost. Therefore, an intelligent Put buyer should not risk more than s/he is willing to lose.

As strong as these points are in favoring the Put purchase over the short sale, they become even stronger when considering LEAPS. Yes, there are people who hold short positions for a long time. They might not have always planned it that way, but it does happen. And all of the negative impingements acting on a short seller—financial and psychological—become both more likely and more threatening as time ticks against him or her.

We will analyze LEAPS Put purchase shortly (pun intended). First, we want to finish examining motivation. There is another and very different reason to buy Puts. That is protection. We have seen illustrations of that in Chapter 15 on protective LEAPS Puts. There we saw results that put (pun intended) the lie to critics of options: trades that were totally nonspeculative. Now let's see about buying Puts for a down move.

Example (January 2)
YZX @ 61   No stock position
Buy Apr 60 Put @ 3¾

On April 1 (no fooling) YZX, which has been falling steadily, reaches 50½. The Put, which has about two more weeks of life, is trading just above its intrinsic value (9½) and you sell it, realizing 9¾. You have made a nice profit of $600 from a downwardly moving stock.

Can we do this with LEAPS? And is it a good idea? We can and it is, with some comments. First, we must observe that there is nothing wrong with this type of trading. It goes against the grain for some. We are almost brainwashed: "Invest in America." "Own your share of American business." Stocks can go only up. And so forth. But stocks do go down. Sometimes they go very far down. Sometime companies go bankrupt. Often shareholders who have believed and hung on, take terrible losses. There is nothing unpatriotic in taking a stance that a stock will decline. Unless you are so good that you pick only risers, you should benefit from the knowledge of how to exploit fallers as well.

That said, which LEAPS Put do we buy? How far out in time and which strike? Exactly the same concepts dealt with in the chapter on buying Calls (Chapter 10) apply here. That is, we must match expectations with expirations and strikes. There is one crucial difference. Stocks do tend to fall faster than they rise. This does not apply to every fall.

It is not at all unusual for a stock to fall a good distance in half the time it took to make that rise. When the expectations that have supported the stock's price diminish, the market often wrecks vengeance on that issue. A shortfall in earnings, a cut in dividends, poor sales reports, or nonapproval by a regulatory body can slash the stock's price with extraordinary rapidity.

Examples

- On September 25, 1992, Medical Care America announced that it would not do so well in earnings as had been expected. It fell that day from 58 to 25, a staggering loss of 56.9 percent.
- On November 11, 1992, Medco Containment cancelled its merger with Diagnostek. The latter fell 5⅞ to 9⅛ in one day.
- On November 25, 1992, Comptronix announced that its earnings had been inflated for three years, and that the top three officers might have been involved in the deceit. The stock fell from 22 to 6 ⅛ that day.
- On January 1, 1993, Centocor suspended enrollment of new patients in trials of its HA-1A/Centoxin after detecting an excess of mortality in some patients. The stock fell 10⅝ from 17½ to 6 ⅞ that day, losing over 60 percent of its value on almost 10 million shares. To see what that might mean to you, its January 1994 20-strike LEAPS Put rose 5⅜ to 13¾ and its January 1995 10-strike LEAPS Put increased 1¼ to 4¼. These one-day gains were percentage rises of 155 percent and 340 percent, respectively.

For those who think that the blue chips are immune to this type of action we offer the following example:

- In mid-December 1992 IBM announced horrible charges to earnings. The stock fell 11 points in two days (down 17.5%).

Of course, not all stock falls are this devastating to stockholders and enriching to Put owners. Still there is ample evidence for our view that stocks fall faster than they rise. Because of this phenomenon, we maintain that OTM strikes are appropriate selections for LEAPS Put purchases. The long life of LEAPS is additional buttressing for OTM strike selections. A stock can fall a long way in a long period. Before giving examples, we urge you to go back to the chapter on buying LEAPS Calls (Chapter 10), and reread the section on matching strike selection to stock expectations. It is just as pertinent and relevant here as it was there.

Examples

Stock	Price	LEAPS Put	Strike	Premium
XYZ	37	Jan (1½ year out)	45	10
XYZ	37	Jan (1½ year out)	30	5
XYZ	37	Jan (1½ year out)	25	2½

These are, respectively, ITM, moderately OTM, and FOM. It is a real-life example. One strike OTM would conventionally be 35 here, but that LEAPS strike did not exist.

Before continuing, we want to preach against inappropriate size. We will not do this at any length. Just go back to Chapter 10 and reread the warning there. Exactly the same applies to this strategy.

If you buy a LEAPS Put with a firm conviction of a stock decline, that does not end your commitment. You must always monitor the position and be alert to changes in the stock that would alter your view on it. If that should occur, you can close (wholly or partially) the position. There are other alternatives here; we will discuss them in the repair chapter (Chapter 40).

But assuming all goes well for you (and ill for the stock), what should happen then? You will reach a point where you must consider whether to hang on for more profit or be content with what has accumulated. Suggestions for this are given in the Enhancement Chapter. Another possibility is scaling out. We saw this maneuver in the Covered Call Writing Chapter. There, an astute investor used LEAPS to get out of a position in partial units and at better and better prices. You can do the analogous here. You can use some of the techniques discussed in Chapter 39 on enhancement. You can also simply sell out your LEAPS Puts at successively higher prices as the stock falls. One guide here should be the time value left in the LEAPS Puts. As that gets lower, you should be more inclined to get out.

If you do sell out a long LEAPS Put position that you have held for over a year, you may reap an added benefit from taxation rules. The details are in Chapter 42 on taxes. We must give here the caveat that we are not tax advisors. That said, selling out a profitable LEAPS Put after a holding period of over a year is the only way we know to make a long-term profit on a declining stock.

SUMMARY

Buying Puts is a good strategy to know about. While it is not unpatriotic, it should not be used indiscriminately. Nor should you do so with any other technique, including buying stock. Buying LEAPS Puts takes advantage of the reduced (per unit of time) cost, gives good leverage, eliminates the terrors of short selling, and allows a lot of time for a stock to fall. A possible tax benefit adds to the pleasure.

CHAPTER 20
WRITING UNCOVERED
LEAPS CALLS

He who sells what isn't his'n
Must buy it back or go to pris'n.

STRATEGY	Writing Uncovered LEAPS Calls
OUTLOOK	Extremely bearish
ADVANTAGES	Short well above market, money inflow, lower collateral
DRAWBACKS	Unlimited risk
DEGREE OF RISK	Extremely high

The opening advice is short and simple: *Don't do it!* Why so vehement? Isn't this strategy just the inverse of writing uncovered Puts? Well, maybe it is, but that doesn't really speak to the risk involved. Some people write uncovered equity Puts with the view that they will "get away with it." That is, the stock will not decline below the strike, and they will keep the premium. In that sense, **Writing Uncovered Calls,** that is, writing Calls without the stock to back them up, is the inverse of uncovered Put writing, but that's only half the story. The other half is what happens if the expectation is erroneous. In the first case—the Put is assigned—that is, stock must be bought. That is hardly a catastrophe. Buying stock is a familiar and comfortable position to participants in the marketplace.

In the second case, however, everything is reversed.

Writing uncovered Calls can lead to a disaster. If the stock rises above the strike and the Call is assigned, what results is a very different position: short stock, instead of long stock. And that is neither a familiar nor a comfortable position for most.

Examples

1. XYZ @ 40 No stock
   position
   Write XYZ 40-strike Put

2. XYZ @ 40 No stock
   position
   Write XYZ 40-strike Call

1. XYZ ends at 36, the Put is assigned, and you now own stock with a built-in loss of four points. That's not the end of the world; indeed, it might even have happened to you without benefit of options.

2. XYZ ends at 44, the Call is assigned, and you are now short stock with a built-in loss of four points. Sound familiar? Then why are you shaking and quaking? Possibly because it has been brought home to you that you are in a position for which you are not really prepared: *POSSIBLE UNLIMITED LOSS* (even the words are quivering).

One could safeguard somewhat against the unwelcome outcome by buying back the written Call if the stock rose to some predetermined level. This would prevent losses from increasing indefinitely, but it almost surely would still result in a loss.

Example

XYZ @ 40 No stock position
Write XYZ 3-month 40-strike Call @ 3

Decide beforehand that if the stock reaches 45, you will close the written Call position. The stock does get there, and you are steadfast in your commitment. You buy back the Call @ 6 ½ and vow never to do it again. The avowal was not from the loss, which was comparatively low, but from the terror you experienced. Just think how much worse that would have been without your mental closeout point. And just think what would have happened to you if you had not remained resolute.

What is to be gained by taking this sort of risk? Only the option premium—that's the dollar return. What about the percentage return? To obtain it, we have to refer back to Chapter 9 on margin. The initial collateral requirement given there for an uncovered call is 25 percent of the market price less any out-of-the-money amount, but with a minimum of 10 percent of market. (You must leave the premium in the account as well.) The maintenance requirement is the *current* premium plus the same percentages of the *current* market price of the stock.

Examples
XYZ @ 40 No stock position
Write XYZ 6-month 40-strike Call @ 4½

Initial collateral requirement is $1,000 (25 percent of $4,000 stock value) plus the 4½ premium.

Stock later rises to 44 and the Call moves to 7⅜. The new requirement is $1,837.50 (7⅜ premium plus 25 percent of $4,400). If you posted $1,000 originally (along with the $450 premium), you will now have to add $387.50.

XYZ @ 36 No stock position
Write XYZ 18-month 45-strike LEAPS Call @ 1½

Initial requirement is $900 (25 percent of $3,600) less $900 (OTM amount) or $-0-/*No good! Can't do that!*

The rules specify a 10 percent *minimum* after subtracting the OTM amount, so that the correct calculation would be: $360 (10% of $3,600) and leave the $150 premium. If the stock subsequently rose to 45 and the Call to 6, the new number would be $1,125 (25 percent of $4,500) with nothing to subtract as the Call is then ATM. With the 6 point premium addition, the total would be $1,725. You need another $1,215.

Before we continue, two observations are in order. One is the quotation at the head of Chapter 9: "Minimum margin is a sign of minimum intelligence." Don't be coy. You must know, even if you're proven correct later, that if you post the absolute minimum, you're likely to be asked for more dollars. Deposit a little extra at the beginning so you won't have to worry about being on vacation, your faithful broker doing the same, and so forth.

The second is a very old rule borrowed from the commodities crowds: "Never answer a margin call!" This doesn't mean you should skip town. It means that if you posted sufficient margin originally and then you get a margin call, it implies that the stock is doing what you thought it wouldn't do. While we do not approve of this concept as an unequivocal rule, we certainly do endorse the notion of rethinking your outlook under these circumstances.

We have shown an ATM conventional write and a nine-point OTM LEAPS Call write. Obviously, the former is much more risky than the latter. Let's assume you do choose the latter. Your return would be 150/360 or 41.7 percent. This calculation assumes that you never had to post additional collateral, that you held the position until expiration, and that you let it expire rather than buying it back. Now, however, as we always do for comparison purposes, we have to annualize that return.

If we adhere to our standard assumption that the lifetime of your chosen LEAPS call is 18 months, that means the *annual* return was 27.8 percent. Now think of what you would be risking to earn this return. For most, this risk/reward ratio (both conceptually and numerically) is badly askew. In general, someone with this outlook would be better off purchasing Puts instead. We say this because that latter strategy could earn a handsome multiple on invested capital (as we saw in Chapter 19 on buying LEAPS Puts), without the terrible risk of the former technique. "Wait a minute," says Mr. Mischief, you could lose 100 percent of your money. Isn't that a 'terrible risk' "? Yes, it is, and you should try to avoid it by monitoring the stock's behavior. *But,* if that's a terrible risk, what name should we give to the risk of *unlimited* possible losses with the uncovered Call strategy? No answer is necessary: the question makes the point.

All this being said, there are still some to whom this strategy has an appeal. For them we say: "It's your funeral; be very careful on the way there."

Now, is this strategy with LEAPS any different? Yes, it is. First, you can get a much higher premium (in absolute terms) for the written Call. Second, you are at risk for a much longer time. Obviously, these two differences play off against each other.

Perhaps one way to use this strategy is to plan on closing the position quickly. This would be profitable if the stock had a bad fall. It would be at a loss if the stock moved rapidly upward. One advantage here with LEAPS is that there are strikes quite FOM. By using one of these rather than a closer-to-market-level strike, you would make the usual trade-off: less profit and less risk.

Our final word is to repeat the warnings above, and to suggest two alternatives. First consider writing uncovered straddles or combinations rather than just Calls (see Chapters 23 and 24). Second, consider ratio writing rather than outright uncovered Calls (see Chapter 28).

SUMMARY

This is not a recommended technique. Even with the improvements offered by LEAPS, its risks are very high compared to potential profit. For those who feel they must do it, we provide guidelines to mitigate the risk.

CHAPTER 21
BEAR SPREADS WITH LEAPS PUTS

If I were a bear. . . .

STRATEGY	LEAPS Bearish Put Spreads
OUTLOOK	Limited bearish
ADVANTAGES	Leverage; limited dollar risk
DRAWBACKS	Limited profit; possible complexities
DEGREE OF RISK	Moderate

We first define a **Bear Put Spread** (also known as a **Bearish Put Spread**) as buying and writing equal amounts of Puts on the same stock with the same expiration. The Put we buy will have a higher strike than the one we write.

Example
Buy   4-month 95-strike ZYX Puts
Write 4-month 85-strike ZYX Puts

We have looked so far only at bull spreads. Now, just as we analyzed buying Puts after buying Calls, we want to do the analogous thing for bear spreads. It is an apt analogy: You will reduce your cost by writing one option against another; you will lower your risk in the same way; and you will limit your profit in the same way. Let's turn the bullish Call example upside down and look at a bear spread.

Examples

Bull Call spread		Bear Put spread	
Buy 85-strike ZYX Calls @ 6		Buy 95-strike ZYX Puts @ 5	
Write 95-strike ZYX Calls @ 2		Write 85-strike ZYX Puts @ 3	
Net debit	4	Net debit	3

We can also generalize the implied analysis above to obtain the theoretical B/E point for a Put bear spread. It is the debit subtracted from the upper strike.

Example
Buy   95-strike ZYX Puts @ 5
Write 85-strike ZYX Puts @ 2
Net debit   3

B/E is 92 (upper strike 95 less debit 3). Think of the stock at that 92 price at expiration. The written Put will not be assigned, as nobody would insist on selling you the stock at 85 if it's at 92. You will sell out the 95 Put for its intrinsic value of 3 (95–92) and make back your debit, thus breaking even. Of course, we also know what the maximum profit will be. This spread can never be worth more than the separation between the strikes.

Example
In the above example, picture the stock ending at some arbitrary number less than the lower strike of 85. In that case you will exercise your long Put and sell out the stock at 95. You will be assigned on the written Put at 85 (buying the stock there), thus getting the 10-point differential. Of course, that difference is not really profit; it is the maximum outcome. Profit is the difference between what we paid for the spread and what we get out. So the maximum profit would be the separation between the strikes less the original debit.

Example
As above, you make 10, but you paid 3. Your profit is 7. As with all option strategies, we can approach this with a stance that is conservative, moderate, or aggressive. We can also match strikes to this expectation.

Examples
With ZYX @ 90
Buy   95-strike ZYX Puts
Write 85-strike ZYX Puts   Moderate, long ITM, written
                                                OTM

Buy   105-strike ZYX Puts
Write 95-strike ZYX Puts   Conservative, both legs ITM

Buy   85-strike ZYX Puts
Write 75-strike ZYX Puts   Aggressive, both legs OTM

Now for the LEAPS experience or even transformation. As we have observed several times before, LEAPS's life and LEAPS's premiums make possible an alteration of strategic choices without abandoning your own attitudes about risk. Thus, continuing the analogy, we would suggest the purchase of a DIM Put and the writing of an OTM.

Example
With ZYX @ 90
Buy   105-strike ZYX Puts
Write 85-strike ZYX Puts

We note that the DIM LEAPS Put is somewhat similar to a stock short sale without many of the attendant risks. For documentation, see Chapter 19 on buying LEAPS Puts. The writing of the other leg really defrays the cost. How FOM a strike you choose depends on how bearish you are. Remember, you will not realize the maximum profit unless the stock goes below the lower strike. This warning applies with even more force if you elect to have both legs OTM.

Example
With ZYX @ 90
Buy   85-strike ZYX Puts
Write 75-strike ZYX Puts

This last example is the most aggressive we have looked at in this context. In order to realize the maximum profit at expiration, the stock would have to be under 75. That would be a decline of almost 17 percent, but we must remember that the context here is one of a limited risk type of strategy. Rephrased, we are taking an aggressive stance within a relatively conservative technique. Once again we see how valuable options (and LEAPS) can be. We just used the phrase: *a relatively conserva-*

tive technique. Remember that to keep it that way, you should not overleverage yourself.

SUMMARY

Bearish LEAPS Put spreads fill a particular need very well. Their utilization should be confined to only that narrow use. With a limited risk, a good percentage return is attainable. With appropriate cautions in mind, this strategy can be rewarding to those whose expectations correspond to its outcomes.

CHAPTER 22
BEAR SPREADS WITH LEAPS CALLS

I play with the Bulls and the Bears.

STRATEGY	LEAPS Bearish Call Spreads
OUTLOOK	Limited bearish
ADVANTAGES	Leverage; limited dollar risk
DRAWBACKS	Limited profit
DEGREE OF RISK	Moderate

A gentle note to the (possibly) exhausted reader:
Please read on. The author sympathizes with you. You have read about bull spreads with Calls, bull spreads with Puts, and bear spreads with Puts. The last one was the most complex. Relax. We will make this chapter short and simple.

Recapitulation

Buy   5 3-month 60-strike XYZ Calls @ 4
Write 5 3-month 65-strike XYZ Calls @ 2
Net debit per spread   2

Buy   5 3-month 50-strike YZX Puts @ 2
Write 5 3-month 60-strike YZX Puts @ 6
Net credit per spread   4

Buy   5 3-month 95-strike ZYX Puts @ 5
Write 5 3-month 85-strike ZYX Puts @ 2
Net debit per spread   3

Above, we have three different types of spreads. They are, in order, a bull Call spread—you are bullish and pay a debit; a bull Put spread—you are bullish and get a credit; a bear Put spread—you are bearish and pay a debit.

Now we have the last link: **Bear Call Spreads** (also known as **Bearish Call Spreads**). Here you buy and write Calls on the same underlying with the same expiration. You are long a higher strike and write a lower one.

Example
Buy   5 3-month 95-strike ZYX Calls @ 6
Write 5 3-month 85-strike ZYX Calls @ 9
Net credit per spread   3

To complete the analogy, we advise against this technique. It is preferred by some because it is done for a credit rather than a debit.

Just as before, with bull Put spreads, we demur on the same grounds. You would be buying more time value and writing less. You might even be writing a lot of intrinsic value. We suggest you return to the section on bull spreads using Puts to see the negative details. In fact, that covers a lot of other material that is relevant here. All the discussions on strike selection, initial collateral, maximum profits, and indeed our general philosophy are covered there. We need not repeat them here.

That leaves us with the familiar transition to LEAPS. As we have seen for all the previous strategies, the essential LEAPS difference is long life—and that operates here as well. If you are right in stock selection, this gives the stock more time to move down and away from the strikes. If the stock moves down far enough, it will go beneath the lower strike. At expiration, this will mean that both Calls will expire, and you will keep the original credit. Let's look at some possibilities:

XYZ @ 50   No stock position   All the LEAPS Calls are
                                 1½ years out
Buy XYZ 45 Call @ 12   Write XYZ 35 Call @ 19
Credit 7 Both ITM

or

Buy XYZ 55 Call @ 7   Write XYZ 45 Call @ 12
Credit 5 1 ITM, 1 OTM

or

Buy XYZ 65 Call @ 4   Write XYZ 55 Call @ 7
Credit 3 Both OTM

These examples exhibit the usual trade-offs. The highest credit (and the lowest collateral) come with both sides ITM. But this is also the highest risk, for the stock has to move down much more for you to avoid a loss, and then to make a profit, and finally to make the maximum profit. In the first example, you would need a 30 percent move at expiration to realize the maximum. If you are the aggressive type and very assured about your outlook, this might be for you.

These results occur when the position is held until expiration. What about closure before that? We already have these answers. They are exactly the same as in the previous discussion on bull Call spreads. If you change your mind, you can close the position. You could change because you thought the stock had gone about as far as it was going to or because something happened that made you completely reverse your outlook on the stock. These changes and closings could lead to either a profit or a loss. While we hope it would be a profit, we want to emphasize that any losses would come, not from LEAPS, but because you started out with a longer-term negative stock opinion and then reversed that view.

SUMMARY

Bear spreads using Calls are inferior as a strategy to their Puts companion. Although credits are generated in this technique, there are sound considerations against this strategy, which is greatly improved with LEAPS. For those who insist (because of credits or other reasons), some suggestions are made to decrease risk. For both this strategy and Bull spreads with LEAPS Puts, we amend the famous quote: "Pay the cash and let the credit go."

Neutral Strategies

CHAPTER 23
WRITING UNCOVERED
LEAPS STRADDLES

We have stood apart, studiously neutral.

STRATEGY	Writing Uncovered LEAPS Straddles
OUTLOOK	Neutral
ADVANTAGES	Profit over broad range
DRAWBACKS	Needs monitoring; large loss possible
DEGREE OF RISK	High, but can be reduced

This is a very different strategy from writing *Covered* straddles. It is so dissimilar because it is intrinsically different in outlook. The writer of covered straddles is, as we have seen, bullish. Someone who is **Writing Uncovered Straddles** is not only neutral, s/he is extremely neutral. What does that phrase mean? It means that the expectation is for the stock to remain confined within quite narrow ranges.

Example

XYZ @ 40	No stock position
Write XYZ	6-month 40-strike Call @ 4
Write XYZ	6-month 40-strike Put @ 3

This writer expects the stock not to go up or down much from 40. Another way to analyze the strategy is to break it down into its component parts. Writing uncovered Calls=bearish; writing uncovered Puts=bullish. The amalgamation of the two produces neutrality. One advantage of combining the two is that you collect two premiums, which reduces the risk. It must be noted that even this reduction will not help if the stock explodes or collapses. While technically you would lose less than if you had written just one (losing) side, the loss could still be unpleasantly enormous.

XYZ @ 40   No stock position
Write XYZ   6-month 40-strike Call @ 4
Write XYZ   6-month 40-strike Put @ 3

If the stock ends @ 60, you will be called at 40. You will have to pay 60 to obtain stock to meet the assignment, losing 20. The loss is reduced to 13 by the 7 points total premium received, but that's only minor consolation. Even less consolation comes from the thought that you would have lost 3 more if you had not written the Put. If the stock ends @ 20, the results will be almost exactly the same.

Now let's see what the best result could be with this strategy. This "best" is quite fictive. To achieve the best result, the stock would have to close at exactly the strike with no assignments on either side. Further, there could not have been any previous assignments on either side. Only then would you make the sum of the two premiums received.

Example
XYZ @ 40   No stock position
Write XYZ   6-month 40-strike Call @ 4
Write XYZ   6-month 40-strike Put @ 3

If the stock ends @ 40 and there are no assignments (then or before), you keep the 7 points.

What would this be on a percentage basis? We need to know the necessary margin. Chapter 9 on margin gives it to us as the greater requirement of the two single sides (and leaves both premiums in the account). That's an out-of-pocket cost of 25 percent of $4,000 = $1,000. This is, of course, only the initial collateral needed. But we will be kind and assume that no further funds were ever needed. In that case your return would be 700/1,000 or 70 percent. Not so bad, but we think all will agree that there's extraordinarily little chance of actually achieving that. Let's make a more practical, albeit arbitrary, assumption: the stock ends 10 percent away from the strike, and you receive an assignment on the losing side.

Example

XYZ @ 40	No stock position
Write XYZ	6-month 40-strike Call @ 4
Write XYZ	6-month 40-strike Put @ 3

The stock ends at 44, and you are called at 40. You buy stock @ 44 to satisfy the assignment. You lose 4 in doing this. Now the returns look like this: premiums 7, stock loss 4, net 3—300/ 1,000 = 30 percent.

That's still pretty good, especially as it's the period return. But the danger is becoming more apparent. If we encountered a move of 20 percent (up or down) the stock loss would more than wipe out all of our option premiums. This leads us to another, very real problem associated with this technique. A position like this, once initiated, needs extremely close attention and monitoring. When you take a one-sided option position (LEAPS or otherwise), you do have to keep your eye on it. But once it starts moving your way, all you have to watch out for is a directional reversal. With the two-sided straddle position, you (or your faithful broker) have to keep watch in both directions. And that's no exaggeration in the type of markets we have had in the last five or so years. They have been characterized by very frequent whipsaws, that is, very frequent flip-flops in prices.

How about implementing the strategy with LEAPS? As we have said before, you get much (absolutely) larger premiums, which helps you. But you are exposed to risk for a substantially longer time. As we said in Chapter 20 on writing uncovered Calls, perhaps the technique should be used with the outlook of an early closure. For most very volatile stocks, there comes a time when premiums just get "out-of-sight." (When that does happen, both Puts and Calls are affected.) If this sort of trading appeals to you, wait until a stock that has LEAPS trading behaves like this. Then pounce quickly. Be prepared to close the trade just as quickly when the volatility has dampened and the extra juice has come out of the premiums.

Warning! We mention this technique, not as an endorsement, but in the recognition that it might be suitable for a small number of pretty nimble traders. It represents one extreme in the spectrum of types of trading that LEAPS offers. We will discuss an alternative that is similar but safer in the next chapter.

SUMMARY

As with many option strategies, the conversion to LEAPS improves the outlook. Writing uncovered straddles is a good fit for some traders whose viewpoint might be described as very neutral. They also must be blessed with agility. More conservative (and less peripatetic) investors with similar views should examine writing uncovered combinations in our next chapter.

CHAPTER 24
WRITING UNCOVERED
LEAPS COMBINATIONS

Home on the range.

STRATEGY	Writing Uncovered LEAPS Combinations
OUTLOOK	Neutral
ADVANTAGES	Profit over broad range
DRAWBACKS	Large loss possible; needs monitoring
DEGREE OF RISK	Less than uncovered straddle writing

We have to compare **Writing Uncovered Combinations** with two other strategies that share similar names. First is writing covered combinations; the second, writing uncovered straddles. Our current strategy has more in common with the second; it is neutral in outlook (the covered version is very bullish), and profits are made when the stock remains within a fixed range.

The difference between the straddle version and the combination can be summed up simply. You write a Put and a Call (with the same expiration) in each. For the straddle, the strikes are the same; for the combination, they are different. In the combination, you will probably make less money, but you have a higher probability of making it. To see why this is so, let's look at a direct comparison.

Examples
XYZ @ 40   No stock position
Write XYZ   6-month 40-strike Call @ 4
Write XYZ   6-month 40-strike Put @ 3
Total premium for straddle   7
or
XYZ @ 40 No stock position

Write XYZ   6-month 45-strike Call @ 2
Write XYZ   6-month 35-strike Put @ 1
Total premium for combination   3

We spoke above about the absolute dollar result, but we must consider that money in terms of a return. Now let's look at the two strategies again, this time noting what the collateral requirements are. Again, from Chapter 9 on margin, the initial collateral needed is the margin for one side or the other— whichever is greater—and leaving *both* premiums in the account.

Examples
XYZ @ 40   No stock position
Write XYZ   6-month 40-strike Call @ 4
Write XYZ   6-month 40-strike Put @ 3
Total premium for straddle   7
Initial collateral requirement is $1,000 (25 percent of $4,000) and leave the $700.

or

XYZ @ 40   No stock position
Write XYZ   6-month 45-strike Call @ 2
Write XYZ   6-month 35-strike Put @ 1
Total premium for combination   3
Initial collateral requirement is $500 ($1,000 less OTM amount of $500) and leave the $300.

Now let's assume that the stock does not vary much during the life of the options. It ends (up or down) 10 percent away from its original 40 price. Note that we are being fair; this is the same assumption we used in the previous chapter. As we saw then, for the straddle you would have to give back $400, keep $300 and make a return of 300/1,000 or 30 percent. With the combination, you would make 300/500 or 60 percent. More important than the higher return is that you will get that profit if the stock ends *anywhere* between the strikes. In the example above, the same result would have happened if the stock closed at 38½, 42, 39⅝, etc.

How about this strategy with LEAPS? While you will be at risk for a longer time period (assuming you keep the position open until expiration), there are two other factors to help. One, the high LEAPS premiums; and two, the farther OTM strikes that can be used. We emphasize that to get the maximum from the straddle write, the stock must do the almost impossible— close exactly at the strike (and with no assignment then or before). The combination, in contradistinction, produces all of the premiums just by having the stock stay between the strikes. Indeed, it is possible for the stock to move outside of this range and then back within it. If there were no assignment made and the stock did end within the limits, you would make the maximum. It is also worth noting—especially with the large dollar LEAPS premiums—that the stock might end outside of the strike-prices range and you could still make money.

Example
YXZ @ 80   No stock position
Write YXZ Jan (1½ year out)   100 LEAPS Call @ 8
Write YXZ Jan (1½ year out)   60 LEAPS Put @ 6

YXZ spend the eighteen months meandering. Near expiration it starts climbing and ends @ 105. You are assigned on the Call and sell stock @ 100. Since you do not own the stock, you buy shares at 105 and lose 5 points. Your original intake of 14 is reduced to a final profit of 9.

You do not make the maximum projected profit, but you do make *some* money. We can easily deduce a break-even range at expiration (assuming no prior assignments). It is simply the sum of the two premiums received—first added to the upper strike, and then subtracted from the lower strike.

Example
YXZ @ 80   No stock position
Write YXZ Jan (1½ year out)   100 LEAPS Call @ 8
Write YXZ Jan (1½ year out)   60 LEAPS Put @ 6

Expiration break-even range is 114 (14 plus upper strike 100) to 46 (60 lower strike less 14).

Note that this range can be extremely wide. There is a spectrum of choices available here. We start (mentally) with the uncovered straddle and move on through wider and wider uncovered combinations. As indicated in the beginning, the wider the range, the greater the probability of keeping all of the premium (or, for that matter, keeping some of it). Once again, we have a trade-off—as the range gets wider, the *amount* of potential profit gets smaller.

Examples
YXZ @ 80   No stock position
Write YXZ Jan (1½ year out)   100 LEAPS Call @ 8
Write YXZ Jan (1½ year out)   60 LEAPS Put @ 6
Expiration break-even range 114 to 46. Profit potential 14

YXZ @ 80   No stock position
Write YXZ Jan (1½ year out)   110 LEAPS Call @ 5
Write YXZ Jan (1½ year out)   50 LEAPS Put @ 3
Expiration break-even range 118 to 42. Profit potential 8.

Obviously this process has a limiting point. We could widen the strikes more and more but expect to make less and less. We want to make an observation here. With short-lived options, especially very short-lived ones, some do just that.

Example
YXZ @ 80   No stock position
Write YXZ Jan (1½ weeks out)   90 Call @ ⅜
Write YXZ Jan (1½ weeks out)   70 Put @ ¼

No, there are no misprints in our example. This is a written combination with only about seven or eight trading days to go, and it is being written for a combined premium total of ⅝ths of a dollar! This practice is an attempt to take advantage of time. With so few days left, the theory is that the stock couldn't move enough to get outside of the winning range. The people who do this type of trading try to do it every month as that month's expiration approaches. They reason that they are replicating the returns consistently and thus will have annualized returns in the stratosphere. We say that's where their heads are now. This type of trading may succeed 10, or even 11 times out of 12. The two or even one other times, there will not be a profit. There will be a loss, and that loss could wipe out *all* of the other profits. Or more.

We compare this technique to systems players who double up after each losing bet at roulette. Each of these methods is guaranteed to succeed with just one little catch: You need to have more money than the house! Since nobody does, there are fewer of these players all the time. Their ranks diminish because they are carried away to another house—the poorhouse! Why have we so furiously fulminated against this practice? Because it is the exact opposite of what we are trying to explicate with LEAPS. We want to take advantage of the *long* time these instruments have. In some strategies we have made use of that time to allow the stock to have a large move (up or down). Here, for those with a strong view that the stock will be confined to a predictable (and not too wide) range, we take advantage of the high-dollar LEAPS premiums to make money.

The lecture is over. Now, which combination should be selected? You, the perspicacious reader, already know what we're going to say about that: Match the strikes to your stock expectations. Right you are. In the usual trade-off between more money and less risk, we suggest no more than two strikes OTM on either side. The more daring (who might be looking at early closure) might go in closer. Even for them we suggest a modicum of moderation: one strike OTM on one leg and two on the other.

We can approximate an objective check on the selection made. Calculate the break-even range, and then see what the actual range was for the last 52 weeks. These numbers are found in the stock tables in the *Wall Street Journal, Investor's Business Daily,* and many other newspapers. They are usually just to the left of the stock's name. Many desk-top quotation terminals (Quotron, Automatic Data, etc.) also carry annual ranges, but be very careful. Sometimes the terminals carry the calendar-year range. That is not what we want. The 52-week range in the papers is updated every week and shows the high-low range going back a full year from the current date.

Now compare your projected break-even range to the 52-week one. Keep in mind that your position may be open for a longer time. If your range is not in line, discard that selection and try another. Of course, there is an assumption here that should be made crystal-clear. The assumption is that the stock will continue its trading pattern or, at least, that it won't become much more volatile. Think about that extremely carefully before you enter into this technique. After all, an expected neutral behavior over a long period of time is the basis for choosing this strategy. If you do pick a good combination of strikes and a stock that behaves in line with your predictions, you will indeed be "home on the range."

Suppose though, that while you do have a good range, the stock starts to change its character. *Be careful!* Watch the stock very closely and be prepared to make adjustments or even to close the position. We will cover this aspect more fully in Chapter 40 on repair.

SUMMARY

Writing uncovered LEAPS combinations is a good concept in certain circumstances. It provides a way of making money without the need for a stock to move up or down more than moderately. We emphasize that while many stocks in many periods do just that, none of them do it perpetually. This implies the need for careful, if not constant, monitoring. It may also require closing the position early. That said, this is in our view a much superior strategy for this type of action than writing uncovered LEAPS straddles. In that strategy only one price out of all possible ones lets you keep all of the premiums originally received. It could be compared to winning first prize—$1 million—in the "ethnic" lottery. Its payoff is a dollar a year for a million years!

CHAPTER 25
BUYING LEAPS STRADDLES OR COMBINATIONS

To buy dear is not bounty.

STRATEGY	Buying LEAPS Straddles or Combinations
OUTLOOK	Expect big move; don't know direction
ADVANTAGES	Profit from large moves in either direction
DRAWBACKS	Needs large move; needs monitoring
DEGREE OF RISK	High, but can be reduced

Let's do the definitions immediately. **Buying Straddles** means buying equal numbers of Puts and Calls on the same underlying with the same expiration and the same striking price. **Buying Combinations** is exactly the same except for the last clause. Take that out and substitute "and different strikes."

When we looked at the writing side, we dealt with straddles first, and then with combinations. Here we will dismiss straddles almost out of hand. The exposition of these two techniques will be just a little bit different than usual. Instead of an explicit description of the strategies using equity options and then a skip to LEAPS, we will start directly with the LEAPS. As we go along, we will discuss the distinctions between the two types of options within the strategies.

The entire theory of LEAPS trading is that, given enough time the underlying can move far enough to produce a profit for you or that, if the stock remains relatively nonvolatile, the big-dollar premiums will produce a profit with a neutral strategy. We saw how that worked in Chapter 10 on buying LEAPS Calls and in Chapter 19 on buying LEAPS Puts. If we combine the two techniques, that is, buy a Call and buy a Put, we will have two premiums to make up. If we buy a straddle, both premiums will be relatively high. Just as in the single option buying, we can look to buying both LEAPS options OTM.

Example
YZX @ 80   No stock position
Buy YZX Jan (1½ year out)   90 LEAPS Call @ 7
Buy YZX Jan (1½ year out)   70 LEAPS Put @ 4

Wait! Why should we do this? Didn't we say that you needed the conviction of stock price direction and magnitude before buying LEAPS? Who could have the conviction that a stock will move either up or down? That's not so far-fetched as it might seem at first view. There are many instances where that might indeed be a reasonable view. One example might be a pharmaceutical or a biotechnology company that is awaiting Food and Drug Administration (FDA) approval for a wonder drug. You might have the expectation that if approval comes, the stock will soar. And if it is disapproved, the stock could collapse.

Caveat! This is an extreme view and is not generally applicable, but it is not impossible either.

Example
The price action of Centocor, a biopharmaceutical company, fits the above description as though it had been genetically engineered for it. Having gone to a high above 60 on January 15, 1992, it drifted down to the low 30s in April. On April 15 there was a negative ruling from the FDA, and the stock tumbled from 31¼ to 18½.

Still, even if stocks do move like this, why implement this strategy with LEAPS rather than conventional options? First, because as always with LEAPS, the additional time can be very helpful. It is easy to construct examples on paper, but in the real world it can take a long time before the expected event materializes. Even the maximum length (eight months) of conventional options may not be long enough, and, by the time you are considering an eight-month option purchase, you should look at the premiums for that and for LEAPS.

Example
Stock @ 45   50-strike Calls
 1-month $ 75
 2-month $125
 5-month $300
 8-month $425
18-month $700

For an additional $275 you get another 10 months for the stock to go your way. We want to emphasize the time factor here. It's not just a question of dollars paid or dollars per time unit. It can be an all-or-nothing proposition. That is the familiar risk of option buying. The hoped-for story comes to pass. But not until after the option expires. Some very high-flying stocks have come down to earth with a thud, but only after soaring even higher first.

Example
Centocor closed @ 35¼ on August 15, 1991. If you had bought an eight-month ATM Put, you probably wouldn't have held it for the full time. The stock went to 60 in January 1992. If you did hold on, you would have had absolutely incredible luck. As we said, the stock crashed on April 15. If the FDA opinion had come a scant three days later, the option would have gone out worth only $375 as opposed to $1,650.

Second, you might get the type of large move you are looking for without a specific watershed event. Many of the underlying stocks with LEAPS are very volatile, and in time they could rise or fall greatly by themselves in conjunction with an industrywide reevaluation or even on an overall market move.

There is another aspect to examine here: You might make money on both sides of the combination! The stock might move up greatly, enabling a profitable trade on the Call side of the LEAPS combination.

Example
YZX @ 80   No stock position
Buy YZX Jan (1½ year out)   90 LEAPS Call @ 7
Buy YZX Jan (1½ year out)   70 LEAPS Put @ 4

Six months after the purchase, the stock has risen (without any great, specific news) to 98. The LEAPS Call is trading @ 17 (the large 9-point time value is because it still has a year to run). You sell it there, not only have you made a profit on the Call, you've more than recovered the entire combination cost.

That still leaves you with a LEAPS Put. In the example above, it would probably be trading for only a nominal amount, but you would be risking very little by not selling it out. Since in our example it still has a year left before expiration, there's no telling what might happen.

Example

The stock continues up after your LEAPS Call closing sale. It reaches 104, and the story that has carried it so high finally emerges. Almost immediately that story is shot down and the stock starts to retreat. It does more than retreat. Over the next four months it declines more and more, picking up downward momentum. One day it goes almost into a free-fall. You (or your ever-so-faithful broker) are watching closely. When the stock reaches 77 on very heavy volume, the LEAPS Put trades @ 5 ½. You sell it out there. If this seems like only a self-serving extrapolation (if not a fantasy), we can say only that much stranger things than that have actually transpired in the market. The above illustration shows something very important. You sold out the LEAPS Put at a profit despite the fact that the stock never went to the strike—let alone below it.

Watch out! Here's Mr. Cynic ready to belabor us. "Who are you kidding?" he asks. "You said the Put was at 5 when the stock was 80. Then when the stock was 77, but with only eight months left, you claim the Put could be 5½."

Yes, we do. And we claim it because something very important happened. When the stock was at 80, it was deemed not very volatile. After that we had evidence in the opposite direction. The stock went to 104, then reversed and had a very sharp fall to 77. This type of action made the options much more valuable, and you reaped the results and rewards of the reevaluation.

"You're not getting rid of me so quickly," Mr. Cynic continues. "I saw what you did with the premiums in the examples.

When you were talking about writing combinations, you made them big; then when you started in on buying combinations, you made them small. I'm wise to you!"

Poor Mr. Cynic! He thinks he's wise to us. Maybe so, or maybe not. But he surely isn't wise to the market. It was the *market* that did these things. It valued the combination we wanted to write in such a way that we found it attractive. In an analogous manner it placed a value on the other combination that we liked. Of course, these were different stocks with different histories. In the first case, we approached the stock because we thought it had potential for the buying combinations maneuver. When we saw the premiums, we pounced. Good for us! Cynicism is a very good trait to possess when viewing the market. Just make sure that it's not a mask for jealousy!

Now let's look at a similar scenario for the opposite side. That is, the stock goes down and the LEAPS Put becomes profitable. You could sell out both sides, otherwise known as: Take all the money and run (often a wonderful method). Or you could hold on to the LEAPS Call and see if the stock reverses and rises.

Example
YZX @ 80   No stock position
Buy YZX Jan (1½ year out)   90 LEAPS Call @ 7
Buy YZX Jan (1½ year out)   70 LEAPS Put @ 4

Very soon after you bought the LEAPS combination, the stock starts falling. It falls slowly at first. After several weeks it rallies, but then it starts falling again. Rumors swirl; there are more rallies and more stories. The stock starts approaching 50 and you feel there would be good support there. With the stock @ 51 you sell your LEAPS Put for an incredible 22 points (a fairly large 3-point time value). You are delighted. You paid 11 and doubled that on only one side. You now expect to make some more money on the LEAPS Call.

Alas! It never happens. Terrible news finally comes out and the stock does nothing but go down. It goes through the alleged support and keeps going down. It never really recovers, and eventually you sell out the LEAPS Call for a pitiful 1 point. Well, maybe it's not so pitiful. It's important to see that not every hope materializes, and this time you were doubly wrong. You expected (or maybe hoped for) a reversal. You cashed in the LEAPS Put far too soon.

Isn't LEAPS trading truly wonderful? How many other methods do you know where you can be doubly wrong while you're doubling your money?

These examples enhance our previously stated view. For those who find this technique attractive, we note that had you bought the LEAPS straddle instead of the combination, you would be faced with a difficult question. If one side became successful, the other would probably be selling at far more than a nominal amount. That would vitiate our statement above about "risking very little by not selling it out." That would leave you impaled on the horns of a dilemma.

Example
YZX @ 80   No stock position
Buy YZX Jan (1½ year out)   80 LEAPS Call @ 13
Buy YZX Jan (1½ year out)   80 LEAPS Put @ 10

Only two months after you buy the LEAPS straddle, the stock runs up to 96. Should you cash in the LEAPS Call (now @ 19)? Should you hold on for more? Should you keep the LEAPS Put (now @ 6)? In this example it is very easy to make the wrong choice. It's an additional reason for buying the LEAPS combination over the straddle.

There is also another reason for preferring the LEAPS combination to the ordinary option combination. If you do reach a point where you want to close out one side of the position, the LEAPS Call or Put will not have decayed (in percentage terms) so much as the shorter-lived option. Of course, that goes double if you should change your mind and want to close out both legs.

Before we leave the subject of LEAPS combinations, we want to talk about an amazing phenomenon. Let's go back to the LEAPS combination example above when the LEAPS Call became profitable.

Example
YZX @ 80   No stock position
Buy YZX Jan (1½ year out)   90 LEAPS Call @ 7
Buy YZX Jan (1½ year out)   70 LEAPS Put @ 4

Six months after the purchase the stock has risen (without any great specific news) to 102. The LEAPS Call is trading @ 19 (still a hefty 7 points above its intrinsic value). The LEAPS Put is at only 1½. We spoke about cashing in the Call. There is another possibility: We could buy a Put at that point. It wouldn't have to be a LEAPS Put.

Example

Keep the long LEAPS Call (90 strike with a year to go)

Buy the four-month 110-strike conventional Put @ 8½ (its mere ½ over intrinsic value is characteristic of shorter-term ITM Puts). Sell out the LEAPS Put @ 1½ to defray the cost of your Put purchase. Why would we want to invest additional capital here? Especially when we had just reached a point of profitability? And very good profitability too. Because you have become options-oriented. And you know how good options can be. You know from the previous chapters that a Put can be used to guarantee a profit. Now you are about to find out that options (and LEAPS) can do even more than that. They can work miracles! That extreme statement is made with beneficence beforehand. What is the miracle? It is that you have created a position with sensational characteristics.

Position

Long 1-year 90-strike LEAPS Call
Long 4-month 110-strike ordinary Put

This position cost you 18 (initial investment 11 + new investment 8½ less closing sale 1½). It is now worth 20. It will always be worth that much (up until the Put's expiration). To see that, just think: If the stock is above 110, the LEAPS Call will be worth 20; if the stock is below 90, the Put will be worth 20; if the stock is between those two numbers, you could call the stock at 90, put it at 110, and get the 20 points.

"You guys are crazy," screams Mr. Know-it-all, jumping into the fray. "Just cash it all in: 19 for the Call, 1½ for the Put, and you got 20½ right away. Why are you making such a commotion about always getting 20 later on?"

Mr. Know-it-all has jumped in, but he doesn't know about LEAPS. The 20 points we're talking about is just the *minimum* value of this position. If the stock were to go above 110, the LEAPS Call would be worth *more* than 20. If the stock declined below 90, the Put would be worth *more* than 20. In each case we assumed that the option on the other side would be worth zero. It probably would be worth more than that. So you have a position that has a guaranteed minimum value. It could become worth more than that. In fact, there is no limit at all on the upside. On the downside, the only limit is that the Put can never become worth more than 90 because the stock cannot fall below zero.

The author thinks that a position with a *guaranteed* minimum value that can increase *without limit* on the upside (where the LEAPS Call would have a long time to run) and that can increase greatly on the downside (with four months to go), certainly deserves to be labeled a miracle! Our intruder may know it all, but we have all the know-how!

Further Comments

Obviously you could do this type of trade in the other direction as well. That is, if the stock declined to a point where the LEAPS Put became very profitable, you could consider buying a Call. In each case you could sell out your existing side to help defray the cost of the new purchase. Believe it or not, there are even more miracles. We will see the next one in Chapter 35 entitled "Time Is of the Essence."

SUMMARY

LEAPS combination buying starts by paying two premiums. That is its big disadvantage. Both must be made back to produce a profit. But LEAPS run for a long time and profits generated can be amazingly and even miraculously multiplied.

ADVANCED LEAPS STRATEGIES

CHAPTER 26
SYNTHETIC STOCK
WITH LEAPS

How much stock should I own?

Up to the sleeping point.

STRATEGY	LEAPS Synthetic Stock
OUTLOOK	Very bullish
ADVANTAGES	One leg helps pay for other; magnifies leverage
DRAWBACKS	Downside leverage magnified
DEGREE OF RISK	More intense than stock

What in the world is synthetic stock? Are we to clone or create stock à la Dr. Frankenstein? Maybe! **Synthetic Stock** is the technical name for a combining of two previously seen strategies: writing Puts and buying Calls. If we do both the Put and the Call ATM, their combined deltas will result in the position closely duplicating the stock performance.

Example
XYZ @ 40   No stock position
Write XYZ 6-month 40-strike Put @ 3   delta −42
Buy   XYZ 6-month 40-strike Call @ 4   delta 58

Long 58 delta and short −42 delta becomes $58-(-42) =$ 100. As the stock rises, the combined movements of the Put and the Call should produce profits and losses fairly close to the stock itself.

Should this technique be used with LEAPS? The answer has to be a highly qualified assent. It is suitable for some but not for most. It gives very high leverage, but it carries very high risk as well. Simply phrased, if the stock price goes against you, you may find yourself in an unenviable stance. That is, you will have a long Call (albeit a LEAPS Call) that is declining in value and a written Put (again a LEAPS instrument) on which you may face increasing collateral requirements. Still, isn't this the risk that any stock buyer takes, that is, that the stock will decline? Yes, *but.* . . . Because of the leverage, the risk becomes magnified. A stock price decline becomes a much higher percentage decline in the LEAPS Call value.

Example
XYZ @ 40   No stock position
Write XYZ 6-month 40-strike Put @ 3   delta −42
Buy   XYZ 6-month 40-strike Call @ 4   delta   58

If the stock goes down 10 percent to 36, the Call would probably fall about 2 points from 4 to 2. But that's a 50 percent loss of value.

Still this strategy is not unusable if we make two qualifications. First, this technique should be used only by someone who is familiar with, and comfortable with, the type of risk involved. Second, we can adjust the strikes involved to reduce the risk. For the Call, don't stretch, that is, don't buy a FOM; and for the Put, write only a reasonably far-out-of-the-money strike.

Example
XYZ @ 40   No stock position
Write XYZ Jan (1½ year out) 35-strike LEAPS
   Put @ 4   delta −25
Buy   XYZ Jan (1½ year out) 45-strike LEAPS
   Call @ 6   delta   50

This will give you a lower return but make the strategy safer.

There is a question that should be considered here. How much profit is enough? That is, why are you doing both sides of this strategy? If you buy the LEAPS Call and you are right, you have low dollar investment combined with leverage. If you write the LEAPS Put and you are correct, you will obtain a high return on a low capital investment. Isn't either of these sufficient?

We will now hear from Mr. Ares (named for the Greek god of war):

"Hey, wait a minute. You taught me all these terrific things about LEAPS and now I want to use them to make a killing." We have to reply: Go ahead, if that's your style, but one of the things we have tried to teach about options and LEAPS is that they are vehicles for the transfer of risk. If you use either half of this strategy—that is, buy a LEAPS Call or write a LEAPS Put— you have good potential. *But* if anything goes wrong, there are methods that you can use to repair your position. We know what can go wrong with a synthetic stock position: The stock can go down. And if it does, you will have to deal with *two* separate positions going against you.

Overall, we think it's smarter to choose which half of the strategy you like better and stick with just that part. In each of them, you can elect to be aggressive if that is what you want. For buying LEAPS Calls you can choose a FOM. And for writing LEAPS Puts you could select an ITM or even a DIM. As we discussed in their respective chapters (Chapters 10 and 12), each of these is quite aggressive.

One of the lessons LEAPS have taught us is to stretch the imagination. If we do that here, we can come up with a somewhat startling suggestion. We just advised the very aggressive among us to drop one-half of the LEAPS synthetic stock strategy and stay with the other, favored half. Well, let's turn that whole concept around and see what the very mild-mannered but shrewd LEAPS player might do.

Answer: Combine the most conservative stances of the two separate legs. Buy an ITM LEAPS Call and write an OTM LEAPS Put.

Example
ZXY @ 38   No stock position
Buy   ZXY Jan (1½ year out) 30 LEAPS Call @ 10¾
    delta   80
Write ZXY Jan (1½ year out) 30 LEAPS Put @ 6
    delta −40

Mr. Stickler arrives on the scene. "Hey, wait up there! That's not really synthetic stock." This interrupter is the most right of all the characters who have invaded our analyses, but he's not totally right. Synthetic stock has two characteristics: First, the Put write should pay for the Call purchase (or nearly so); second, the combined deltas should make the combined position emulate the underlying stock's performance.

On the first count, we plead *nolo contendere*. Our write doesn't pay for our long leg. On the second charge, it is now we who say: "Wait up." Our combined deltas will outdo the stock! In the previous example we didn't have a perfect delta sum either. That added to 75; this to 120.

Of course, this can work against us as well. The position will outperform negatively if the stock goes down instead of up. That is the nature of synthetic stock positions, and it is why only the most bullish and bravest (dare we say "the brave bulls"?) among us should employ this method. But it is still another example of how *any* LEAPS trading technique can be implemented across a very wide spectrum. You can use a given strategy in a stance that is very conservative, conservative, moderate, aggressive, or very aggressive. You pays yer money and you picks yer option!

Who's this shouting at us? Why, it's Mr. Super-Stickler! "I still say that's not synthetic stock." We will reply in a way we think is both appropriate and deserved: "That don't make me no nevermind!" What we mean is that it's a waste of time to worry about the *name* of the maneuver. We want it to hold out the desired result for you—bullish, bearish, or neutral. We want it to fit your stance—leverage, protection, or a compromise thereof. We want it to fit your style—conservative, moderate, or aggressive. If you read this book and become proficient with LEAPS, we suspect that you will become indifferent to the labels attached to approaches. You might like this last modified form of LEAPS synthetic stock even if it were known as "the leaping lizards LEAPS!" We recapitulate our posture: If the strategy fits, use it.

SUMMARY

Synthetic stock is not for the novice. When you add LEAPS, you can structure the strategy so that some risks are lessened or you can modify the method to be closer to your own specifications. Still it seems that greed is the predominant motive for this technique. We recommend, except for the aggressive sophisticate, using only either half of this strategy.

CHAPTER 27
SYNTHETIC SHORT
WITH LEAPS

A Bull makes money, sometimes.
A Bear makes money, sometimes.
But a Hog; never.

STRATEGY	LEAPS Synthetic Short
OUTLOOK	Very bearish
ADVANTAGES	One leg helps pay for other; leverage magnified
DRAWBACKS	Losing leverage magnified
DEGREE OF RISK	Similar to short stock

Synthetic Short is just the inverse of synthetic stock. We buy a Put and write an uncovered Call to mimic a short stock position's performance. *Stop!* This may be just the reverse, but it is much more dangerous. We saw the danger in Chapter 20 on writing uncovered Calls. The danger is similar to the difference between long stock and short stock. In the latter the potential for loss is *unlimited*. Who would want to assume such a dangerous position? Someone who was totally convinced of the stock's decline. Still, that stance can be implemented by purchasing a Put without taking on the terrible risk of an uncovered Call as well.

Why also go short an uncovered Call? Should anybody do this with LEAPS? The reply is the same as in the chapter referred to above. Most of us should not get involved in this type of trading. But again LEAPS and strike selection can decrease the danger.

Example
XYZ @ 40
Buy   XYZ 18-month 35-strike LEAPS Put @ 6   delta −25
Write XYZ 18-month 45-strike LEAPS Call @ 4   delta 50

In the discussion of synthetic stock, we said that the strategy was too aggressive for most. That goes more than double here. A long Put has it all over a short sale. That was extensively covered in Chapter 12 on buying LEAPS Puts. A LEAPS Put is even better. That should be enough for all but the option Rambos among us. Even for them we repeat our suggestion made in Chapter 20 on writing uncovered Calls. Consider using this technique with an eye toward early closure.

We could also modify this method as we did in the previous chapter. For the uncovered LEAPS Call, write use a FOM. For the LEAPS Put purchase, try an ATM. And good luck to you (and your heirs)!

Despite all of our negative comments, this technique does have a good use, but that is not by itself as a surrogate short sale position. Rather it is designed as a particular type of protection for a long stock position in certain circumstances. All of the details are in Chapter 32 on LEAPS Fences.

SUMMARY

Even with the advantages of LEAPS, synthetic short is not a recommended method. Maybe it is for hotshots who want to magnify downside leverage several times over. For the rest of us, however, we suggest taking the previous proscriptive interrogatory: "How much profit is enough?" and adding to it the new inhibitor, "How much risk is too much?"

CHAPTER 28
RATIO WRITING WITH LEAPS

All life is six to five against.

STRATEGY	LEAPS Ratio Writing
OUTLOOK	Limited bullish
ADVANTAGES	Extra profit potential
DRAWBACKS	Extra risk; needs monitoring
DEGREE OF RISK	Moderate to high to very high

As always, we must start with a definition. **Ratio Writing** is the writing of more than the equivalent number of Calls than you are long (or currently buying) stock. The word *ratio* refers to the mathematical expression of the number of Calls divided by the number of round lots of stock. Another way of saying this is that you write more Calls than you would have if you were doing covered Call writing.

Example
You buy 500 shares of stock and write six Calls. The ratio here is 6/5 or 1⅕ or 1.2. By now we know the questions we have to ask. What are the risks and rewards of this strategy? What is the motivation for it? To answer these questions we will do what we did in the related technique in Chapter 11 on covered Call writing. That is, we will look at the profit-and-loss potentials first. That will lead us to the motivation.

Example
Buy 500 @ 40   Write six 40 Calls @ 4

If the stock does not rise above 40, you will make $2,400 (versus $2,000 with five covered Calls). Your initial investment would have been $20,000 for the stock, reduced to $17,600 by the option premiums. To that we would have to add $1,000 as collateral for the one uncovered Call: 2400/18600 = 12.9 percent (for the period). This return is questionable except as theory. With the stock "not above 40" you will presumably have an unrealized loss in the stock component of the position.

If the stock rises above 40 and all the Calls are assigned, you may lose money. You have an assignment on one uncovered Call and your obligation on it is to deliver stock at 40. You will have to purchase stock in the market at whatever price it is then trading. Since the stock is above 40, you will lose money on that part. Will you lose money on the entire transaction? In our example 500 shares are a washout. That is, you originally bought the 500 shares at 40 and you will sell them on the assignment at 40. So whether or not there is an overall loss depends on what price you have to pay for the extra 100 shares.

Example
Buy 100 @ 51	Sell 100 @ 40	loss	$1,100
Premiums from Calls written			2,400
Net result		Profit	$1,300

Example
Buy 100 @ 71	Sell 100 @ 40	loss	$3,100
Premium from Calls written			2,400
Net result		Loss	$ 700

We can generalize from these example. The overall profit or loss will be the total premium less the stock covering cost minus the strike. But these two examples dealt with only *one* uncovered Call. Let's look at a higher ratio.

Example
You buy 500 shares of stock and write 10 Calls. The ratio here is 10/5 or 2. This ratio produces more profits at substantially higher risks.

Example
Buy 500 @ 40   Write 10 40 Calls @ 4

First the good news: If the stock does not rise above 40, you will make $ 4,000 (versus $ 2,000 with 5 covered Calls). Your initial investment would have been $20,000 for the stock, reduced to $16,000 by the option premiums. To that we would have to add $5,000 as collateral for the five uncovered Calls, 4000/21000 = 19 percent (for the period). Again, there is a presumptive unrealized stock loss here.

The good news is that we have increased the theoretical return dramatically. The bad news is absolutely awful. It shows what a terrible risk is being taken here. In the example, remember that there are *five* uncovered Calls.

Example

Buy 500 @ 51	Sell 500 @ 40	Loss	$5,500
Premium from Calls written			4,000
Net result		Loss	$1,500

Example

Buy 500 @ 71	Sell 500 @ 40	Loss	$15,500
Premium from Calls written			4,000
Net result		Loss	$11,500

Hoping to make $4,000 and risking losing over $11,000 is not a good way to trade. In fact, the risk was much higher than that. It was absolutely *unlimited*. Making a greater profit sometimes at the risk of unlimited losses at others is, to state it kindly, D-U-M-B. For the rest of us mortals, the moral is more important than the mathematics: the higher the ratio, the higher the risk.

There is another point to be made here. In the ratio = 2 examples, the dreadful losses should never have been allowed to happen. The stock did not go from 40 to 51, let alone 71, while you were sleeping. The position should have been altered or closed long before this eventuation.

We chose a very simple scenario to start off our comprehension of ratio writing. We had both the market price and the strike price at the same level of 40, but no reasonable person would want to do ratio writing under those circumstances. Now that we have some understanding of the process, let's look at some more realistic (and more sensible) examples.

Example
Buy 500 @ 38   Sell six 40 Calls @ 3

In this example, you will make less money with no assignment (compared to the ATM write). If the stock does not rise above 40, you will make $1,800 (versus $ 1,500 with five covered Calls). Your initial investment would have been $19,000 for the stock, reduced to $17,200 by the option premiums. To that we would have to add $750 as collateral for the one uncovered Call (25 percent of 3,800 less 200 OTM); 1800/17950 = 10.0 percent (for the period). This return is just theoretical. The stock could be below 40, but you might have an unrealized loss or an unrealized profit.

But if the stock rises above 40 and you are assigned, you will make some additional profit on the covered portion of the position. That will go to improve the uncovered part. As in the very first example above, we need to look at only the 100 shares that are not covered.

Example

Buy 100 @ 51 Sell 100 @ 40	Loss	$1,100
Premium from Calls written		1,800
Profit from strike differential		1,000
(500 bought @ 38, sold @ 40)		
Net result	Profit	$1,700

Example

Buy 100 @ 71 Sell 100 @ 40	Loss	$3,100
Premium from Calls written		1,800
Profit from strike diffferential		1,000
(500 bought @ 38, sold @ 40)		
Net result	Loss	$ 300

We can generalize from these examples. The overall profit or loss will be the total premium less the stock cost minus the strike, plus the profit on the covered part. Let's redo our examples with the same numbers, but in a different format.

Example

Buy 500 @ 38	Buy 100 @ 51	Cost	$24,100
Sell 600 @ 40		Proceeds	24,000
Premium from Calls written			1,800
Net result		Profit	$ 1,700

Example

Buy 500 @ 38	Buy 100 @ 71	Cost	$26,100
Sell 600 @ 40		Proceeds	24,000
Premium from Calls written			1,800
Net result		Loss	$ 300

A gentle note to the reader:
We note, passim, that in trying to work out what might happen at different points, it's usually a good idea to look at the total money involved.

Now let's look at the higher ratio with some new numbers and in the new format.

Example

Buy 500 @ 38	Buy 500 @ 48	Cost	$43,000
Sell 1,000 @ 40		Proceeds	40,000
Premium from Calls written			3,000
Net result			$ —0—

Example

Buy 500 @ 38	Buy 500 @ 58	Cost	$48,000
Sell 1,000 @ 40		Proceeds	40,000
Premium from Calls written			3,000
Net result		Loss	$ 5,000

This is surely an improvement from our ATM example, but it is certainly still not a good way to trade. The bottom line is that ratio writing is not suitable for many. For those who do find it acceptable, we emphasize the desirability of keeping the ratio low.

We said in the beginning that we would look at profit and loss potentials in order to divine the motivation for this strategy. We think that the motivation for the (sensible) ratio writer is not too dissimilar to that of the covered Call writer. The outlook for both is a bullish one, but limited in nature. There is a crucial difference between them, however. The difference is that the covered Call writer takes on only an opportunity risk if the stock rises more than expected, while the ratio writer pays in dollars for that error. Of course, the ratio position must be watched like a hawk. In exchange for those extra risks, there is a larger cushion on the downside and a greater return if the stock rises but does not greatly exceed the strike.

We need to reexamine the last sentence. The first half can be given an unqualified approval; not so for the second. What is missing is the role of the ratio. We have said before that the ratio should be kept low. Now let us quantify that sentiment.

Examples/Table
Buy 500 @ 38   Sell X# 40 Calls @ 3

Number of uncovered Calls	Profit or loss @ 58
1	+$1,000
2	−$ 500
3	−$2,000
4	−$3,500
5	−$5,000

The table should make clearer the idea of a low ratio being more desirable. We can express that in a conceptual analogy. If the ratio is 1:1 (1 Call:100 shares), we are dealing with covered Call writing; if the ratio is 1:0 (1 Call:0 shares), we are talking about uncovered Call writing. We gave that strategy short shrift (deliberate pun) in Chapter 20. Here we observe that as we move the ratio upwards from 1, we move from a conservative technique to a very dangerous one. What seems at first like only a quantitative distinction becomes a qualitative difference of a high order of magnitude. In brief, we think that (low) ratio writing has its adherents, but that almost all should shun (high) ratio writing.

We have spent an atypically long time expounding this strategy before we mentioned LEAPS. That is because it is a more complex and potentially more dangerous technique. It is unquestionably more risky if you don't have a clear comprehension of its workings. That said, now what about LEAPS ratio writing? As we have seen many times before, the strategy improves with LEAPS. You get paid a premium that is much larger (in dollars) than with ordinary options. And you can get that high-dollar number on a moderately OTM LEAPS Call.

Example
Buy 500 YXZ @ 38
Write six YXZ 18-month 45-strike LEAPS Calls @ 7

That higher dollar premium is one of the keys to the successful implementation of this technique. Still we must keep the ratio low enough to still promise profit without escalating the risk beyond acceptability. We venture to state that very few of our readers will guess the upside break-even point at expiration for the above position. Is it 60 or 80 or 99? The correct answer is 122!

Buy 500 @ 38	Buy 100 @ 122	Cost	$31,200
Sell 600 @ 45		Proceeds	27,000
Premium from Calls written			4,200
Net result		Upside break-even	$ —0—

"Hey, that's great!" For goodness' sake, look who's talking: It's Mr. Converted LEAPSman (né Skeptic)! "I want some of that action! You were just kidding about the dangers, right? Let's do it with 10 LEAPS Calls." They say that recent converts make the most ardent proselytizers. Why don't we take a look:

Example
Buy 500 YXZ @ 38
Write 10 18-month 45-Strike LEAPS Calls @ 7
Here the expiration B/E is 66.

Buy 500 @ 38	Buy 500 @ 66	Cost	$52,000
Sell 1000 @ 45		Proceeds	45,000
Premium from Calls written			7,000
Net result		Break-even	$ —0—

The sound you hear is the cheering of Mr. LEAPSman.

We make it a point never to cheer before we check. A B/E point of 122 doesn't seem at all frightening. It seems so good, let's worry about what's wrong. The catch is that it's the B/E *at expiration*. A $38 stock could reasonably be deemed quite unlikely to reach 122, even in 18 months. But during that long period of time, it could easily get to 66 well in *advance* of expiration. And that wouldn't be so good! If, in our second example, it did get there (or seemed likely to be well on its way), that position should be altered or closed immediately. Better still, it should never have been created. LEAPS are great and there is enough money to be made on the writing side. That could be with writing Puts, covered Call writing, or (low) ratio writing. (High) ratio writing is actually a different strategy. Let's leave it to those who need to learn from experience.

SUMMARY

We are not so negative on ratio writing as we were on uncovered Call writing. We distinguish between low and high ratios as really being two different methods. Even low ratio writing should be practiced only by those who are quite experienced. Sensibly handled (at initiation and with monitoring), LEAPS low ratio writing can be very rewarding and considerably less risky.

CHAPTER 29
RATIO SPREADING
WITH LEAPS

. . . increases in the ratio. . . .

STRATEGY	LEAPS Ratio Spreading
OUTLOOK	Limited bullish
ADVANTAGES	Leverage to high leverage
DRAWBACKS	High percentage at risk
DEGREE OF RISK	High, to very high

A gentle note to the (perhaps exhausted) reader:
Relax. The author knows that you have just been through a long and extremely complex chapter. We will try to keep this one relatively short and simple.

Ratio Spreading is the sale of more Calls than purchased Calls on the same underlying and usually with the same expiration.

Example
Buy   5 40-strike Calls
Write 6 50-strike Calls

We could say that this is a bull Call spread with some additional Calls written. Ratio spreading is very similar to ratio writing. In the latter, one buys stock and writes more Calls than would be covered. In the former, one buys options and writes more than the number bought. We can express this as a formal analogy:

Ratio spreading is to ratio writing as bullish Call spreads are to covered Call writing.

Just about everything we said in Chapter 28 on ratio writing applies here as well, but there is a kicker which is easily grasped through the analogy. Because options (or LEAPS) are being bought instead of stock, the outlay is substantially lower.

Example

Buy 500 @ 38	Buy 5 35-strike Calls @ 5
Write 6 40-strike Calls @ 3	Write 6 40-strike Calls @ 3

The initial investment in the first case is $19,000 for the stock, reduced to $17,200 by the option premiums. To that we would have to add $ 750 as collateral for the one uncovered Call. That gives us a total of $17,950. In the second case we need the same $750 for the single uncovered Call, but the rest is only the collateral for 5 bull Call spreads. That is five times the two-point debit or $1,000. Thus the ratio spread needs only $1,750 at first, in comparison to the $17,950 for the ratio write. That's good, because it will lower your cost, lower your risk, and give you greater leverage.

> *A gentle note to the reader:*
> *Watch out! Leverage is appealing, but it is always accompanied by higher risk. Don't be seduced. Keep the size of your position in line. And don't forget that leverage cuts both ways.*

That last warning line can be checked in Chapter 17 on bull Call spreads. In addition to keeping a rein on leverage, the proscription against high ratios is in force here as well. Keep the ratio low if you want to employ this method in the market.

Examples

Buy 5 35-strike Calls @ 5	Buy 5 35-strike Calls @ 5
Write 6 40-strike Calls @ 3	Write 10 40-strike Calls @ 3

We have already seen the initial collateral requirement for the first case. It is $1,750. For the second (with 5 uncovered calls) it would be $4,750. The first position is suitable for few, but for some. We wouldn't want to see anybody take on the second.

There is one difference between the two techniques. You can utilize ratio spreading for Puts as well as for Calls.

Example

ZYX @ 40   No stock position

Buy   5 ZYX 40-strike Puts @ 3

Write 6 ZYX 35-strike Puts @ 1

In line with the analogy we made before, this is like a bear Put spread with some additional Puts sold. All the same warnings apply to ratio spreading with Puts as they did with Calls. Do this only if you are completely convinced of the stock's direction. Do it only in reasonable size. And keep the ratio low.

Reminder

These, like all the other spreads we have mentioned, must go in a margin account.

We have the basics and the warnings; let's move on to LEAPS ratio spreading.

As we have seen many times before, this strategy improves with LEAPS. You get paid a premium that is much larger (in dollars) than with ordinary options. And you can get that high-dollar number on a moderately OTM LEAPS Call.

Example

ZYX @ 38   No stock position

Buy   5 YXZ 18-month 35-strike LEAPS Calls @ 12

Write 6 YXZ 18-month 45-strike LEAPS Calls @ 7

That higher dollar premium is one of the keys to the successful implementation of this technique. As we said in the previous chapter, we must keep the ratio low enough to still promise profit but not to escalate risk beyond acceptability.

Example

Buy 500 @ 35, buy 100 @ 77	Costs	$25,200
Premium for Calls bought		6,000
Sell 600 @ 45	Proceeds	27,000
Premium from Calls written		4,200
Net result	Upside break-even	$ —0—

This B/E point is much lower than the corresponding one in the ratio writing example. That is because there is an initial debit incurred from doing the spread. We don't think we have to provide more examples and fulminate against a high ratio. The reader has surely gotten the point. Just as with ratio writing, ratio spreading is really more than one strategy. If the ratio is low, it has some risks and should be done sparingly and carefully. But if the ratio is high it turns into a totally different technique and should be avoided.

SUMMARY

LEAPS ratio spreading, like LEAPS ratio writing, has a place in the pantheon of option strategies, but that place is reserved for those who are very sophisticated. Further, as the ratio rises, risk rises as well, and the use of high ratios is strongly discouraged. If LEAPS are used and the ratio is kept rational, the technique becomes more reasonable.

CHAPTER 30
AVERAGING DOWN
WITH LEAPS

Just let me get out even and I promise never to do it again.

STRATEGY	Averaging Down with LEAPS
OUTLOOK	Bullish despite decline
ADVANTAGES	Leverage to high leverage; limited dollar risk
DRAWBACKS	High percentage at risk
DEGREE OF RISK	High, but can be reduced

Averaging down is a standard and well-known method for stock investors and traders. It simply means buying more of a stock that has declined. If the stock rises suitably, the double position may then be sold. This allows "getting even" without the stock returning to its original purchased price.

Example

You bought 500 shares of XZY @ 90. It has gone down to 70, but you feel sure it will retrace some of this decline. You buy a second lot of 500 @ 70. The stock does rebound, and when it reaches 80, you sell out all 1,000 shares.

500 @ 90 cost $45,000
500 @ 70 cost $35,000
Total $80,000   1,000 @ 80   Sale $80,000

Another way of looking at what happened is to say that (per 100 shares), when you sold @ 80, you lost 10 points on the first lot, but gained 10 points on the second lot, breaking even. You have accomplished your objective. You have broken even without the stock returning to its original cost level of 90.

We make several observations:

1. The second purchase should be an amount of stock equal to the original.

2. The technique allows you to get a lower break-even price.
3. The procedure should be used only if you retain some bullishness on the stock. That might be only the expectation of a rebound. Like many market strategies (stock, options, or LEAPS), it should not be used for its own sake but solely as a method to implement financially your expectations. There are two obvious and relevant proverbs here: "Put your money where your mouth is" and "Don't throw good money after bad."
4. Many people are more aware of and use this method near the year's end, looking for a tax benefit as well as a better break-even point.
5. Some realize that Calls can be substituted for the second lot of stock. That last concept has a lot going for it.

Example

You bought 500 shares of XZY @ 90. As we saw above, it goes down to 70. But this time your purchase is 5 XZY 60-strike Calls @ 11. The stock goes to 80; you sell out the stock @ 80 and the Calls @ 20 (no time value at all).

500 @ 90 cost	$45,000	500 @ 80 sale	$40,000
5 Calls @ 11 cost	$ 5,500	5 calls @ 20 sale	$10,000
Total cost	$50,500	Total sale	$50,000

Viewed alternatively, you lost 10 points on the stock and made 9 on the Calls, losing 1 point 5 times or −$500. Either way you did not break even, or rather you did not break even perfectly. You missed out by $500.

If, in our realistic example, we finished a little shy of the target, why did we say this method had a lot going for it? Because it does. With the stock you reinvested $35,000; with the Calls only $5,500. You could have invested the difference—$29,500—in Treasury securities during that time.

We have illustrated averaging down using options instead of a second lot of stock. If we substituted longer-term options, we would have **LEAPS Averaging Down.** Note that in our example we used an ITM example and an equal number of Calls. One of the well-known ways of implementing this method is to buy ATM Calls and to buy enough of them to give a delta of 100 so as to mimic the stock. You still would invest substantially less than the cost of a second stock lot. If you do this and the stock continues its fall instead of rebounding, your loss would be limited to the Call premium. The stock could produce a larger loss than that.

Obviously we could expand on this interesting technique. We could compare OTM, ATM, and ITM Calls, look at different deltas, see what leverage could do, etc. But that is not our intention here. We want to see what the advantages might be of substituting not conventional Calls, but LEAPS Calls in this strategy.

The primary risk using options instead of stock is that the stock won't move up enough before the expiration date. Obviously with LEAPS that is far less of a problem. You may not want to hold on for such a long time. But if the stock does rebound, the LEAPS will carry more time premium than a shorter-term option and you will profit by that difference.

Caveat: The tax-related information in this chapter has been obtained from sources we consider reliable, but we do not guarantee it. Tax laws, and the regulatory and judicial interpretation of such laws, are subject to change. Before entering into any tax-related strategy, investors should consult with a competent tax adviser.

Now let's look at the delta idea that could be employed in averaging down with LEAPS. Buy approximately 2 ATM LEAPS Calls for every 100 shares of XYZ you already own.

Example
Long XZY @ 90
XZY now @ 70
Buy eight XZY 18-month LEAPS 70 Calls @ 8 ½

After a relatively short time (one to three months), XZY rebounds and reaches 80. You sell out the LEAPS Calls @ 15 and the stock @ 80.

XZY	$5 \times -10 \ (80–90)$	$= -\$5,000$
XZY LEAPS Calls	$8 \times 6½ \ (15 - 8 \ ½) =$	$+\$5,200$
		$\$ \ \ 200$

You have broken even in the 90–70–80 move. Using LEAPS instead of stock for the averaging-down purchase cost you 8 × 8 ½ or $6,800 instead of 500 × 70 or $35,000. As we have always advised, these saved dollars could be invested in Treasury securities in the interim. But why did we buy eight LEAPS Calls instead of five or 10? We started by saying "approximately two" for every 100 shares. We wanted to replicate the performance of a second lot of stock. We get that by dividing the number of shares by the LEAPS Call's delta (in this case 62), 500 / 62 = 8 (rounded).

It's important to be aware of the Internal Revenue Service's *wash sale rule* when you use options/LEAPS strategies. We will give you our understanding of that so long as the reader knows that we are not tax experts. For more details, see Chapter 42 on taxes. Under the current provisions of the wash sale rule, a loss resulting from the sale of stock will be deferred if within 30 days the same security, a substantially identical security, or an option to purchase such a security is bought. The 30-day period specified by the rule refers to both the 30 days prior to a stock sale and the 30 days afterward. Since XYZ LEAPS Calls are options to acquire XYZ stock, they are considered to be an equivalent of it. Therefore, if you bought LEAPS Calls and subsequently sold your stock at a loss without waiting at least 31 days, the rule would affect the tax treatment of your loss. The disallowed loss on your stock would be added to the acquisition price of the LEAPS Calls, creating a higher cost basis for them. The ultimate result would be a reduction of the gain (or an increase of the loss) on the LEAPS Calls when there was a taxable disposition of them. Were the LEAPS Calls to be exercised, their higher basis is added to the cost basis of the new stock. In addition, the holding period that had accrued on the stock before it was sold would be "tacked on" to the holding period for the LEAPS Calls.

A gentle note to the taxed reader:
We're sorry this got so complicated. We really tried to simplify it, but with the IRS there are limits to what you can do.

If the stock moves up and the overall stock/LEAPS Calls position is profitable there are several ways you could handle it. For example, let's assume the stock is trading below your purchase price, but has moved up enough to make your LEAPS Calls profitable. Let's also assume that the gain in the LEAPS Calls exceeds the loss in the stock. You could take advantage of this opportunity to "clean house" and get out of the entire position at a profit by simultaneously selling the stock at a loss and the LEAPS Calls at a profit. Here the wash sale rule would not result in a continuing deferment, since the position triggering the rule was sold as well. Alternatively, you could keep the stock if you believed it could go even higher and view the LEAPS Call's profits as a cushion against the risk of continuing to hold the stock.

Summary
It must be emphasized that this strategy should be used only by an investor who remains strongly bullish on the stock involved and is aware of the risks attending Call buying. Within this framework averaging down with LEAPS rather than additional stock could prove rewarding. LEAPS averaging down has possible tax benefits and consequences that should be checked carefully, but the technique is not limited to tax advantages.

CHAPTER 31
DOLLAR-COST AVERAGING
WITH LEAPS

It's my own invention.

STRATEGY	LEAPS Dollar-Cost Averaging
OUTLOOK	Bullish, bearish, or hedged
ADVANTAGES	Systematic investing at lower cost
DRAWBACKS	Untried technique; needs discipline
DEGREE OF RISK	Depends on stock/sector selection

Caveat. This is a new and theoretical strategy that—to the author's knowledge—has never been publicly analyzed. Perhaps some brave individuals have inaugurated this technique on their own. Still there is no evidence—statistical or even anecdotal—on the efficacy of this stratagem.

What is **Dollar-Cost Averaging?** Dollar-cost averaging—henceforth, we will say DCA—consists of systematically buying equal *dollar* amounts of a stock you favor strongly. Note that you do buy equal dollar amounts, *not* quantities of stock. We will look at investing every quarter.

Start	Stock @ 60	Buy 500 shares = $30,000
3 months later	Stock @ 50	Buy 600 shares = $30,000
6 months later	Stock @ 40	Buy 750 shares = $30,000
9 months later	Stock @ 50	Buy 600 shares = $30,000
12 months later	Stock @ 60	Buy 500 shares = $30,000
15 months later	Stock @ 75	Buy 400 shares = $30,000
18 months later	Stock @ 60	Buy 500 shares = $30,000

Over the course of a year and a half, the stock started and ended at 60. In between, it went up and down. You bought a total of 3,850 shares and invested a total of $210,000. That means you had an *average* cost of 54.54 per share. The reason this method works is that it makes you buy more stock when the price is lower and less when it is higher. Of course, we have to stipulate that the stock should not fall into a continued downtrend. Our illustration is somewhat idealized in order to demonstrate the mechanism.

How can we use this technique with LEAPS? Take the stock of choice and start buying the farthest-out LEAPS Calls. Some warnings are appropriate here. The stock should be one on which you have an absolutely unqualified longer-term bullish view. That would probably imply that it should be a superior growth stock. Do not spend all your money at once. Plan on investing equal dollar amounts at periodic intervals. If you start with LEAPS at, or close to, a two- to two-and-one-half-year life and invest monthly, you will make somewhere between 16 and 24 purchases. By then the LEAPS will be approaching their changeover to conventional options, and that is probably a good point to stop.

Which strike should you use here? All the previous comments about matching strike to expectation and to risk attitudes apply with intensified force here. This writer thinks that, notwithstanding this comment, you are probably best-off with a DIM call. That provides a straight surrogate for the stock at a lower cost. Those whose bullishness cannot be restrained could lower the cost further by picking a less DIM, an ATM, or even a slightly OTM LEAPS Call.

Should you stop if the stock goes down? This sounds like a difficult question. We need to walk a tightrope here, balancing the need to maintain the investment at lower prices with the necessity of avoiding adding money to a losing investment. This is why we prefer a DIM call. If that is selected, the question becomes much easier to answer. Simply substitute in your mind the stock for its LEAPS surrogate. The whole idea of implementing the strategic concept is to keep on buying even when the stock is lower.

So keep on buying when the LEAPS Calls are lower. Of course, you might change your fundamental attitude about the stock. If you would halt when buying the pure stock, then you should do the same with LEAPS. Even here, there is an option alternative. You could keep the purchased LEAPS Calls and hedge that position by writing other options or LEAPS against them.

LEAPS Dollar-Cost Averaging

1. Start	Stock @ 60 18-month LEAPS 45 Call @ 18½.	Buy 10 = $18,500
2. 1 month later	Stock @ 60 17-month LEAPS 45 Call @ 18.	Buy 10 = $18,000
3. 2 months later	Stock @ 50 16-month LEAPS 45 Call @ 10.	Buy 18 = $18,000
4. 3 months later	Stock @ 50 15-month LEAPS 45 Call @ 9⅞.	Buy 19 = $18,763
5. 4 months later	Stock @ 45 14-month LEAPS 45 Call @ 6½.	Buy 28 = 18,200
6. 5 months later	Stock @ 40 13-month LEAPS 45 Call @ 4.	Buy 45 = $18,000
7. 6 months later	Stock @ 45 12-month LEAPS 45 Call @ 6.	Buy 30 = $18,000
8. 7 months later	Stock @ 50 11-month LEAPS 45 Call @ 9.	Buy 20 = $18,000
9. 8 months later	Stock @ 60 10-month LEAPS 45 Call @ 17.	Buy 11 = $18,700

Over these eight months the stock started and ended at 60. You bought a total of 191 LEAPS Calls and invested a total of $164,162.50 for an average cost of 859.49. Two months later, if the stock is @ 60, you could sell them all (for between 15 and 16).

You could also buy the stock at a discount by exercising the Calls (giving up any time premium). Finally (our choice), you could sell out the Calls and buy the stock; 191 Calls sold @ 16 = $305,600. Subtracting the cost leaves $141,437.50. This would give you an approximate average cost of 52⅝ on your 19,100 shares.

COMPARISON

	Time	$ Invested	LEAPS/shares	Average cost
Stock	18 months	210,000	3,850	54½
LEAPS Calls	8 months	164,163	191 (= 19,100)	52⅝

We hasten to point out that both examples were idealized constructs to demonstrate the old and new techniques. Intellectual honesty compels us to say that in the (exaggerated) LEAPS fluctuations we might not have held on. Still we believe if you believe. That is, we believe in the system if you believe in the stock.

Some additional comments: Should your investments be at a lower frequency than monthly? Probably not. That is easy to follow and provides discipline without difficulty. Should you invest more frequently? We say definitely not. This is an *investment* method, and we don't want to turn it into a trading technique. Should you invest at the same time every month? And which time should it be? Yes, we think you should. It adds to the disciplinary devotion that is so important. As for which time, pick whatever is convenient for you and stick with it. There is one exception here. Try to avoid days within "expiration week." In Chapter 41 on LEAPS and program trading, we describe how you can use this aberrant phenomenon to your advantage. But for long-term investment there is no reason to subject yourself to the wacky whipsaws that often occur in that period.

Should you invest with other than straight LEAPS Calls? Some who are comfortable with the alternative method could use bullish LEAPS Call spreads as described in Chapter 17. We think that for most investors KISS is appropriate: "Keep It Simple, Sweetheart."

You could also buy Puts rather than Calls if you had a severely longer-term negative outlook on the stock. You could invest in more than one stock either way. In fact you could play *mix and match*. That is, you could dollar-cost average with LEAPS Calls on one stock and with LEAPS Puts on another. Expanding the number of stocks leads us to our final comment. You could implement this technique using index LEAPS. Dollar-cost averaging for the entire market—or a substantial section of it—has never really been available as a direct investment before. Of course, people have done the equivalent by using DCA with a broad-based mutual fund or even an indexed fund. Here you can do it for yourself. You will find more details on this method in Chapter 38 on index LEAPS.

SUMMARY

Although this is not a time-tested technique, we think LEAPS dollar-cost averaging has great promise for patient and disciplined investors. Those with faith in their stock can be rewarded with LEAPS DCA. The possibility of using both LEAPS Calls and LEAPS Puts speaks to the type of markets we have been in. The ability to transfer this technique to the entire market or to market sectors is an exciting development. Further, there is the potential to play off one group against another or versus the entire market.

CHAPTER 32
LEAPS FENCES

Good fences make good neighbors.

STRATEGY	LEAPS Fences
OUTLOOK	Protective
ADVANTAGES	Guarantees an "out"
DRAWBACKS	Complex; limits profits
DEGREE OF RISK	Extremely low

This strategy has several different names. Many call it a *hedge wrap* or a *hedge wrapper.* Some describe it as a *collar.* Another name is *fence.* This last name is fairly widely used in the commodities business. The author's favorite is *two-way stretch,* but that never caught on. We will stay with *fences.*

Now that we have the title, what is the technique? Consider an investor who is nervous about holding onto a stock that has appreciated in value. S/he knows that a Put could be purchased that would protect the accumulated profit. More precisely, after making allowances for the Put's cost, a high percentage of the profit would be guaranteed for the life of the Put. We saw this in Chapter 15 on LEAPS protective Puts.

S/he is also aware that writing a covered Call against stock held at a profit can hedge that position. Here money is received rather than paid. But it gives a cushion, not a guaranteed out. Which strategy is better? Many people have pondered this problem and a long time ago it was solved. The solution in certain circumstances is to do both! Write an OTM call and use the proceeds to finance the purchase of a protective Put. That is what's called a **Fence.**

Example
ZXY cost 33, now @ 47
Write ZXY 50 Call   Buy ZXY 45 Put (approximately equal
                    dollars)

Let's be specific about what this double-barreled maneuver accomplishes. If the stock rises, you will get out at a better price than where the stock was when you hedged it. If the stock should fall, you do have a guaranteed "out price," and the downside protection costs little to nothing.

Example

Long ZXY, now   @ 47
Write ZXY 50 Call @ 3
Buy   ZXY 45 Put @ 2⅝
Net credit   ⅜

If the stock rises and ends above 50, you will be out at an effective price of 50⅜. If the stock falls and ends below 45, you will be able to exercise the Put and sell at 45 (and gain ⅜ from the net credit). These two exit points are, respectively, 7.2 percent above and 3.5 percent below the stock's price at the time of hedging.

Some people might implement this technique but feel disappointed at its fruition. The stock might rise further than expected. Of course, this is a drawback of covered Call writing. Because the Put's strike is below the market, more could have been gotten by simply selling out. We note impassively that these two objections contradict each other. That is, the first would be relevant if the stock continued on upward. The second would apply if the stock fell. This is the rationale for the strategy: You are worried and/or nervous about which path the stock might take. This method speaks to both problems, albeit with some limitations. Enter LEAPS to the rescue!

The objection about not getting enough on the upside is taken care of by selling the first OTM strike. Because the Call written is a LEAPS Call, a large dollar premium will be received, and adding the distance from market price to strike results in an even higher "out" price.

Example

Long YZX, now @ 90
Write YZX LEAPS 95 CALL @ 12½

If the stock is called, you will be out @ 95. You will also gain some of the 12½ premium as well. We say "some" because the rest of it is going to be used for the LEAPS Put purchase. For the LEAPS Put, select the strike as close as possible to market. The LEAPS Call premium will sometimes pay for this in full.

Example

Long YZX, now   @ 90
Write YZX LEAPS 95 Call @ 12½
Buy   YZX LEAPS 80 Put @ 6½
Net credit   6

Why did we choose an 80 Put, rather than an 85? Simple. There was no 85. However, we still will have some good news here in a moment. Let's recapitulate: If the stock ends above 95, you will be out @ 101 (95 strike plus 6 credit). If the stock ends below 80, your out price will be 86 (80 strike plus 6 credit). That's the good news we referred to. Even though we are using an 80 strike, the credit generated got us out above the level of an 85 strike. In percentage terms, this technique got us out on the upside 12.2 percent above the stock's price.

This also captured most of the built-up profit by producing an out price on the downside only 4.4 percent below the stock's price. These figures are theoretical in order to explain the process. In practice, they would be altered by considering what to do with the two options. Specific illustrations are coming in a moment.

Whether the stock went up or down after you erected your fence, you were able to generate and guarantee an out price for your stock. You guaranteed a profit without paying any money (or only a small sum) to accomplish that guarantee. We think that's wonderful. It is one of many option techniques that reward the investor for using options rather than dismissing them as mere speculation.

This strategy is certainly not for all. It might be deemed too complex for some. Others would prefer one leg or the other, but not both. But for those who have the expectation/fear, it fills the bill very nicely. We note that the position of long Put with written Call is our old friend *synthetic short*. It's no surprise then that the theoretical equivalent of a short stock position can be used as a hedge for a long one. It shows us that we should never dismiss a LEAPS strategy out-of-hand. Synthetic short was one we advised against as an initial position; here we have used it to protect a profitable, but worrisome, position. For the majority of our strategy expositions, we have reserved follow-up action—whether enhancement or repair—for a separate chapter. For LEAPS fences, we will speak about it in its home chapter.

Suppose, after you build the fence, the stock falls—fast and furiously. What to do? Remember that we implemented this technique in order to preserve profit.

Example
Long   YZX, now   @ 90
Write YZX LEAPS 95 Call @ 12½
Buy   YZX LEAPS 80 Put @   6½

When you established this fence, let's say both the LEAPS Put and Call had 14 months to run. Now, five months later, we find the following prices:
YZX   @ 79
YZX LEAPS 95 Call @   3½
YZX LEAPS 80 Put @   8½

What should be done with this position? There are many possibilities, but we will examine only the simplest: Close all. Buy back the written LEAPS Call, sell the stock, and sell out the LEAPS Put. (Of course, we don't exercise the Put; that would abandon all of its time value.) You would get a 5 credit here, plus the 6 credit earlier. That would produce an effective sale price for the stock of 90. Thus, even though the stock fell 12 percent, you got out even, and you didn't pay any dollars to achieve that protection.

Now, let us postulate for the same time frame that the stock rises well above the strike of the written LEAPS Call.

YZX   @ 100
YZX LEAPS 95 Call @   14½
YZX LEAPS 80 Put @   3½

While there are many avenues open here, once more we will observe the total closure. Sell the stock, sell out the LEAPS Put, and buy back the LEAPS Call. A debit of 11 is created from the last two transactions. We subtract our previous 6 credit for a 5 net debit. That brings the stock sale down to an effective price of 95. So in this scenario you got all but the last 5 points of the stock's additional increase. Phrased another way, you captured 50 percent of the stock's rise. The important aspect here is to remember that you didn't know the stock was going to rise. You were worried that it might fall.

In both extrapolations, we examined only the complete closure of the positions. As always, whether this was the best move would have been up to you to decide. And your decision would be based on your expectations and attitude for the stock at those points. The point about LEAPS Fences is that this technique allowed you to cope with *both* the fear of falling and the worry about missing more profits. Being able to accomplish this with little to no dollar expenditure is one more example of the amazing abilities of LEAPS.

SUMMARY

Using a LEAPS fence is a relatively complex option strategy. It is still satisfactory for many investors, but only if its mechanism fits their expectations. While we have said that about every LEAPS strategy, it is probably most applicable here. Fences should not be built just because the position is there. The technique also has the greatest drawback from nonexistent strikes. Still LEAPS fences are superior to conventional ones giving rise to our quote improvement: "Good fences make good protection."

STRATEGIES
UNIQUE TO LEAPS

CHAPTER 33
LEAPS SURROGATE THERAPY (DIM LEAPS CALLS AS STOCK SUBSTITUTE)

... substitute for inner worth.

STRATEGY	DIM LEAPS Calls as Stock Substitute
OUTLOOK	Bullish to very bullish
ADVANTAGES	Leverage to high leverage; limited dollar risk
DRAWBACKS	Higher percentage at risk
DEGREE OF RISK	Comparable to long stock

In Chapter 10 on LEAPS Call buying we referred to an additional method. That technique we label **LEAPS Surrogate Therapy,** which consists simply of buying DIM LEAPS Calls as a surrogate for straight stock purchases. Since all Call buying might be regarded as a substitute for the stock, what distinction are we making here? Let's go back—first in time, and then to basics—to see what is involved.

Listed options trading started on the CBOE 20 years ago. Almost from day one, savvy participants understood that there could be a lot more to Call buying than outright speculation. While the traditional vehicle for this strategy—buying out-of-the-money Calls—offers the lovely lure of leverage, this is certainly not the entire story.

Our previous considerations were for LEAPS ATM and OTM. We want to espouse a different viewpoint here. That viewpoint is for a different person. It is intended for a very low-risk-profile person. Such an investor or trader can find an advantage to substituting the in-the-money LEAPS Call for a straight stock purchase. This is similar to *leveraging up*—buying the stock on margin instead of cash. For the same dollars, you could control roughly twice as much stock.

Example
ZYX @ 75

ZYX 4-month	55 Call @ 21	time value 1
ZYX 14-month LEAPS	55 Call @ 22½	time value 2½

Notice the favorable comparison between the 4- and 14-month time values of 1 and 2½. On a monthly basis you would be paying for time value at rates of, respectively, .25 and .18.

Buy stock—cash	$7,500
Buy stock—margin	$3,750; 50 percent of cash cost (pay margin interest)
Buy LEAPS DIM Call	$2,250; 30 percent of cash cost (no margin interest)

There are both advantages and drawbacks to this technique. First and foremost, you are investing fewer dollars and will get a movement very similar to that of the stock itself. This implies that while you could still lose money on such trades, it would not be for the all too frequent reason. You might lose because you chose the wrong stock or timed the purchase incorrectly. You would not lose because you selected an option with a relatively short period until expiration.

Drawbacks. No dividends. As a Call owner, you will not be a stockholder and will not collect any dividends. You also will not be eligible to go to the annual meeting or receive the annual report. Of the 127 stocks now trading LEAPS, all but 20 currently pay some dividend; the mean yield of these is 2.7 percent. For those that pay no dividends, this is not currently a factor. We will see below that perceived "loss" of dividends from switching strategies (outright stock ownership to long DIM LEAPS) can be offset by other financial factors.

Advantages. As alluded to above, you are investing fewer dollars. You could control more than 100 shares or you could buy LEAPS on more than one security. If you stuck to one unit of stock, the amount "saved" could be invested elsewhere as discussed previously. Indeed, if the alternate investment were made in Treasury securities, you would generate additional risk-free dollars that might partially offset (or occasionally exceed) the dividend loss. For those who invest on margin, there would be a saving of margin interest. This is a not inconsiderable amount over the time involved.

The purchase of the LEAPS 55 Call in place of the stock "cost" you the two-and-one-half-point time value. You may miss as many as five projected dividends, say, $175. You would "save" $5,250, which invested at 7 percent in Treasury securities would generate about $360. You would "save" $950 versus buying ZYX on margin, but you would pay no margin interest on the Call purchase. This would "save" about $460.

Obviously, this strategy is not a panacea. It certainly has benefits for investors who understand the risks involved. It allows an investment surrogate at a fraction of the stock's cost. That gives leverage or allows diversification.

SUMMARY

LEAPS Surrogate therapy—buying DIM LEAPS Calls as a substitute for stock—is very different from buying OTM LEAPS Calls. That's OK. The two techniques are appropriate for different people and at different times. For those with a pronounced bullish expectation and a strong degree of risk aversion, this strategy must ring the bell. We deliberately said *must* rather than *might* because of reports we have seen that say this is the most popular LEAPS strategy.

CHAPTER 34
LEAPS REPLACEMENT THERAPY

You can't eat your cake and have it too.

STRATEGY	LEAPS Replacement
OUTLOOK	Nervous about longs
ADVANTAGES	Profit and capital out of market; participate in strong upmoves
DRAWBACKS	Need to make up LEAPS premium
DEGREE OF RISK	Low

Our quote is one of the most venerable in the English language, and we should respect its wisdom about the inability to do contradictory things. But, as we have seen before, with options and LEAPS you can do a lot of things that would have been impossible otherwise. What can you do akin to the title with LEAPS?

Suppose you own a stock and you are growing increasingly nervous about holding onto it. Still, you don't want to sell it. What to do? We have seen that in such a situation, you can buy a Put to protect accumulated or potential profits. We have also seen that you can write a Call for a downside cushion. We have looked at doing both—fences. There is still another strategy that can be employed: **LEAPS Replacement Therapy.** You sell out the stock and replace it with a LEAPS Call.

Example
XYZ @ 64   Jan (1½ years out)   LEAPS 60 Call @ 10¾

In this example we replace the stock with a DIM LEAPS Call. This is a twist on surrogate therapy. There we bought the LEAPS Call *instead* of the stock. Here, while we still expect something good from the stock, we have lowered the original cash investment. This still allows a profit from up moves. What can be done with the saved funds? Anything you want. They could be used to buy Treasury securities, another stock, or another LEAPS Call.

Do we have to use a DIM? No. When you sell out the stock, you could replace it with OTM, ATM, ITM, or DIM LEAPS. Indeed, you can replace the stock on other than a 1:1 ratio. If you are buying an ATM LEAP with a delta of 50, you could buy 2 of them and see the equivalent rise (or fall) as with the stock.

Example
XYZ @ 64   Jan (1½ years out)   LEAPS 70 Call @ 8
                                       (delta 50)

There is also a completely different way to accomplish a similar end. That consists of selling out the stock and writing a LEAPS Put.

Example
XYZ @ 64   Jan (1½ years out)   LEAPS 55 Put @ 4

There are two negatives here: If the stock goes down, and you are assigned and if the stock continues down you may lose money. That would be the same as holding on to the stock originally. Rather, it would be similar, but not the same.

Example
XYZ @ 64 (stock retained)   Sell XYZ, write Jan 55 LEAPS
                                  Put @ 4

XYZ drops to 50
Stock loss $1,400   Put position loss $500
                                  (less 400 premium)

XYZ drops to 40
Stock loss $2,400   Put position loss $1,500
                                  (less 400 premium)

A gentle note to the reader:
  We note in passing that probably the first stock position and surely both the stock and the LEAPS Put in the second position should have been altered or closed before these losses grew.

There are a variety of viewpoints to consider in this apparently simple scenario. We showed the losses as lower with the

LEAPS Put positions; that was for dollars but not for percentages. If you held onto the stock, the losses would have been 22 percent and 38 percent. The LEAPS Put losses (based on the initial collateral posted) would have been 71 percent and 214 percent. We wish we had a interrupter here who would say something like: "You're being unfair to yourself. Those are, at worst, the percentages on only a part of the position. You freed $6,400 and reinvested only $700 collateral for the LEAPS Put. What did you earn on the rest of the money? Even if you lost it all (or about twice it), that would be a smaller dollar amount than the losses sustained on the retained stock."

We have only negative interrupters in this book, so we'll make our own case. We say that with the LEAPS Put position, these aren't losses at all! They would be losses if you bought back the written LEAPS Puts, but you don't have to. You were uncomfortable with the stock at 64. You sold it out there; now you're in position to buy it back at 51 (LEAPS Put 55 strike less 4 premium). If you keep the LEAPS Put position open, it's because you're not averse to that stock repurchase. If you monitor the written LEAPS Put properly, you should be pleased with the result.

Now we must consider the other "risk": that the stock doesn't go down at all. More precisely, if you were never assigned, you would never buy the stock back and not participate in upmoves. Actually you would have some participation: the LEAPS Put premium. This could be a worthwhile return on the collateral needed for the position.

Example
Sell XYZ @ 64   Write Jan 55 LEAPS Put @ 4
Initial collateral 25 percent $6,400 = 1,600
   less 900 OTM = $700
(and leave the premium in the account).

$400 on out-of-pocket $700 (over 50 percent period return) is a nice sop for "not participating in upmoves."

It is worth noting that you have choices in which LEAPS Put you write. As in the Call, you could write 2 ATM Puts with a delta near −50 to replicate the stock's behavior or you could do OTM or ITM. As always, you could choose a conservative, a moderate, or an aggressive stance.

How about combining these two techniques? Sell the stock, buy the LEAPS Call, write the LEAPS Put. The answer here has to be a qualified "maybe." This would result in your replacing stock with the position—written Put, long Call—which we studied in Chapter 26 on synthetic stock with LEAPS. That can be a good technique in the right circumstances.

Example
Sell XYZ @ 64
Write Jan 60 LEAPS Put @ 6
Buy   Jan 70 LEAPS Call @ 7

But we don't think that this is the right choice with the premises we have posited. You are afraid to hold the stock because you fear it will decline. If you replace it with synthetic stock, you will have less capital tied to that stock's behavior, but you will lose about as much if it does decline.

Example
Initial Put collateral 25 percent $6,400 = 1,600
  less 400 OTM = $1,200
XYZ at expiration @ 50
Buy back Put   @ 10 (intrinsic value)
Call expires   @ 0
Net loss 10 plus 1 debit (pay 7, get 6) = 11 = $1,100
Stock loss (if retained)   = $1,400

As an incremental benefit, when you replace the stock sold at a profit with a LEAPS Call, you do not trigger the IRS's wash sale rule. That's because you are selling the stock at a profit, not a loss.

SUMMARY

Once again we have a LEAPS strategy that is not for all nor for use at all times. If it fits the time and person, it will be wonderful. LEAPS replacement therapy speaks to both fear and greed. It allows you to realize profit and to release a substantial percentage of capital—all this while still permitting participation in strong upmoves.

CHAPTER 35
TIME IS OF THE ESSENCE (LONG LEAPS/WRITE SHORTER-TERM)

O time, arrest your flight!

STRATEGY	Calendar LEAPS Spreads
OUTLOOK	Moderately bullish
ADVANTAGES	Many writes versus one long
DRAWBACKS	Needs monitoring; needs new decisions
DEGREE OF RISK	Moderate, becomes reduced

The most distinctive feature of LEAPS is their very long time horizon. We have commented on this quite often. The theme has been that there will be enough time for the underlying stock to appreciate (or to decline). This has resulted in suggesting buying OTM Calls (and Puts), writing OTM Calls, etc. There have been other strategies—for example, surrogate therapy—where the long length of time is linked to the basis for the strategy.

Now we want to speak of a strategy that takes direct advantage of the long-lived LEAPS and their brethren—shorter-term conventional Calls. The heart of the strategy can be described succinctly: Buy a LEAPS Call and write a shorter-term conventional Call on the same underlying.

This technique (although usually employed with two conventional Calls) is generally known as a **Calendar Spread** or a **Time Spread.** In distinction to bullish or bearish spreads, which are also known as **Vertical Spreads,** the calendar spread also goes by the name **Horizontal Spread.**

Be it calendar, time, or horizontal, what is the basis and outlook for this strategy? Although there are other uses, we will be concerned with only the simplest type. The theory here is that the written Call will expire worthless. This can happen even if the stock rises during the life of the written option. In fact, the best possible outcome would be for the stock to rise to just under the written strike right at the expiration of the shorter-lived option.

Example
Long 18-month LEAPS 60 Call
Written 3-month conventional 60 Call

If the stock is @ 59⅞ at the three-month Call's expiration, you will not be assigned, you will keep the received premium, and you will retain a 15-month LEAPS Call that is right ATM.

If ever there was a strategy custom-made for LEAPS, this is surely it! That is because when we are using conventional Calls, the long side will also suffer some premium erosion due to time decay, but this will be far less true with LEAPS.

Example
Long   6-month conventional 60 Call
Written 3-month conventional 60 Call
                or
Long   24-month LEAPS 60 Call
Written 3-month conventional 60 Call

In the first case the 6-month call might have declined from 7 to 4. For the long LEAPS Call, the decline would probably be only from 18 to 16½.

Let us recall what was said in Chapter 18 on bull spreads with LEAPS Puts. We explained that this was inferior to its Calls cousin. We argued that the best way to do spreads was to write an option with much time value and to buy one with as little as possible. That led us to buy ITM and write OTM. Here we can improve on that. Let us buy a DIM LEAPS Call and write a fairly short-term OTM conventional call.

Example
XYZ @ 72
Buy   60-strike XYZ LEAPS Call @ 17
Write 2-month conventional 80-strike XYZ Call @ 2

Here comes a new entrant. Mr. Doubter complains: "Why do you always have to get so complicated? I could have done the same thing—just buying a plain Call—or even simpler—just buying the stock. Who needs your fancy LEAPS?"

Chacun à son gout. Let him do whatever he wants. We are comfortable with our cheaper (than the stock) LEAPS Call. We note that even the small premium from writing becomes a greater percentage of protection for the reduced-cost stock surrogate. We have also noted that the LEAPS Call has not been very much impacted by time passage.

Example
Long XYZ @ 72
Written   2-month conventional 80-strike XYZ call @ 2
or
Long   24-month 60-strike XYZ LEAPS Call @ 17
Written   2-month conventional 80-strike XYZ call @ 2

The written call premium is a 2.8 percent cushion for the stock, but it is an 11.8 percent cushion for the LEAPS Call.

But we're not finished here—not by a long shot (LEAPS pun intended). We still own a LEAPS Call with much of its life remaining (the conventional Call expired). What are we going to do with it? We are going to write *another* shorter-term Call.

Example
XYZ @ 76
Long 22-month 60-strike XYZ LEAPS Call
Write   1-month conventional 80-strike XYZ Call @ 1½

We wrote the same strike here. It was still OTM and we wrote it for only one month. While having the written Call assigned to us would not be the end of the world, in general we want to avoid this. Let us postulate again that the written Call is not assigned.

Example
Long   22-month 60-strike XYZ LEAPS Call
Written   1-month conventional 80-strike XYZ call @ 1½
At the ordinary call's expiration, XYZ ends @ 79.

There is no assignment and you are now long a 21-month LEAPS Call. The discerning reader probably has begun to suspect where we are going. Our intention is to keep writing OTM shorter-term calls and keep collecting those lovely premiums.

Example

You started with a 24-month 60-strike LEAPS Call. So far you have written twice against that and taken in 3½ in premiums. You continue, writing 1- or 2-month Calls and collecting more dollars.

Let's pause here for some reflection. First a note of caution: We do not want to write every month and we must be prepared for two eventualities. One, that the stock will have a fairly sudden move that results in a significantly higher probability of assignment. Two, that the stock can go down as well as up. With these two possibilities in mind, we see that this is not a technique to be fashioned mechanically. Every time a written option expires, we must make some judgments. Should we write again immediately? How far out of the money should we write? Or should we—this time—write ATM or even ITM?

The basic context here is that although we made comparisons above to bull spreads, that is not what we are doing. Although this chapter opened with an introduction to calendar spreads, that is not really what we are doing either. Yes, it does have the form of a calendar spread. But what we are essentially doing is (disguised) covered Call writing! The DIM LEAPS Call is, as we know, a stock surrogate. We are writing shorter-term Calls in a way that would be ordinarily dangerous. We alluded to the premium intake as a higher percentage protection. It is that, but it is something else as well.

In order to see that and to clarify the situation generally, we need to describe explicitly the expiration system for conventional options.

When listed options first started trading, they were on a quarterly cycle. The nearest three of January, April, July, October were traded at any time. Later February, May, August, November were added and finally March, June, September, and December. When OEX (and other index options) started with a sequential, rather than a quarterly system, the public liked that. Now, for equity options a "hybrid" system is used. Each underlying stock has four months trading. These are the nearest two, plus two additional taken from one of the original quarterly cycles. A chart will make all of this clear.

When Spot Month Is			Expiration Months Will Be		
			(Newly Added Month Is Underlined)		
January	Jan Feb Apr Jul		Jan Feb May Aug		Jan Feb Mar Jun
February	Feb Mar Apr Jul		Feb Mar May Aug		Feb Mar Jun Sep
March	Mar Apr Jul Oct		Mar Apr May Aug		Mar Apr Jun Sep
April	Apr May Jul Oct		Apr May Aug Nov		Apr May Jun Sep
May	May Jun Jul Oct		May Jun Aug Nov		May Jun Sep Dec
June	Jun Jul Oct Jan		Jun Jul Aug Nov		Jun Jul Sep Dec
July	Jul Aug Oct Jan		Jul Aug Nov Feb		Jul Aug Sep Dec
August	Aug Sep Oct Jan		Aug Sep Nov Feb		Aug Sep Dec Mar
September	Sep Oct Jan Apr		Sep Oct Nov Feb		Sep Oct Dec Mar
October	Oct Nov Jan Apr		Oct Nov Feb May		Oct Nov Dec Mar
November	Nov Dec Jan Apr		Nov Dec Feb May		Nov Dec Mar Jun
December	Dec Jan Apr Jul		Dec Jan Feb May		Dec Jan Mar Jun

This structure assures us of always having two "spot months." That is, when we are ready to write, we know that there will be a one-month and a two-month expiration available for our plucking!

Let's recapitulate a series of trades:

Examples
Jan 20   XYZ @ 72
Buy XYZ 24-month LEAPS 60 Call @ 17
Write 2-month XYZ 80 Call @ 2   Call expires
Mar 22   XYZ @ 76   Write 1-month XYZ 80
   Call @ 1½   Call expires
Apr 19   XYZ @ 79   Write 1-month XYZ 85
   Call @ 1   Call expires
May 17   XYZ @ 84   No Write
Jun 21   XYZ @ 88   Write 1-month XYZ 90 Call @ 2½
Jul 1   XYZ @ 92   There is too great a probability of
   assignment.

Jul 1   Buy back XYZ 90 Call @ 4; write XYZ 95
    Call (same month) @ 2; Call expires
Jul 19   XYZ @ 94   Write 2-month XYZ 100
    Call @ 4   Call expires
Sep 20   XYZ @ 89   Write 1-month XYZ 100
    Call @ 2   Call expires
Oct 18   XYZ @ 81

Now we see the amazing advantage of this strategy. We have made up for the time value of the long LEAPS Call. In fact, we have more than made up for it.

Example
You took in a total of 11 in shorter-term Call premiums (including one loss from a repurchase). You made up for the time value of your long LEAPS Calls after the July expiration. After the October expiration (despite the 1-month, 10 percent decline), you own a 60-strike LEAPS Call with 15 months until expiration. It is 21 points ITM and your (reduced) cost is 6! In theory, if you were adept enough (and maybe a little lucky as well), you might end up with a zero (or even less) cost for your LEAPS Call! We are constrained to point out to Mr. Doubter that our fancy LEAPS have wrought another miracle!

Let us not have any misunderstandings here. The strategy is a good one, but it does necessitate frequent market decisions. Still, if you have selected the right stock and don't get too greedy, you will have a good thing going for you.

SUMMARY

"Time is of the essence" is a strategy with a cute, but clumsy name. In order to practice it, one must be deft, not clumsy. But if you can pick the right stock and maneuver dexterously, you can make money with greatly reduced risk. This LEAPS strategy is among those that require extremely close attention to the performance of the underlying stock. As an added benefit, if all goes well, you will have a lot of fun with this technique!

CHAPTER 36
LEAPS AFFIRMATIVE ACTION
(SELL HALF POSITION, WRITE
LEAPS STRADDLES)

Our minds are naturally affirmative.

STRATEGY	LEAPS Affirmative Action
OUTLOOK	Worried bullish
ADVANTAGES	Establish partial profit
DRAWBACKS	Complex position
DEGREE OF RISK	Lowered

We have run the gamut of titles. We've had simple declarative descriptions. We've had some intriguing names and some open to the charge of cuteness. What in the world is a strategy named *Affirmative Action?* For the moment, let's evade the titular interrogation and examine what the strategy does.

The discerning reader may have noticed something by now. In the advanced strategies section, we have dealt a lot with the posture we could label *worried bullish.* That's not too surprising. The basic techniques will do to establish a position—bullish or bearish. If you own stock and regard it with equanimity, there isn't any problem. There is also no problem if your conviction does a complete about-face: You simply sell the stock. It's when some degree of ambivalence enters that something else is required. And LEAPS fill the bill quite well, as we have learned. We saw several strategies suitable for this end. For different desires and fears we explored:

1. Hold stock; buy LEAPS Puts.
2. Hold stock; write LEAPS Calls.
3. Hold stock; write LEAPS Calls and buy LEAPS Puts.
4. Hold stock; average down with DIM LEAPS Calls.

5. Sell stock; replace with LEAPS Calls.
6. Sell stock; write LEAPS Puts.
7. Sell stock; write LEAPS Puts and buy LEAPS Calls.

We're getting closer to our goal. Let's restate your attitudes (deliberately plural) here. You really like the stock, you are nervous about a decline, you would consider selling it here, and—overall—you just don't know what to do. You can overcome your ambivalence and take **Affirmative Action with LEAPS.**

Example

You own 2,000 YXZ bought @ 40. It has climbed to 70 and you are nervous. You view the stock as a longer-term holding but are concerned about the immediate prospects for the company. You sell out half of your holdings—1,000 shares @ 70, and simultaneously write 10 LEAPS 70 straddles for 24 (14 for the LEAPS Calls and 10 for the LEAPS Puts). Your position is now.

Long   1,000 YXZ
Written   10 YXZ LEAPS 70 Calls
Written   10 YXZ LEAPS 70 Puts

What has been accomplished here? Very simply, if the stock (at expiration) is above 70, you will be out of the second half of your position @ 94 (70 + 24). If it declines, you will be assigned on the LEAPS Put. Then, in effect, you will buy back the half position you sold, but at a much lower price—46 (70−24). Unless the stock ends at exactly 70 (and with no previous assignments), one of two situations will result. First, you will be out of all of your stock, half @ 70 and half @ 94. That's an average price of 82—more than double your original 40 cost. Second, you will still own the 2,000 shares, but your cost basis will be lowered to 28. That comes from total premium of 24 on half position = 12 on full position, 40 − 12 = 28.

So you either double your dollars or lower your cost by 70 percent (from 40 to 28). Those two outcomes seem pretty good to us. Technically, there are some other possibilities. You might receive two assignments (first the LEAPS Call and then the LEAPS Put, or vice versa) and/or you might alter your basic viewpoint on the stock. We cannot analyze all the possible permutations. The basic concept is that the technique will get you out of your quandary. It will bring in two large-dollar premiums that will protect you in both directions. It will also allow you to sit with a stock position without the fear of either missing an upmove or holding on too long.

SUMMARY

LEAPS Affirmative Action is not for all. It is a complex technique intended for some investors at a time of indecision. It provides protection in both directions with a good price—either as an exit point or for a reacquisition. It could be described as "a medicine for melancholy" or "an antidote to ambivalence."

CHAPTER 37
REDUCED-RISK EQUITY TRADING WITH LEAPS

. . also there's a worth that brings no risk.

STRATEGY	LEAPS Reduced-risk Trading
OUTLOOK	Alternating; trading viewpoint
ADVANTAGES	Leverage to high leverage; limited dollar risk
DRAWBACKS	May lead to excessive trading
DEGREE OF RISK	Much lower than stock trading

"Different strokes for different folks" is certainly a truism in the marketplace. So far we have shown strategies for the investor (conservative through aggressive) and for the trader (with an equally wide spectrum). Now we want to expound on a technique for "scalpers."

"Just a darned minute," interrupts Mr. Tory. "You have told us several times that LEAPS are longer-term investments; that, if we wanted to "scalp," we should do it away from LEAPS. Now you say to use them. You're talking out of both sides of your mouth." We certainly see where this criticism is coming from. We did say something like that, but not exactly that. What we did say was that if you were a scalper you should not look to buying LEAPS Calls. And we still do believe that. But we also believe (and think we have shown you) how incredibly versatile LEAPS can be. We have shown you how to make money with LEAPS in up markets, in down markets, and even in flat markets. We have shown you how LEAPS can offer large leverage and powerful protection. We have even described miracles wrought with LEAPS. Now we will ask Mr. Tory to temporarily suspend judgment on us until he hears the strategic specifics.

The modus operandi for **LEAPS Reduced-Risk Trading** is pretty easy to follow. Start by buying a LEAPS combination.

Use the technique with both legs OTM (you might want to go back and scan Chapter 25). We showed how to use this technique to profit from a large move in *either* direction. Now we will employ it in a related, but distinct method.

Assume that after your double purchase, the underlying moves down to a point below your LEAPS Put strike and then hesitates. If you believe it is about to turn up, you could buy the stock at that point. If you were correct, you could then sell out the stock at a point when you again thought it might reverse direction. Similarly, if the stock first rose, you could short it and buy it back after a decline. Yes, some people do trade like that. It can be very risky, but not so for you. You will have the protection of the LEAPS Call or the LEAPS Put. Either of these will prevent any losses from getting out of hand.

Example

Date	XYZ Price	Action	Profit
January 3	50	Buy XYZ 18-mo. 60 LEAPS Calls @ 6 Buy XYZ 18-mo. 40 LEAPS Puts @ 4⅜	
4	49½		
5	49¾		
6	48¾		
9	47⅝		
10	47		
11	46½	Buy XYZ @ 46½	
12	47		
13	47½		
16	48¼		
17	49	Sell XYZ @ 49	2½
18	49⅞		
19	50½		
20	51¼		
23	51		
24	52⅜		
25	53⅝	Sell short XYZ @ 53⅝	
26	54		
27	54⅛		
30	53½		
31	53		
February 1	52⅝		
2	52⅛		

Date	XYZ Price	Action	Profit
February 3	51½		
6	51¼	Buy XYZ 51¼	2⅜
		cover short	
7	51		
8	52½		
9	52⅞		
10	53¾		
13	54⅞		
14	55⅝	Sell short XYZ 55⅝	
15	55¼		
16	54½		
17	54¼		
20	55		
21	54¾		

We're going to interrupt our presentation because we are being assailed by two different commentators:

Mr. Eager: "You call *that* scalping? A whole 2½ trades in two months? I could have done that in one week. Why are you making such a fuss?"

And Mr. Sharp: "It's *déjà vu* all over again! I saw that before, and without any LEAPS. I think you're stealing it!"

For our eager talker, we say that we do call it scalping. Trading to make about two points deserves that description. While it may not be everybody's way, we're satisfied with it. Even in scalping, one has to be careful, and we're making a fuss because every time we took a position, it was protected by a LEAPS Call or a LEAPS Put. Not everybody who scalps (at whatever rate of speed) can have protection like that.

As for our sharp-eyed and sharper-tongued friend, he's partially right. He did see it before and without LEAPS. He saw it in a great book: *"Options / Essential Concepts and Trading Strategies,* edited by The Options Institute and published by Business One Irwin. It was in the chapter entitled "Options for the Small Investor" and written by your humble author. While it didn't use LEAPS (not yet trading), it did use options. Let's resume our trading.

Wait! We have yet another voice to be heard from:

"I knew it, we could have done it cheaper. If you did it with options, why should we spend more for the other? I think you're LEAPS-nuts!" So shouts Mr. Miser.

This time we'll say in our reply that maybe he's partly right. Sure, you could have done it cheaper. In the example in the other book, only 2⅜ was spent. But the purchased options in that example expired in one and a half months. If you wanted to do this type of trading for a longer period of time, you would have to buy new combinations or originally buy longer expirations that would have cost more money. Even then, after a while those also would have expired (or been exercised), requiring additional expenditures. Still, Mr. Miser is entitled to trade in his own manner. We are allowed to do our thing as well. As for the accusation, well, yes, we are nuts about LEAPS. We think they are wonderful and have been trying to persuade you of that.

Now, everybody, SSHHH! We want to see what happens.

February 22	54¼		
23	54		
24	53¾	Buy YXZ @ 53¾	Cover short 1⅞
No more trades in February.			
March 1	53		
2	52⅜		
3	52		
4	51⅝		
5	51	Sell short XYZ @ 51	
8	50⅛		
9	49½		
10	48⅞		
11	49¼		
12	48⅛		
15	47¾		
16	47		
17	46⅝		
18	47⅜	Buy XYZ @ 47⅜	cover short 3⅝

This time *we* will be the one who does the interrupting. Why? Because now we have another demonstration of LEAPS's wonderfulness (if not another miracle). If you add up the accumulated profits, you will see that they total 10⅜. What's wonderful (or miraculous) about that? Simply, that it's the sum total we invested in LEAPS at the beginning of the year! After not quite three months we have completely recovered that investment. We have either seven more months (if we stop when the LEAPS become conventionals) or 15 more months (if we trade right to the expiration). During this time there is no limit (other than our own prudence) on how frequently we can trade. And there is no theoretical limit on how much money we might make.

Before you get carried away at the thought of unbounded wealth, let's make some practical observations. No matter which time interval you choose, it is exceedingly unlikely that you will keep trading up to that point. That's because none of us are that good. Sooner or later, one of the positions you take— long or short—will go against you. Then you will have to be rescued by your long LEAPS (Call or Put). For example, in October or November you might buy stock at about 43½. After terrible news emerges, the stock breaks 40, drops to 36, and never recovers. It keeps drifting lower and you abandon ship. You use the LEAPS Put to get out at 40 (losing $350) and sell out the long LEAPS Call. Any price you get for it is "gravy."

We must note that you did have an alternative. When you saw the stock about to break 40, you could have sold out the stock (and maybe even the LEAPS Call), preserving your now precious LEAPS Put. That would have kept you alive for a few more trades. Either way, we doubt that you could trade for another seven months. If we're wrong, we say, "Good for you!" and "Good for LEAPS, that made it possible for you to do so well."

We are not going to finish our calendric tabulation; we have made our point. But we are going to do another one and make an even more sensational point! What? Is there no limit to what LEAPS can do? No comment. Let's just look at the presentation:

Date	Action	Profit	
January 11	Sell XYZ Feb 40 Put @ 1½		
January 17	Buy XYZ Feb 40 Put @ ½	Close position	1
January 25	Sell XYZ Feb 60 Call @ 2⅞		
February 6	Buy XYZ Feb 60 Call @ ¾	Close position	2⅛
February 14	Sell XYZ Feb 60 Call @ 1⅜		
February 17	XYZ Feb 60 Call expires	Close position	1⅜
March 5	Sell XYZ Mar 55 Call @ 2⅜		
March 18	Buy XYZ Mar 55 Call @ ⅛	Close position	2¼
		Total profit	6¾

What have we done here? We have done exactly what we always advocate: think about substituting options (or LEAPS) positions for stock positions. The dates are the same as in the previous presentation. The stock prices (not shown here) are also the same. What is different is the action taken. Where formerly we bought stock, here we substituted the equivalent—writing a Put. Where we sold stock short, we instead wrote a Call. And when the stock positions were closed, we closed the option positions. We won't let Mr. Stickler (or Mr. Miser) speak this time. We all know what either would say—that we didn't make as much money this time. Right. And we didn't risk as much either. Instead of paying roughly $5,000 (for a long stock position) or posting $2,500 (for a short), we needed only the order of magnitude of $1,000 for the written Put or Call and we had a better position. We were short above the market (for example, a 60 Call when the stock was 53⅝ or we were committed to a long below the market.

Before we leave this augmented version of LEAPS reduced-risk trading, we must comment about size. In the augmented version we had to post fewer dollars. The temptation is to do more options than we did stock in the original. We have always said no to inappropriate size. Here we will surprise some by not saying no. When you do as many options as you would have bought (or sold) stock, you are protected by your LEAPS position. If you do more options, it would seem that you are not protected on the additional options. But in fact, you might be. You are protected by the fact that the delta of the chosen options is not 100. If you select an option with a delta of 50 (that is approximately what most of them will be), you are entitled to write two of them rather than one (for each long LEAPS). If we wanted to be really technical, we would say that the correct number of options to write would be found by dividing the delta of the appropriate LEAPS (Call or Put) by the delta of the option.

Example
Long LEAPS 60 Call   delta 80
About to write one month 60 Call   delta 50
Write 1.6 Calls   (80/50 = 1.6)

Under these circumstances we think there is nothing wrong with writing two Calls. Now let's go back to the total money we made in the augmented version. It was 6¾. If we had done two each time, instead of one, we would have ended up with 13½. We will remind you that we made only 10⅜ with the stock version. We will also get the good news out to Mr. Miser. We trust he will be thrilled. Not to kill the thrill, but we would look aghast at any increase in the size past this point.

Which of the two strategies is better? By now, we know that you know the answer: whichever one you are more comfortable with. Either way, we think it's a great system.

SUMMARY

Reduced-risk LEAPS trading is a technique that allows its practitioners to trade many times over the LEAPS's life. Many of these trades will be scalps, but all are protected. Smart and/or lucky traders will recover their initial investment and have the freedom to trade with their capital tucked under the mattress (or wherever else they consider it safe). This technique is certainly not for all. But for those who are comfortable with it and nimble, it holds out great potential/low risk in either of two versions.

CHAPTER 38
INDEX LEAPS

The Navigator has reached the New World.

How did he find the natives?

Very friendly.

STRATEGY	Index LEAPS
OUTLOOK	All
ADVANTAGES	"Economy of size" = Deal with entire portfolio/sector/market, not individual stocks
DRAWBACKS	Some strategies more dangerous than ordinarily
DEGREE OF RISK	Varies with technique

Because we dislike being interrupted at the start of a new chapter, we will preempt our critics. Yes, we know that the "E" in LEAPS stands for Equity. Therefore, there can't be any such thing as index LEAPS. "There ain't no such animal" is what the man said when he saw the giraffe. But there was, and there are longer-dated index options. We will go along with the paradoxical, if not contradictory, label and refer to them as index LEAPS. Forget the name, there's great stuff here to be learned.

Like the Navigator, we reach a new world with the subject of **Index LEAPS.** Index LEAPS are the same type of longer-term options we have seen with equity options, but here they are index options. First we have to define and explain **Index Options.** An index option has many characteristics in common with an equity option, but the differences are essential and important. We want to highlight these differences. We will use as a paradigm the first index created for options trading—the S&P 100—generally known by its ticker symbol OEX. OEX consists of 100 blue chip stocks selected from the S&P 500. In general, index options are traded in the same way as equity options. What makes the index fluctuate is not an underlying stock, but the movement of all the stocks that make up that index.

A very large difference arises when we come to exercises. The exercise of an equity option results in the delivery and receipt (to different parties) of 100 shares of stock. There is *no* delivery of stock upon the exercise of an index option. Instead, the exercisor receives (and the assignee is debited) an amount of money. This amount is 100 times the in-the-money amount of the option.

Example

You are long five OEX 380 Calls expiring in a few days. If you exercise with OEX @ 383.33 you will receive $333 for each Call exercised. The reference point for this calculation is the *closing* value of the index on the day the exercise is made.

Example

If you had written OEX 390 Puts and received an assignment before the opening on Wednesday morning, you would be debited based on the in-the-money amount at *Tuesday's close.*

Warning Note

All indexes that now have options trading use this system on every day but one. That day is the day before expiration—usually a Friday and commonly called *expiration Friday.* That exception provides that for many indexes the basis for calculating an option's intrinsic value (the ITM amount) will be the *opening* price of the index on that day.

Example

You own SPX (the S&P 500) 400-strike Calls which you exercise on the day before expiration. You receive the in-the-money amount based on Friday's *opening,* not Friday's closing.

This type of index is referred to as having an **Opening Settlement** or an **AM Settlement.** OEX and others sharing its parameters are known as a **Closing Settlement** or **PM Settlement.**

While we are distinguishing among indexes, we will take note of some other differentiations. Indexes come in two exercise styles: American and European. The **American Style** is the one we have become familiar with in observing equity options. That is, these options can be exercised at any time after purchase. The **European Style**—cannot. They can be exercised *only* on the day before expiration. We note that no early exercises means no early assignments. This can be beneficial in certain strategies. For example, if you write uncovered combinations and the underlying moves out of the safe range (even greatly so) and then back into it, staying there for expiration, you will not be assigned if the index on which you wrote was a European one.

The last difference we will look at here is the broadness of an index. OEX is a **Broad-Based Index,** which means that it represents a broad spectrum of the market. The other type is a **Narrow-Based Index.** Narrow-based indexes would have component stocks from a narrower section of the market. Broad-based indexes are also known as **Market Indexes** and narrow-based ones are also referred to as **Industry Indexes** or **Sub-Indexes.**

Examples
Broad—OEX, SPX, XMI, etc.   Narrow—Biotech Index, Bank Index, Oil Index, etc.

The *minimum* margin requirements for narrow-based index options are the same as those for equity options. Broad-based index option requirements are set lower (see Chapter 9 on margin). Broad-based index options also have a different tax treatment (see Chapter 42 on taxes).

Strategies with Index Options

Most of the strategies we have looked at with equity options can be carried over into the world of indexes. Some cannot be translated in the same form as, for example, covered writing. Others are basically different. One glaring difference can be seen if we look at writing uncovered Puts.

Example
ZYX @ 93
Write 5 ZYX 85 Puts for 3

Example
ZZZ Index @ 393
Write 5 ZZZ 385 Puts for 9

Both underlyings decline and all the Puts are assigned. Now let's posit that after some time has elapsed the two instruments in our examples both recover nicely. In fact, we will have them recover to a point above the original strike.

Example
ZYX @ 81 at assignment
ZYX bottoms at 79,
rebounds to 83, and
months later sells at 90.

Example
ZZZ Index bottoms at 379,
rebounds to 383, and
months later sells at 390.

In the equity example, a profit is actually made after holding on (although it would probably have been better to take the loss and move on to a different investment). But in the index example there was *no* delivery of securities. All that was placed into the account was a debit, which did not change no matter how much time passed and no matter how high the index subsequently went. This is one of the two strategic reasons why some people lost so much money in 1987. They wrote uncovered Puts on index options. The other was the size in which that was done. Now you know why we have inveighed so forcefully against inappropriate size in LEAPS/options trading.

We cannot go into any extensive discussions for each strategy. It's enough to say that the general concepts also carry over. Match index to portfolio (real or desired), strategy to expectations, and strikes to risk attitudes. We will give thumbnail sketches for almost every strategy. In these sketches, we will mostly assume that you can make the jump to index LEAPS. We will also emphasize the differences and/or dangers that arise from the change. If in the sketch we say: Read (or reread) the equity chapter, we mean the equity LEAPS chapter corresponding to the index strategy you're reading about.

Buying LEAPS Index Calls

People buy index Calls for the same reasons they buy equity Calls: a smaller amount of money, a known maximum loss, and the lure of leverage. All can be carried over to index calls. Depending on the index of choice, you will have as "underlying" the market, as measured by the bluest chips, a smaller group of blue chips, the middle-cap sector, the small-cap segment, or a particular industry group. For index LEAPS Calls, just reread the equity chapter with the idea that you are not taking a stance on a single stock. The market, as we have described it above, is considerably less volatile than most individual stocks. Still it has made major moves over one- and two-year periods. If this is your game, rather than trying to select and predict single stock performance, OK, be careful, be alert, and monitor the position. Also read Chapter 39 on enhancement and Chapter 40 on repair.

Buying LEAPS Index Puts

We have here the same as above, with one exception. Start by rereading the equity chapter. The comment there about stocks frequently falling faster than they rise is applicable here as well. What's the exception?

If you go back to the Chapter 2 on the big secret, you will find a discussion of the fundamental difference between Puts and Calls. That difference can come into play in this strategy. Suppose that you are right in your bearish stance, and that the underlying index does indeed decline significantly. Moreover, it occurs well in advance of expiration, say, with a year left to run. Suppose further that in its decline it has gone DIM and is coming close to the first mental target you have for it. (It is not unusual to have more than one target for a stock or index.) You have to evaluate whether to sell out or hold. A negative surprise can occur here. The index LEAPS Put may very well be trading at a discount, and the size of that discount could be very troubling.

Example
ZZZ index @ 370
ZZZ 400-strike index LEAPS Put @ 28

You bought this index LEAPS Put @ 14 when the index was at 400. Now, six months later and with a year to go, the index has tumbled to 370, and the index LEAPS Put is trading at 28. This is two points below its intrinsic value of 30.

We said that the index "may very well be" and "could be" above. Are we waffling? Aren't we sure of our ground? We are sure and we are not waffling. The reason for the hedgelike language is not that we don't know about the discount. It is because we don't know about the interest rate! Once again, we urge you to page back in the book. This time go to both Chapter 8 on beating the experts and Chapter 2 on the big secret. This will serve to remind you that (1) the prevailing interest rates two years out may not be predictable, and (2) the level of interest rates is a significant determinant in options pricing theory.

Is all of this some academician's fantasy? *No, no, no!* Besides the various theoretical aspects, it is known to be empirically true. The author has seen many cases of successful index Put purchasers who ended up both baffled and frustrated by this sort of denoument. Those who retain any degree of skepticism here, need only consult old issues of *Barron's*. Issues published during times of high interest rates are the most pertinent.

We have here two very cogent questions to answer. First, are all LEAPS Puts impacted in the same way? Second, does this mean we shouldn't employ this technique?

Answer to the first question: There is not a lot of documented history here, but there is enough for us to know that there will certainly be a problem. The problem will be most acute as rates go higher, but it will happen only to European style index LEAPS Puts. Why? Because, if we could exercise at any time, we would do just that. If we wanted to get out and realize the intrinsic value, we could simply exercise on any day when we liked the value, as measured at the closing price level. We cannot do that with European index LEAPS.

Answer to the second question: No, it does not mean that at all. It means that we have to use our imaginations to deal with the problem. First though, let's make the problem very explicit. If we are going to wait until expiration when we expect the index to be lower, why should this phenomenon disturb us at all? Because that was our *original* expectation and plan. If the index has gone down farther and faster than we thought it would and we are worried about a reversal to the upside, we should take prudent steps. The simplest step to take is to close the position. "Aye, there's the rub." We don't want to sell out the long index LEAPS Put for less than its intrinsic value and we can't exercise. What to do?

Example
ZZZ index @ 370
ZZZ 400-strike index LEAPS Put @ 28

As always, the course to take depends upon your evaluations and your risk tolerances. One procedure is to keep the index LEAPS Put, but write another with a lower strike. In the example you could write the 375 LEAPS Put @ 14. If you did that and the index stayed level or went down, you would end up with the strike differential as profit.

You exercise @ 400, you are assigned at 375, and you make the 25. That would be all profit as the sale of the 375 Put recovered your initial investment of 14. If the index did reverse to the upside, the 14 points taken in would provide "equivalency protection" up to an index level of 386. That is, if you held on and the index was 386 at expiration, you would make the same "double" you could get right now by selling out your 14-cost LEAPS Put @ 28.

We understand the reluctance to sell out something for less than its intrinsic valuation. Why should you give away the 2 points? A practical possibility is to enter an order between the 30-point intrinsic value and the actual 28 bid (in this case, say, 29). But if you really want out, we have one more proverb quote to add to the others in this book: "Pay the two dollars!"

Writing Covered Calls with Index LEAPS

The title is self-contradictory (unless you own all the stocks in the index and in the same proportion and/or weight). Still you could write LEAPS index Calls against a portfolio that moved in concert with the underlying index. If your stocks moved down, you would have the familiar cushion from the LEAPS sale. If the index rose and you received an assignment (creating a debit), the presumption is that the index rise would produce a greater credit from the increase in value of your portfolio. How many index LEAPS Calls would be covered? Remember that the value of the index is 100 times the index level. With the index at 400, its valuation is $40,000. A portfolio that moved in synchronization with that index and was worth $400,000 could have up to 10 index LEAPS Calls written against it. We emphasize that this covered status is tactical only. There still will be no delivery of securities, and you will have to post collateral as though you had written uncovered calls.

Writing Uncovered Index LEAPS Calls

Don't do it. Period.

Writing Uncovered Index LEAPS Puts

You can do this, but make sure to read the above description about the basic difference here between this strategy and the corresponding one for equity LEAPS Puts. Remember what happened in 1987 to people who wrote too many of these Puts.

Buying Protective Index LEAPS Puts

Sure. Protect a built-up profit in your portfolio. Just make sure that you do want LEAPS here. You might want shorter-term protection or you might be pleased with a one-time purchase that won't have to be rolled or replaced. When it comes time to be sold, that purchase will retain a good deal of its value. To see how many index LEAPS Puts to buy, go back three paragraphs. Which strike you should use will be determined by what you are trying to protect against. Absolute and total protection would suggest an ITM (although here, you should certainly consider selling out and maybe apply the replacement therapy). The next level would require ATM or a slightly OTM. If you're willing to sustain small-to-medium losses but want protection against a catastrophe, try further OTM. This would be akin to buying insurance with a "deductible." You pay the first part of the loss yourself; then the "insurance" of the LEAPS Put takes care of the rest.

Buying Married Index LEAPS Puts

The situation is the same as above, except for the different initial motivation. If you are yearning but frightened about entering the market or a sector thereof, this could be the answer for you.

Buying Index LEAPS Straddles and Combinations

When we discussed this technique with equity LEAPS, we said that it really was reasonable at some times to expect a stock to move sharply up *or* down. Can we say the same thing about the market? Maybe. Certainly far less often. However, don't go away. We can say the same thing about some specialized sections of the market. Biotechnology is a case in point. Just as we saw examples of stocks from that incredible industry, we could focus on the industry as a whole or at least on the component stocks in the two Biotechnology indexes. This strategy should be used sparingly. But if you can accurately predict the approach of a major move (even if you don't know the direction), this could be for you.

Writing Index LEAPS Straddles and Combinations

This technique translates favorably into our new arena. This endorsement is warranted only if you keep in mind all the previous warnings, most especially the warning about size. Also remember that even the dullest markets can break out or break down. Be alert! A wide strike differential should be preferred here, as should a European style for exercise.

Synthetic Stock/Synthetic Short with Index LEAPS

These tactics have to be renamed *synthetic markets*. Just as we did before, we urge avoidance of such methods. As before, we counsel that for either of the two you pick the half—LEAPS index Calls or LEAPS index Puts—that you want and eschew the other.

Ratio Writing/Ratio Spreading with Index LEAPS

Even if you keep the ratio low, we say a clear *no* to these investments. For the second, we realize that we haven't even discussed plain spreads yet. We will, but the dangers versus the rewards and the existence of alternate, more sound strategies, make us say: Stay away.

Surrogate Therapy/Replacement Therapy with Index LEAPS

These "therapies" are the purchase of a DIM LEAPS Call either as a surrogate for stock or to replace stock sold. Each technique can be carried over into the index domain. The first would be to buy DIM LEAPS index Calls instead of buying a portfolio. This could be done as an initial market entry. An example would be LEAPS index Calls on an industry index for someone who had no position in that sector. Another example would be a broad-based index for somebody who had left the market and wanted to reenter. The second technique would be for the other direction. Let's take, for example, someone who wanted to sell out (a broad- or narrow-based portfolio) but was nervous. S/he could make the sale but replace the stocks with LEAPS index Calls.

LEAPS Index Fences

Write the OTM LEAPS index Call and buy an ATM LEAPS index Put if your view is that you would sell out your portfolio at about a 10 percent increase and you are worried about a market/sector fall.

Dollar-Cost Averaging with Index LEAPS

Absolutely yes. The only caveat is the one we made in Chapter 31 on dollar-cost averaging. This is the author's invention and an untested strategy. The theoreticals argue for it, and there is no reason you can't employ it for the overall market or an industry sector as well as on individual stocks. Just keep reappraising your fundamental market/sector outlook. It is yet again a demonstration of what LEAPS can do: DCA on the entire market!

Time Is of the Essence (Long Index LEAPS/ Write Shorter-Term)

You can certainly change this method from equity LEAPS/ options to index LEAPS/options. Just refresh your recollection with Chapter 38 on index LEAPS. There is one big problem, though. We have looked at just about every LEAPS technique but until now we have not discussed spreads. Because there is a fundamental divergence (as well as a peril) here, we will give it a very special, unusual treatment.

Index LEAPS Spreads

These fall into the category of being tolerable translations with a very major point to be carefully noted. These spreads—bullish or bearish—will do what their equity LEAPS counterparts did. They will reduce your cost and your risk while limiting potential profit. There is, however, an added peril in American-style index LEAPS spreads. To make this clear we go now to the LEAPS Playhouse to see:

A Mini-Drama in Three Acts

Act I: Set on January 2 of this year
Place: Your broker's office
ZZZ index @ 390
Buy   ZZZ index LEAPS 375 Call
Write ZZZ index LEAPS 400 Call
    We have not indicated prices. For this illustration they are irrelevant (except for the obvious fact that the spread incurred a debit).

Act II: Date: Halloween, October 31 of this year
Place: Your broker's office
Prices: ZZZ index—434

ZZZ index LEAPS 375 Call—56
ZZZ index LEAPS 400 Call—34

You are very pleased with your acumen in taking this position. You are holding on to make more of a profit (it's worth 22 and could go to 25). Something is disturbing you though, and you don't know what it is. You think about it and finally perceive it as an unknown fear, which you put down to the Day.

Act III: Date: All Saints' Day, November 1 of this year
Place: Your broker's office
Time: Before the market opening

AAAGH! You have just found out that you have been assigned on the 400 Call. Even more disturbing is the specific bad news that has occurred and will impact the market negatively. You valiantly shrug it off, secure in the knowledge that you own an index LEAPS Call that was 59 points ITM yesterday. Alas! The market opens down 40; you try to sell your long Call but the market keeps declining and the Call is consistently bid at a discount to intrinsic value. At the end of the day, you say the hell with it and give your broker instructions to exercise your index LEAPS Call. ZZZ index closes at 419. You get $4,400 (100 × [419 − 375]). You are debited $3,400 (100 × [434 − 400]). The assignment and the exercise took place on *two different* days and are based on *two different* closing prices.

Daily Variety Review: Index LEAPS Spreads Lays an Egg

Index LEAPS Spreads, a somewhat eccentric playlet, had a lot going for it. The set was the spitting image of a real brokerage office, the actors were accomplished, the costumes authentic, and the lighting perfect. The only thing wrong was the story line, which was totally unconvincing. Two alleged sophisticates in a complex market maneuver didn't even know a basic fact. The playwright showed promise and maybe his next will be better.

We have been melodramatic in order to underscore the danger here. We showed an expected profit that got chopped down.

It could happen that an expected profit turned into a loss! Even if "all the saints and sages who discussed" the problem agreed, nothing could change. Exercises and assignments on equity options go in opposite directions, but do the same thing. They result in delivery and receipt—but of stock. The same processes with index options results in an exchange of only money. If you are assigned on an equity Put or Call and exercise a corresponding long option, you will then have a flat position. With index options you will have a difference of dollars. The moral is that you must be aware of all the differences and distinctions among the instruments you are dealing with. And you must always be on your guard.

Now that we know about index option structures and strategies, let's move on to another particular about index LEAPS. There is another difference here. Some index LEAPS trade on what is known as a **Reduced Value LEAPS** basis. Again we will use OEX LEAPS for our illustration. OEX LEAPS are set with an index number equal to one-tenth the OEX number.

Example
With OEX @ 400, OBX (= 1995 OEX LEAPS) would have a 40 level. The strikes would bracket this reduced level.

Example
OEX @ 400
OBX @ 40
OBX strikes 35   37½   40   42½   45.

The "reduced value" means that, although we have used the usual numbers in our examples, they have to be changed. For index LEAPS that trade on a reduced value basis, 10 have to be bought or sold instead of one, to keep all comparisons intact. Some strategies, however (buying index LEAPS Calls is a perfect example) could employ less than 10 for reduced exposure. The indices that currently have LEAPS trading and their symbols expirations, styles, and settlements are shown in the Table 38.1.

TABLE 38.1

Index	Symbol	Exch	LEAPS	Settle	B/N[1]	F/R[2]	Expire
S&P 100	OEX	CBOE	OBX	PM	B	R	Dec '94
S&P 500	SPX	CBOE	SPL	AM	B	F	Jun/Dec '94
S&P 500	SPX	CBOE	LSY	AM	B	R	Dec '94
Major Market	XMI	ASE	LTA	PM	B	R	Dec '94
Major Market	XMI	ASE	LTB	PM	B	R	Dec '95
Value Line	VLE	PHLX	WVL	PM	B	R	Dec '94
Value Line	VLE	PHLX	VVL	PM	B	R	Dec '95
Institutional	XII	ASE	XII/XIW	AM	B	F	Mar '94
Biotech	BGX	CBOE	WRG	AM	N	R	Dec '94
Russell 2000	RUT	CBOE	WRU	AM	B	R	Dec '94
Pharmaceutical	DRG	ASE	WRG	AM	N	R	Jan '94
Pharmaceutical	DRG	ASE	VRG	AM	N	R	Jan '95
Japan	JPN	ASE	JAB	AM	B	F	Jun/Dec '94

[1]B = broad-based   N = narrow-based.
[2]F = full LEAPS value   R = reduced LEAPS value.

SUMMARY

Trading or investing with index LEAPS offers a new world of opportunities. It gives you the ability to deal with an entire portfolio. It allows you to take a stance—bullish, bearish, or neutral—on the entire market or on a subset of it. That subset could be a division by size, for example, large caps versus small caps, or by sector, for example biotechnology stocks. It allows you to replicate a portfolio or to protect an existing one. Most of all, it allows you to have time on your side in dealing with these large market areas.

You must be aware of all the index LEAPS characteristics. You must know how they differ among themselves and from equity LEAPS. Armed with that knowledge, you can use index LEAPS for leverage, replacement, surrogacy, profit, and protection.

FOLLOWING UP ON
STRATEGIES

CHAPTER 39
LEAPS ENHANCEMENT

. . . which Providence sends to enhance the value.

STRATEGY	LEAPS Enhancement
OUTLOOK	Winning but greedy
ADVANTAGES	Increase profit
DRAWBACKS	May increase risk
DEGREE OF RISK	Varies with technique

Since LEAPS enhancement is not a strategy, there will be no definition here. We mean merely the common use of this word: to heighten or to magnify. In brief, we want to look at a LEAPS position that is profitable and see if there is a way to increase the profits.

We hope the reader will immediately react by asking: "Are we going to increase the risks as well?" The answer has to be twofold. First, yes and no. That means that some methods will and some won't. Second, it will depend on your outlook at that point. While we will be looking at almost every LEAPS strategy, a general principle will apply. You could nail down the profits by closing (in whole or part). Keeping the position open will, in general, have potential for greater gains along with the possibility of advances ebbing, if not vanishing. We want to speak to that dichotomy. We will do so by dealing with strategies separately.

Buying LEAPS Calls

Like its equity options cousin, this is the most frequent tactic and deserves much commentary. The techniques available here are generally the same as for options, with some restrictions. There are fewer expirations and fewer strikes as possible alternatives.

Examples

Long ZYX 2-month 80 Call   Long 18-month ZYX LEAPS
                                       80 Call

   The first Call could be associated with (i.e., rolled to, or combined with) an 85 strike or a four- or seven-month, or both. The second might have only a 100 strike and/or an expiration a year longer. Still, that doesn't mean that there's nothing we can or should do. It does imply, however, that more weight should be given to closure. Take the money and run! More weight, yes; all weight, no. This chapter is about alternatives. Let's set up a particular situation and examine the possibilities.

Example

ZYX @ 90

Long 24 14-month ZYX LEAPS 80 Calls @ 18

   You bought these LEAPS Calls four months ago when the stock was just a bit above 70. You paid 9 for them because you foresaw a breakout and you were right. You were even more right than you had thought. You weren't sure how long before this upmove might occur, but you were smart and used LEAPS Calls as your investment. Now the stock, having crept up, has suddenly exploded. And only four months have gone by. Deep in your heart, you really think the stock can go higher, but you are very nervous. Your nervousness stems both from its rapid rise and the fact that the stock has been doing much, much better than the rest of the market. You are bombarded both by others and your own inner voices giving you absolutely contradictory advice. *Sell quick! Hold, hold!* You even hear *Buy more!* We know something better than all this. Some have labeled it *the best strategy of all*, but it is widely known as *OPM*. Take a deep breath, close your eyes, and sell out one-half of the position.

Example

Bought 24 18-month ZYX LEAPS 80 Calls @ 9 = $21,600
Sold   12 14-month ZYX LEAPS 80 Calls @ 18 = $21,600

   You have with LEAPS again manufactured a miracle! You have gotten all of your own money out of this position. You now own 12 LEAPS Calls on a rising stock with excellent relative strength. You have 14 months to go with your leveraged position and *none* of your own capital at risk. You are using OPM—other people's money!

Years ago Jerome Weidman wrote a wonderful book with that title (it even featured a female character named Dowie Jones). The book was very good, but we think the strategy is even better. Having no upside limit on a leveraged position with no money of your own at risk is an investor's dream. Moving from miracles back to mundane matters, we note that this type of transaction doesn't always have to use "one-half."

Examples

Bought 24 18-month ZYX LEAPS 80 Calls @ 9 = $21,600
Sold   15 14-month ZYX LEAPS 80 Calls @ 14½ = $21,750

or

Bought 24 18-month ZYX LEAPS 80 Calls @ 9 = $21,600
Sold   18 14-month ZYX LEAPS 80 Calls @ 12 = $21,600

Why did we sell more in these later examples? Why didn't we wait for the LEAPS Call to double as in the first illustration? Because we used this technique, as we have always advised, not for its own sake. We employed it when we felt it was necessary. If you always wait for a Call—option or LEAPS—to double before you take any action, we predict trouble, *tsuris*, and *agida* for you. The point is that when your fear threatens to overtake your greed, OPM is a great maneuver to use.

Incidentally, we did exaggerate the size of the initial position. That was merely because 24 has a lot more divisors than 10, which keeps the examples simpler. That should not deter you from the technique. If you are long five LEAPS Calls and have to sell three instead of two-and-a-half, don't give it a second thought. OPM is not the only technique available here. Let's look at a similar situation but consider a different stock scenario.

Example

ZYX @ 90
Long 10 13-month ZYX LEAPS 80 Calls @ 17

Here we see that you bought these LEAPS Calls five months previously at a cost of 9. The stock has had a slow and steady move, but has never "exploded." You have a fairly firm conviction that the stock will continue upward, but think that it will take time. You also see resistance just above the 100 level. You convert your long position into a spread.

Example
ZYX @ 90
Long 10 13-month ZYX LEAPS 80 Calls @ 17
Write 10 13 month ZYX LEAPS 100 Calls @ 9

You have changed the long LEAPS Call position into a LEAPS bull spread position. That spread has a lot going for it. First it takes one of the classic forms: long ITM, written OTM. Second, the written LEAPS Call has a strike in your perceived resistance area. Last, but perhaps most important, you have recovered your original investment. You bought 10 LEAPS Calls @ 9, and you have just written another 10 LEAPS Calls for 9. We suppose you could say this is another use of the OPM strategy. We say yes and no. Yes, because you did get back the entirety of the initial investment. No, because that wasn't the intent here. If you had gotten only 6 to 7 instead of 9, it would still have suited your objectives. If the stock does end at or over 100, you will make the strike differential—20 points. That 20 points might be all profit (when you got back 9) or mostly so (when you got back 6 or 7). You also might choose to close the position before expiration and take less than the maximum possible potential. The initiation of this technique and the choice over whether or not to seek early closure all depend, as these decisions always do, on your expectations and risk attitudes.

Suppose there were a LEAPS strike of 95, but no 100 strike? Should you use the 95? Or should you wait for a higher one to be created? (Remember that new LEAPS strikes are created at about 20 percent OTM.) We don't know. It depends on you. There is another possibility to explore, however. Look at the strikes in the longest conventional expiration. That expiration will have a duration of six, seven, or eight months. In that month there might be a 100 strike. It won't give you as high a dollar premium as a LEAPS Call, but it is a possibility to be checked. If you want to stay with the long LEAPS Call for a while, this variation is part bull spread. The other part is the technique we covered in Chapter 35, "Time Is of the Essence."

Finally, there is the method of buying an ITM Put (LEAPS or option) against a profitable LEAPS Call that has gone ITM. We covered this in Chapter 35 on buying LEAPS straddles or combinations. Go back; it's worth reviewing. It's one of the LEAPS methods we call "miraculous."

We just said "finally." Aren't we going to consider rolling profitable LEAPS Calls? Some readers might like to do this and we say, "*Wow,* are you ever superbullish!" If you want to be regarded in that manner, it might be right for you. It could even be done with a twist or two.

Examples
I. In the same year:
YXZ @ 42
Long 24 YXZ LEAPS 35 Calls @ 12 (bought @ 8)

You are now convinced that the stock will move substantially higher. If on the basis of your conviction you are very aggressive, you could roll up and double up.

Sell out 24 YXZ LEAPS 35 Calls @ 12   Closing position
Buy 48 YXZ LEAPS 45 Calls @ 6

You have spent no additional funds ($24 \times \$1,200 = 48 \times \$600$), but increased the number of LEAPS Calls you are long. We can quantify what we have named your superbullishness: The stock must, at expiration, be above 55 for the switched position to outperform the original. We call this the **Strategic Break-even Point** (S/B/E). By that we mean the level for the stock at which one strategy (i.e., position) outdoes the other.

If you are not that aggressive, an alternate switch would be:
Sell out 24 YXZ LEAPS 35 Calls @ 12   Closing position
Buy   16 YXZ LEAPS 45 Calls @ 6

The second switch looks almost as aggressive as the first, but there's more here than meets the eye. This switch is really a use of OPM. You have recovered your initial investment ($[24 \times \$1,200] - [16 \times \$600] = \$19,200 = 24 \times \$800$). If you are correct in your stock prediction, you can make a lot of money in the time left. Having that potential with none of your own capital at risk is surely enhancement!

II. In another year:

YXZ @ 42

Long 24 YXZ LEAPS 35 Calls @ 12

Sell out 24 YXZ (one year out) LEAPS 35 Calls @ 12   Closing
    position

Buy   24 YXZ (two year out) LEAPS 35 Calls @ 14½

We have allowed, in this example, for two bid/asked spreads. That is, we recognize that you will be selling on one bid and buying on one offer. Even so, you will have spent only 2½ points per LEAPS Call and given yourself a full additional year for appreciation. We comment, in passing, that this is another year for the position to go wrong, so be careful.

If you are even more aggressive than that you could:

Sell out 24 YXZ (one year out) LEAPS 35 Calls @ 12   Closing
    position

Buy   28 YXZ (two year out) LEAPS 45 Calls @ 10

We think this is dubious and undesirable. While you have eliminated the extra cost, gained an extra year, and gotten long more LEAPS Calls, you have sacrificed the lower striking price. Before you contemplate such action, reread one of our mini-essays on aggressiveness versus greed.

Buying LEAPS Puts

This one is pretty easy after the last example. All the strategies enumerated there can be transferred to this technique. But there is a difference to be carefully observed. We have previously discussed the concept that stocks tend to fall faster than they rise. Now we will tell you that very often when stocks go into a downswing, they will fall farther than expected. There may be pauses and/or countertrend rallies, but the downmove may persist for longer (in price as well as time) than anybody anticipated. If no fast fall has yet occurred but your LEAPS Put is profitable, it is probably good to look at enhancement. Before we do, we state that to do this you would have to have changed your outlook from bearish to superbearish. You would also have to be nimble. If those factors are satisfied, you could go for increased leverage. But if the stock has already had a dizzying decline, pause for evaluation. Let's look at one example from each category.

Example
XYZ @ 70
Bought 10 18-month XYZ LEAPS 70 Puts @ 13
Four months later XYZ @ 60
Sell out 10 14-month XYZ LEAPS 70 Puts @ 18   Closing
    position
Buy   20 14-month XYZ LEAPS 55 Puts @ 9

Here you have spent no more money, but are now long twice as many LEAPS Puts with over a year to go. This is technically enhancement, but it should be done only on two conditions. One, as we said before, you are superbearish. Two, you will monitor the position extremely closely and get out early with a profit. If it goes against you, take quick action.

Example
You bought 18-month, 100-strike LEAPS Puts @ 17

Now the stock is @ 67, you have 11 months to go, the LEAPS Puts are quoted 33–34
If you are really bearish for the longer-term, you could see the 23-month 100 strike LEAPS Put quoted 33½ – 34½. By selling out yours, and buying the one farther out, you would incur a 1½ debit (34½ – 33) but own LEAPS Put with a very long time until expiration.

Writing Covered LEAPS Calls

You bought stock and wrote LEAPS Calls. Now, with the stock giving every indication of longer-term outperformance, you are fretting over the limitation of LEAPS covered Call writing. You have fewer choices than with conventional Calls, but you do have some.

1. You could buy back the written LEAPS Calls and hope to watch the stock soar higher.

Example
XYZ @ 92
Write 18-month 100 strike XYZ LEAPS Calls @ 17
One month later, XYZ is @ 99 (and looking great)
Buy back the LEAPS Calls @ 24

Over the next six months XYZ (with some minor interruptions) keeps going higher. When it hits 124 you sell out (or you take some LEAPS action). You have made 32 points less the 7 loss (17 write less 24 buyback) on the LEAPS Calls. Good work.

That's very nice. What we really mean is that's very nice if it does work. We ask you to recall the informatory question: "How much profit is enough?" If you're not very right, you will learn a very expensive lesson.

Example
XYZ @ 92
Write 18-month 100-strike XYZ LEAPS Calls @ 17

One month later, XYZ is @ 99 (and looking great)
Buy back the LEAPS Calls @ 24

Unfortunately, the next week XYZ reverses and falls like a rock until it reaches 54. We hope you sold out soon enough to limit your losses. The 17 points was originally a cushion; your avaricious action turned that into an additional 7-point loss. We don't know exactly how much you lost, but we do know it was a big loss that could have been avoided.

2. Roll up the written LEAPS Calls to a higher strike.

Example
XYZ @ 92
Write 18-month 100-strike XYZ LEAPS Calls @ 17
XYZ has gone back and forth over a three-month span. Finally, you see that it is about to break out @ 93
Buy back the written XYZ 100 LEAPS Calls @ 18   Closing
    position
Write new   XYZ 120 LEAPS Calls @ 13

Rolling up in this manner could be viewed as halfway between doing nothing and a LEAPS Call buyback. It's certainly less risky than just paying up for the written LEAPS Calls and expecting the stock to pay you back. But it is not without any risks. You paid 5 in the expectation (hope?) of assignment 20 points higher. Great for you if it does happen that way. If the stock declines instead, or even stays flat, you have decreased your cushion by that 5 points.

3. Roll out the LEAPS Calls to a farther time. You can usually do this at either the same strike, or roll into a higher one.

Examples
XYZ @ 92
Write 18-month 100-strike XYZ LEAPS Calls @ 17
XYZ has gone back and forth over a 3-month span. Finally, you see that it is about to break out @ 93
Buy back the written (15-month) XYZ 100 LEAPS Calls @ 18
Write the next year   (27-month) XYZ 100 LEAPS Calls @ 22
or
Buy back the written (15-month) XYZ 100 LEAPS Calls @ 18
Write the next year   (27-month) XYZ 120 LEAPS Calls @ 13

Of these, we much prefer the roll to a higher strike. There you are doing something very right: You are rolling in the direction of the trend and you are not too greedy. We are not too fond of either of the other two techniques. For that view we'll have to accept some admonishment from Mr. Finicky: "You taught us to use our imagination in investing or trading with LEAPS. Now, when we try to do that, you say it's not so hot. What gives?"

We not only accept the criticism; we applaud it. Yes, we do want the reader to stretch the imagination and to look for alternate possibilities. We certainly do not rule out all enhancement—far from it. But we want to make sure that enhancement is the actual goal. Often it's excessive greed that's at work here. "Greed is good," shouts out Gordon Gecko, the character from the movie *Wall Street*. We can only reply: "Moderation in all things," even LEAPS trading.

We see the basic problem present as an investor who learned about a technique involving LEAPS. Now s/he wants *more*. You should learn from every trade or investment you make. We think it's better to learn that you made mistakes and still made profits. In the scrutinized strategy the lesson would be that you chose the wrong stock for a LEAPS covered Call write or rather that would be the lesson if you turned out to be correct. If you were wrong, you would learn a very different and very costly lesson. That is summarized in the quotation at the head of Chapter 27 on LEAPS synthetic short.

Enough of preaching. There are two other techniques to learn about here.

I. Next time you think you see a stock like this, write only half the number of Calls you could do.

Example
Long (or buying) 1,000 YZX @ 50
Write 5 YZX 18-month 60 LEAPS Calls @ 2½

When the stock does move forcefully upward, you can write more LEAPS Calls and with a higher strike.

Example
Position as above
YZX @ 57
Write 5 YZX 70 LEAPS Calls @ 3

You can do this even more aggressively, if you are, as we said, superbullish. Buy back the written LEAPS Calls and write twice as many at a higher strike.

Example
Long 1,000 YZX @ 50
Written 5 YZX 18-month 60 LEAPS Calls @ 2½
YZX @ 57   YZX 60 LEAPS Calls @ 6
Buy back the 5 YZX 60 LEAPS Calls @ 6   Closing position
Write   10 YZX 70 LEAPS Calls @ 3

You have spent no additional money and are now fully written with a 10-point higher strike. That should satisfy Mr. Finicky!

II. Make absolutely any of the moves described above. Pick the one that appeals to you the most. Use even those we inveighed against. But at the same time sell out your stock and replace it with DIM or ATM LEAPS Calls! This last process gives you the potential for greater profit while simultaneously reducing the amount of your capital at work and at risk. Now that's what we call enhancement!

Writing LEAPS Puts

You have written LEAPS Puts and the underlying stock is rising. We ask you to remind yourself that that's what you wanted. If that has become insufficient reward for your acumen, you could consider buying back the written LEAPS Put and writing another—with a higher strike—in its place.

Example
YXZ @ 40
Write 18-month YXZ 35 LEAPS Puts @ 4
Four months later YXZ @ 47
Buy back 14-month YXZ 35 LEAPS Puts @ 2   Closing
   position
Write   14-month YXZ 45 LEAPS Puts @ 5

You will take in more money in this procedure. Obviously you also are exposing yourself to greater risk. Some, seeing this done successfully, might want to repeat the process. To them we say: "No tree grows to the sky." We also say that they have moved far away from the original idea of writing LEAPS Puts. We think rolling once is enough and recall an old story: When Voltaire was invited to an orgy, he reluctantly accepted and then acquitted himself so well that he was immediately reinvited to the next such occasion. He respectfully declined, replying: "Once a philosopher, twice a pervert"!

LEAPS Bull Spreads

You are long a LEAPS Bull spread with two LEAPS legs. You are pleased that the underlying stock is rising but not so pleased with the speed of the rise. You no longer like the limitation the spread places upon you. Once again we have to distinguish between an altered viewpoint and an increase in greed. We repeat: "How much profit is enough?" If the stock does continue to rise at its rapid rate, it will allow you to take most of the money out by closing the position before expiration. Our view here is in that scenario that you would be able to close very early; that would be beneficial.

Example
XYZ @ 38
Bought 10 XYZ 18-month 35 LEAPS Calls @ 7
Wrote   10 XYZ 18-month 45 LEAPS Calls @ 3
                          Net debit   4
Six months later XYZ @ 48   Close both sides
Buy back 10 12-month XYZ 45 LEAPS Calls @ 7   Closing position
Sell out   10 12-month XYZ 35 LEAPS Calls @ 15   Closing position
                          Net credit 8

You have not gotten the maximum possible—10 points—from this spread. But you have doubled your dollars and gotten 80 percent of the maximum a year ahead of time. A LEAPS profit in the hand is worth two in the bush! If this does not satisfy you, what else might you do? We do not have to list and analyze the different possibilities here, because we have already done that. They can be found in the section above on enhancing LEAPS covered Call writing positions. That's because the bull spread is structurally similar to the covered write. That is especially true when one leg of the spread is ITM. As before, we prefer the method that rolls the written LEAPS leg to a higher strike. As before, we do not endorse the other two methods.

LEAPS Bear Spreads
The advice to close early that we gave for LEAPS bull spreads applies here and with more force. An alternative for the super-bearish is to cover the written leg. It is even better to cover that leg and write another lower-strike LEAPS Put in its place.

Writing Uncovered LEAPS Calls

We told you not to do it. If you did it and it's working, we suggest that you should be very happy. Look for protecting the profit that has accumulated, not enhancing it. The obvious methods here are to buy a LEAPS Call with a lower strike, to buy an ITM Put, and to close the position.

Buying Protective LEAPS Puts and Buying Married LEAPS Puts

The enhancement for each of these is very easy to visualize. At some point you decide that you no longer need the protection and sell out the LEAPS Puts. When do you do that? Only you can know that. Your degree of confidence versus worry will allow you to make that decision. What we would counsel here is to remember the admonition about not thinking in all-or-none terms. You could sell out some of the LEAPS Puts rather than all. Bravado would allow the total sale. Caution suggests the partial disposal. You are walking a tightrope and we suggest a little patience. Sell out some and look at the position again later. Barring highly unusual events, you will either get more or just a little less on the balance.

Buying LEAPS Straddles and Combinations

The thought here is very similar to the last strategy. Sell out the nonprofitable side. You could do that in one swoop or you could parcel it out. Before you do either, go back and read Chapter 25 on this strategy. Pay special attention to the section on *not* being too quick to sell out LEAPS.

Writing LEAPS Straddles and Combinations

It could easily be argued that there is no need for enhancement in these techniques. If the stock is staying within your projected range, that implies that you will make the money you expected. If you must look for more, the recommendation is to write additional LEAPS on the less threatening side. If you do this, do *not* write an equal amount. Just do a few.

Example
XYZ @ 50
Written XYZ LEAPS 60 Calls
Written XYZ LEAPS 40 Puts

XYZ rises to 54 without giving any indication that it will rise *substantially* from there. Write two to three additional XYZ LEAPS 40 Puts. Whatever you do, don't let this get out of hand. Remember our diatribes against inappropriate size and remember that this is not a theoretical distaste. People went bankrupt in 1987 because of violating the greed/size proscription.

Synthetic Stock/Synthetic Short with LEAPS

We advised against these two techniques. If you did one and it's working for you, we suggest reading the comments on enhancing writing uncovered Calls. They are equally applicable here. The overriding protocol for any of these has to be wariness for a reversal that could wipe out all profits and even generate losses.

Ratio Writing/Ratio Spreading with LEAPS

We assume that you did either of these in line with our proscriptions against high ratios. Of course, you wrote OTM LEAPS Calls. Here the danger is not so large as in the two synthetics and the straight uncovered, but the danger is of a different character. You should be in fear here, but of an intensification of the trend, not a reversal. Since that is, almost by definition, more likely, we think that here also you should be more interested in establishing profit rather than enhancing it. Fortunately there is an obvious maneuver that speaks somewhat to both issues: Buy back the excess LEAPS Calls. That will allow you to participate in the stock's movement without the risk inherent in the original position. You could make the maximum possible profit from such positions and have no risk at all on the upside.

Surrogate Therapy/Replacement Therapy with LEAPS

In each of these two techniques, you will be long LEAPS Calls. Just ignore how you came to that position and use the methods outlined above on enhancing long LEAPS Calls.

LEAPS Fences

Treat this triple position (long stock, written LEAPS Call, long LEAPS Put) as you would the LEAPS protective/married Puts position. That is, dispose (all at once, or slowly) of the LEAPS Puts. If you are more bullish and more aggressive you can also buy back the LEAPS Calls. The details are given in Chapter 32 on this subject.

Dollar-Cost Averaging with LEAPS

We state with great vigor: Do *not* disturb positions arising in this strategy. It is a long-term and systematic method of investing. The last thing it needs is to have greed interrupt it.

Time Is of the Essence (Long LEAPS/Write Shorter-Term)

If the stock involved in this stratagem starts trending lower, you could consider writing the shorter-term Calls with a lower strike than you had previously planned. This will bring in more dollars and enrich you—if you are right. You should be very aware, however that you are operating with almost contradictory premises. You believe the stock will go up (otherwise you wouldn't be holding on to an ITM LEAPS Call) and also that it is, as we said, "trending lower." That means you must be extremely adept at fine-tuning which strikes to use. You must also constantly review your fundamental attitude toward the stock. Don't you always have to do that with LEAPS investing? Yes, but more so here. As in all the enhancement maneuvers, we say, "Don't get *too* greedy." If you are (doubly) correct in your stock appraisal, be alert to switching back up to higher strikes.

If necessary, you may have to incur a minor loss by rolling one back up. If you have to do that more than once, we think that you should stick to the straight strategy rather than enhancement.

SUMMARY

Enhancing LEAPS positions can be used for almost all LEAPS strategies. It can generate lovely lucre increments. Motivation should be examined to assure that enhancement, not greed, is the primary goal. In this context it would be salutary to recall this interchange: "Baron Rothschild, how did you make all your money?" "I always got out too soon."

CHAPTER 40
LEAPS REPAIR

. . . to repair and perpetuate and keep it alive.

Like enhancement, LEAPS repair is not a strategy but an approach. We think repair is much more important than enhancement. If you didn't know anything at all about enhancement, the worst that would happen to you would be a lower profit. But if you knew nothing about repair, you could lose much more money than you would like.

   We will go right to the strategies. In the first strategy, we will learn some very useful general principles.

Buying LEAPS Calls

We have discussed at length how to select LEAPS Calls for trading and investment. In the previous chapter we went into how to increase profit potential. So what's left to say? What's left to say is that none of us are omniscient: "To err is human." Sometimes the stock you select for buying LEAPS Calls will go down, not up. Don't give up. It has happened to the best of us. What makes the best of us different from the rest of us is that the best investors are more flexible. If they make a mistake, they don't compound it. You can—indeed, you must—learn how to do the same thing in trading and investing with LEAPS. Before we go through this strategy, let's formally declare our assumptions. You know the stock has gone down. What do you think it will do from that point? We assume that you expect, at least, a rebound.

   We will examine four different techniques:
1. *Hold and Hope*
The worst of the lot. Here, you find yourself saying, successively:
   "It will come back, I know it will"
   "It will come back, I think it will"

"It will come back, I hope it will"
and even
"It will come back, I pray it will."

By the time you have reached the hope stage (let alone, the prayer), it is often too late. This is not the way to trade or invest successfully. If you have objective criteria that produce your hopefulness, we wish you well. Let's have the rest of us move on to some more realistic alternatives.

2. *Bite the Bullet*
Sell out. Take what's left of the money and run! Strictly speaking, we ruled this out when we said you expected a rebound, but it is such an important and underutilized method that we want to talk about it. Why is it so underused? Because it entails a double blow—one to the wallet and one to the ego. The notion—let us not mince words, the *stupid* notion—that you have only a paper loss cannot be derided enough. Yes, you have a paper loss now. If that's your approach, you will have a larger loss when you do sell out. Ratiocination is the key, not rationalization. As for the ego blow, it's good to remember the old Wall Street maxim—"The first loss is the best loss."

We said you were expecting a rebound. With that comment in mind, it's good to forget about your original cost. It is no longer relevant. Don't lose sight of the fact that your primary goal has changed. You are no longer trying to make a nice profit; you are trying to repair, or salvage, your position.

3. *Trade In*
The concept here is to trade in your "getting bad" LEAPS Calls for fewer "could-do-it" LEAPS Calls or a smaller number of "more probables."

Example
XYZ @ 44

Long	24 XYZ LEAPS 50 Calls now @ 8½		
Sell out	24 XYZ LEAPS 50 Calls	@ 8½	Closing position
Buy	17 XYZ LEAPS 40 Calls	@ 12	
	or		
Buy	12 XYZ LEAPS 35 Calls	@ 16	

We have not stated the original cost nor how much time until expiration because these factors are irrelevant. What is cogent is your changed perceptions. You are looking for a recovery—both of the stock price and some of your money. The first point here is that you should spend no additional funds; 24 sold @ 8½ = $20,400 = 17 bought @ 12; 12 bought at 16 = $19,200.

Not only did you spend no more money, but you obviously have a lower break-even level and hence less downside risk. As for the upside, just suppose the stock recovers and ends @ 50. Then 17 40-strike Calls would have an intrinsic value of 10 = $17,000; and 12 35-strike Calls would have an intrinsic value of 15 = $18,000. Oh, we must not forget that 24 50-strike Calls would have an intrinsic value of -0- = $-0-. But since you are long many more of them, we'll rewrite it as 24 50-strike Calls will have an intrinsic value of -0- × 24 = $-0-. We're being emphatic, not cute. It does you no good to be long more if the strike is no good.

4. *Better Switch*

The switch advocated here is not of calls, but of strategies. Switch your long LEAPS Calls positions to a LEAPS bull spread position, but not by writing a higher strike. Instead, sell out the longs to close the position. Write an equal number of the same to open a new position, and buy an equal amount of a lower strike.

Example
ZXY @ 44

Long	12 ZXY LEAPS 50 Calls @ 8½	
Sell	12 ZXY LEAPS 50 Calls @ 8½	Closing position
Write	12 ZXY LEAPS 50 Calls @ 8½	Opening position
Buy	12 ZXY LEAPS 35 Calls @ 16	Opening position

New position
Long   12 ZXY LEAPS 35 Calls
Written 12 ZXY LEAPS 50 Calls

In a sort of LEAPS alchemy you have transformed your long LEAPS Call position into a LEAPS bull spread position. You have done it for no cost; 24 × 8½ = $20,400 < $19,200 = 12 × 16. You have lessened your downside risk (and your upside potential). If the stock does recover at expiration to 50 or above, you will retrieve 15 (the spread differential) × 12 = $18,000. In both this and previous example, you might settle for somewhat less and close the new position early.

Buying LEAPS Puts

In this case you wanted the stock to go down, but it's going up. You can take the buying LEAPS Calls repair strategies and construct corresponding ones for long (but wrong) LEAPS Puts. Keep in mind that LEAPS Puts will give up time value faster than LEAPS Calls. And surely keep current the concept that closure can be desirable.

Writing Covered LEAPS Calls

Even though your view for this technique was described as "limitedly bullish," you did want the stock to go up. If it's going down, you have to do something. As always, one of the things you could do is to close the position. There are other possibilities. We presume that you took our advice and wrote an OTM LEAPS Call. Good. That will give you the flexibility to "roll down."

Example
ZXY @ 39
Written ZXY LEAPS 50 Calls

Again it is irrelevant what you got when you first sold the LEAPS Calls. You are interested only in improving your lot.

Buy back the 50 LEAPS Calls @ 4   Closing position
Write   the 40 LEAPS Calls @ 8

Depending on the strikes available on the specific stock, your roll might leave you with another OTM, an ATM, or an ITM as your new written LEAPS Calls. In all of these cases, you have gotten money from the roll, you have stayed long the stock, and you are still in a LEAPS covered Call position. The advantage of the money inflow is that it gives greater protection to the long stock.

There is also the possibility of rolling out in time. That is, buying back the written LEAPS Call and writing another with a year later expiration. This could be at the same strike. It could be at a higher strike—a "diagonal roll"—providing you took in a credit from the roll. It could even be at a lower strike—a downward diagonal roll.

Examples
XYZ @ 39
Buy back the   50 LEAPS Calls @ 4   Closing
                                                position
Write (1 year farther) 50 LEAPS Calls @ 8 *or*
Write (1 year farther) 40 LEAPS Calls @ 12

This type of roll will keep you exposed to the same stock for as much as a year longer. Therefore, we urge that you employ this tactic only with a greater commitment to the stock.

Writing LEAPS Puts

You wrote the LEAPS Puts with a commitment to buy the stock if it declined. Now it is going down, but you no longer feel as enamored. *Get out!* Why are we so abrupt? Why don't we examine other possibilities? Because, while there are repair techniques analogous to those in similar strategies, we don't think you should use them. You certainly can if you want to, and you might be right in so doing. We want you to remember how often we have said that stocks fall faster than they rise, and that they can fall farther as well as faster. There's nothing wrong in making a mistake. Repeating an error is asking for trouble.

LEAPS Bull Spreads

In this strategy, you can adopt the methods used for LEAPS covered Call writing repair. As we said in Chapter 39 on enhancement, these are structurally very similar. But as we said in the technique immediately above, you had better be careful. Give serious consideration to closure.

LEAPS Bear Spreads

The repair methods for these positions are very similar, but inverted, to the LEAPS bull spreads repair techniques. Also look at what we said about repairing long LEAPS Puts as opposed to Calls. The bottom line is to be more careful, to take action sooner and to assign heavier weight to closure.

Writing Uncovered LEAPS Calls

We told you you'd be sorry! If this happens to you—that is, you write uncovered LEAPS Calls and the stock rises threateningly—do *not* wait around. *Get out!* We mean this even more than the same advice for written LEAPS Puts. There you might face large losses. You would be long stock and could see it fall precipitously. Still that does happen to people who buy stock without any LEAPS involvement. But in your strategy of choice (not ours), you would be short stock and see it rising. And you would face the paralyzing prospect of *unlimited* losses. Forget it. Buy back the LEAPS Puts, take the loss, and learn a lesson.

Buying Protective LEAPS Puts and Buying Married LEAPS Puts

♪♪♪   ♪♪♪   ♪♪♪
"It's dee-licious, it's dee-lightful, it's dee-lovely!"

What are we singing about? We're talking about the absolutely fabulous distinction between the terrible tactic above—writing uncovered LEAPS Calls—and the twin techniques here. What's so amazingly different? In the previous case, you faced the specter of unlimited losses. But in these two strategies you were always limited in possible losses from the moment you initiated the LEAPS Put purchases. There will be nothing to repair because nothing can go wrong! That is just a slight overstatement. If the stock moved up but not enough to make up for the cost of the LEAPS Put, then you might be sorry about the LEAPS Put purchase. But that's a pretty slim chance, considering the life of the LEAPS Put. You might say that these two techniques were examples of built-in repair. The same comment applies to LEAPS replacement therapy.

Buying LEAPS Straddles and Combinations

In order to consider repair here, you would have to become convinced that the stock was not going to move enough to make your position profitable. That's more likely with the straddle than the combination. Both are somewhat unlikely but not impossible. If you do feel that way, closure is certainly a choice. Again, the fact that these were LEAPS would leave you with more premium when you did decide to cash in. Another possibility is to see which way the stock is moving and then sell out the LEAPS option on the other side. Then convert the position into either a LEAPS bull Call spread or a LEAPS bear Put spread. The reason for adding another leg is your feeling about reduced movement (we would say volatility). If the upmove or downmove is only temporary, the double cash raised (once from closing one LEAPS combination leg and once from writing a spread leg) will greatly protect the Long LEAPS position.

Example
XYZ @ 39
Long LEAPS 50 Calls now @ 4
Long LEAPS 35 Puts now @ 5

The stock has come down from 43 and has been very quiet. You no longer see the stock as neutral. In fact you think it will go lower.

Sell out LEAPS 50 Calls @ 4   Closing position
Write   LEAPS 30 Puts @ 3

New Position
Long   LEAPS 35 Puts
Written LEAPS 30 Puts

Your position change reflects your altered view on the stock. If it doesn't, then don't make this maneuver.

Writing LEAPS Straddles and Combinations

This strategy was undertaken with a specific stock view: limited range. If you change your mind on that outlook, you will have to take action. Remember our warnings about both the written uncovered LEAPS Puts and the written uncovered LEAPS Calls. Here you have both of them combined. It is true that the combining gives you a second LEAPS premium that will lower any losses, but that might be of scant satisfaction. You could buy back the more threatening side and write a farther out (in price) strike. Too often that just postpones the trouble. Whatever you do, don't try the trick of buying back, as we just described, and writing more of the new strike. You might get away with that temporarily (because there would be, at that time, a lower margin requirement). It is more likely that you not only postponed your troubles but that you increased them. People have gone bankrupt trying that; don't join them. "Go with the flow" and "the trend is your friend" are not just silly statements; they are the distilled wisdom of the marketplace.

If you set yourself up against that wisdom, we think you're not just looking for trouble, you're asking for it! You could take an offsetting position. The most obvious is buying the stock, if the trend is up. That would change your position from uncovered LEAPS straddles or combinations to a covered version of the same. You obviously could use a lower-strike LEAPS Call instead of the stock to achieve the same type of position, and you could take analogous positions if you established the trend as down. Finally, you could close the position. Never forget that line of action. Whether it's for taking a profit or for limiting losses, it should always be kept in mind.

SUMMARY

Much has been written about options and some about LEAPS. These writings always tell you when to buy and occasionally when to sell out. Few, if any, tell you what to do when things go wrong. But that's the most important to know, for "The best-laid schemes . . . gang aft a-gley." LEAPS repair encompasses many maneuvers for different strategies. The theme is constant; close the position (in whole or part) or alter it. The alteration is for salvage, not increased profits. LEAPS repair is far from supererogatory; it is essential. Indeed, we might say: "To err is human, to repair divine." For those who might find elements of sacrilegiousness in that repair quote, we offer the old, but original: "He who fights and runs away / lives to fight another day."

OTHER LEAPS
TOPICS

CHAPTER 41
LEAPS AND
PROGRAM TRADING

We must embark on a bold new program.

STRATEGY	Using LEAPS During Program Trading
OUTLOOK	Applicable to all strategies
ADVANTAGES	Better prices obtainable
DRAWBACKS	Nimbleness needed
DEGREE OF RISK	Varies with strategy selected

A gentle note to the (possibly) frightened reader:
Please read on. The basis for so-called program trading is full of mathematical complexity. You will not have to study that nor are we advocating participation in that technique. We just want to explain how you can use LEAPS to benefit when others use it.

This is a short chapter on a long and complex subject. Happily you will not have to study **Program Trading (PT).** This misnamed technique—it is more properly labeled **Index Arbitrage**—is used when prices get out of line. The prices we are talking about are twofold: first, the price of an index, say, the S&P 500, second, the price of the futures contract trading on that index. Suffice it to say that there are times when these prices are not in balance. This can result in one of two scenarios. Arbitrageurs will either buy the stocks in the index and sell the futures, or just the reverse. (It may be noted, *passim,* that sometimes only a subset of the entire index is used.) It is the reverse that usually scares people. When the futures are low in price, they will be bought and the stocks sold. (The stocks may not only be sold, they may be sold short, although here there are some restrictions.)

This can produce whipsaws in the market on an intraday basis. We have seen many such days where the market (as measured by the Dow Jones Industrial Average) is up, say, 15 points, and then reverses, and ends up down 20 points. "Program trading did it" blare the headlines or "Triple witching hour" made the market collapse.

You don't have to worry about any of that. The rational investor, instead of being frightened off by such occurrences, can make them work for him or her. Placing a bid below the market for a selected stock involved in program trading can bring ownership at a reduced price.

If that is true for stocks, it is even more true for LEAPS. Why isn't it so for options in general? Because, as always, the nearer expiration can wreck havoc. But with LEAPS you can have up to two or even three years for the reduced cost to benefit you.

Of course, the reverse would work if you wanted to buy LEAPS Puts. Wait until PT started operating on the upside. Then your selected stock would be pushed up, and its LEAPS Put would decline correspondingly (measured by delta). Again you could get a bargain which would enhance profits that might accrue from this purchase.

Looked at abstractly, buying LEAPS during PT is only a special case of a general methodology. Buy LEAPS Calls when the stock declines and purchase LEAPS Puts when the stock is rising. This is generally good, but can sometimes be a nuisance to carry out. It might mean placing many orders away from the market and annoying, if not antagonizing, your broker. When PT starts to operate, you can take advantage of it. The time to be most alert is during expiration week (the week containing the third Friday of the month). You should be more alert on Expiration Thursday and most especially on Expiration Friday. It is then that price distortions—which have little to do with underlying trends—are most likely to occur. Note also that large moves occurring at the end of that week are often reversed on the following Monday.

Suppose the market rises (or falls) because of more fundamental reasons, which you have mistaken for PT? If you bought LEAPS Calls during such a downtrend, you will be in a similar position to somebody who bought stock then. You each made a mistake. Just get out. The problem here has nothing to do with

PT, LEAPS, or options. It is one of misevaluating a trend. If you see that you have done that, don't wait around. Fortunately, while you may lose money here, that loss will not be magnified by a premium decay as it would have been with ordinary options. Naturally the same admonitions apply to LEAPS Puts purchased during an apparently artificial upmove that turned out to be real.

If you (and/or your broker) have correctly identified an extremely short-lived, countertrend market movement, however, you can build profits from your acuity. We should note that this technique is not limited to outright LEAPS purchases. For example, if you are long stock and have been contemplating the sale of a LEAPS covered Call, you might find a good opportunity during PT. If your stock (and its LEAPS Call) rose as a result you could exploit that situation. Similar remarks are applicable to almost all LEAPS strategies. So sharpen your pencil, stay at your telephone, and find some LEAPS bargains while others just wail and bemoan program trading.

SUMMARY

Trading LEAPS while others cause turmoil with their artificial arbitrage, summons Kipling to mind: "If you can meet with Triumph and Disaster . . . Yours is the Earth. . . ." Without going quite that far, we observe that "Fortune favors the brave." This technique is not for all. For the brave and nimble, LEAPS positions can be established during program trading at potentially profitable prices.

CHAPTER 42
LEAPS AND TAXES

Nothing is certain but death and taxes.

At various points in this book, we have made disclaimers of one sort or another. Here we cannot emphasize enough how strongly we feel about disclaiming. Tax rules, and the interpretations of them, change. Those interpretations can be by the Internal Revenue Service (IRS), a tax court, or other judicial bodies. The treatment of securities taxations is very difficult. What applies to one reader of this book may not for another. There are some unresolved tax issues relating to options. Further, in some instances there are contradictory opinions, rulings, or precedents.

We have said it before, but we must repeat it here. Nobody should enter into *any* tax-related investment, trade, or position without individual advice from a competent tax adviser. We are not tax advisers. Although we have obtained the information in this chapter from sources previously found reliable, we make no guarantees, and we urge you to consult your own tax adviser.

We have another sort of disclaimer. We cannot possibly cover all options/LEAPS tax rules—let alone try to explain them. We will do something else instead. We will try to discuss most of the tax rules that have a major impact on LEAPS strategic decisions. We will deal first with equity LEAPS.

Long Equity LEAPS Calls or Puts
(as Single, Unhedged Positions)

If these investments are held for more than a year, the gain or loss on selling them out will be a long-term capital gain or loss. If they are sold out in a year or less, the gain or loss is short-term. LEAPS held until they expire are deemed to have been sold out at a price of zero on the expiration day.

Strategic Impact

You should consider bailing out of a losing long LEAPS position before it has been held for over a year, and you should try to hold on to a winning one for at least a year and a day. If you do that successfully, you will have profits as long-term and losses as short-term.

We have noted in Chapter 19 that the selling out of a profitable LEAPS Put after you've held it over a year is the only way we know to make a long-term gain on a declining stock.

If you have held a LEAPS Call or Put until the December preceding its January expiration, you should consider whether you want to take the profit or loss that year (i.e., close the position in December) or next year (i.e., close the position in January).

Exercising LEAPS Calls or Puts
(as Single, Unhedged Positions)

The exercise of a long LEAPS Call will result in adding to the striking price—the LEAPS premium originally paid—to arrive at the cost basis for the stock. The holding period for that stock begins on the day after exercise and does not include the LEAPS Call holding period.

Strategic Impact

Give thought to whether you want to exercise in December or in January. In general, profitable LEAPS Calls should be sold out, rather than exercised (to gain any time value left). You might be willing, however, to sacrifice a small amount in order to establish a stock position with a lower cost basis (strike plus original LEAPS cost) and a built-in profit.

The exercise of a long LEAPS Put results in subtracting the original LEAPS premium from the sale proceeds of the stock sold.

Strategic Impact

See the discussion of married Puts in Chapter 16.

Writing LEAPS Calls or Puts

There is no taxable event from writing a LEAPS Call until one of three following events occur:

1. The LEAPS Call expires. The premium is short-term capital gain, independent of the time involved.
2. The LEAPS Call is repurchased. This will be a short-term gain or loss, depending on how much you pay to close the position.
3. The LEAPS Call is assigned. The LEAPS Call premium is added to the strike.

Loss or gain is computed by subtracting from that total the cost basis of the stock. The resultant loss or gain will be short-term or long-term depending on the holding period of the *stock*.

Strategic Impact

1. Again consider, if applicable, whether you want to close the LEAPS Call position in December or let it expire in January.
2. If you have the choice, decide whether it's better to buy back in December or January.
3. Stock that has long-term status when sold out on a LEAPS Call assignment will, because of the event described under #3 above, in effect, convert the LEAPS Call premium to long-term treatment as well.

Writing a LEAPS Put has a similar treatment. No taxable event takes place until one of the three events described above, occurs:

1. Same as #1 above.
2. Same as #2 above.
3. On the assignment of a LEAPS Put, the cost basis of the stock is the strike, less the premium received when the LEAPS Put was written.

Strategic Impact

1. Same as #1 under Strategic Impact above.
2. Same as #2 under Strategic Impact above.
3. To realize a taxable loss on the stock, the stock must be sold.

Offsetting Positions

This is a very important IRS concept. One or more positions added to another can change the tax treatment. The test is a "substantial reduction of risk of loss." If the position meets that test, there are consequences:

1. The holding period is suspended or terminated during the offset.
2. The wash sale rule applies to defer losses in some offset positions.
3. You cannot take a deduction for losses.

Qualified Covered Calls

The law provides that the initiation of certain covered calls meets the test described above. That is, they are viewed as substantial reduction of risk of loss and as a result you face the consequences. This has led to the specification of *Qualified covered Calls*. These positions will not suffer the consequences listed above. The qualification test is for ITM Calls; others are deemed qualified.

The table below shows which calls will be considered "qualified."

Close means the stock's close on the business day before the initiation of the covered Call. If the opening sale of the stock on the day of initiation is 10 percent or more above the close, that opening price, and not the closing price, becomes the basis for calculations.

Also note that to be qualified the covered Calls must be written with or after the stock purchase. Writing uncovered

Stock Price/Time to Expiration	Lowest Qualified Strike
Less than or equal to 25 More than 30 days	One strike below close; Must be minimum of 85% stock price
Greater than 25; less than, or equal to, 60 More than 30 days	One strike below close
Greater than 60; less than, or equal to, 150 31 to 90 days	One strike below close
Greater than 60; less than, or equal to, 150 More than 90 days	Two strikes below close; Not more than 10 ITM
Greater than 150 31 to 90 days	One strike below close
Greater than 150 More than 90 days	Two strikes below close

Calls and then buying stock might be a good or a bad tactic, but it does not result in qualified covered Calls.

Strategic Impact

It is always important to know the tax implications of trades and/or investments. While the qualified covered Calls concept might impinge on your dealings, it will not impact on much of what we have advocated. This is one more reason to prefer OTM LEAPS covered Calls.

Married Puts

Married Puts occupy a peculiar position in IRS regulations. Internal Revenue Code Section #1233 specifically exempts them from the short sale consequences. This would seem to allow an uninterrupted holding period (if the other rules are complied with). However, it is not clear whether married Puts are exempt from the offsetting position rules of Section #1092. One difference from the usual treatment is clear. If a LEAPS married Put expires unexercized, its original cost will be added to the stock's purchase price. For the other conflicts, we note that when Congress passed the Deficit Reduction Act of 1984, the Treasury said that it would issue interpretations of the new rules. We are still waiting.

Strategic Impact

It is rather difficult to assess the strategic impact when we don't even have a clear view of which rules are applicable. We think the guide here should be whether the strategy fits without any tax breaks.

Example
You want to buy a stock which is very volatile and hold it for a long time. Because of its extreme volatility, you are fearful. If you decide to buy the stock and the LEAPS married Put, we say that's good. The LEAPS Put will speak to your fears and protect you from your nightmares. If you later get a tax benefit, that's even better.

Index LEAPS

We made a distinction between broad-based and narrow-based indexes. This differentiation is all-important when it comes to taxation. Narrow-based index options or LEAPS are taxed in the same way as equity options or LEAPS. But broad-based index options are taxed in a completely different manner. These are known as Section #1256 contracts, and the tax treatment is simple but startling. If you have a position in such an option—long or written; Puts or Calls; LEAPS or not—you will be bound by two rules:

1. Mark-to-the-market. This means that you will be taxed as if you had closed out your position at the last sale price on the last trading day of the calendar year.

Examples
On January 3 you buy 10 broad-based index LEAPS Calls for 3 that expire on January 19 of the following year. The last sale of these (not made by you) on December 31 is 5. On January 18 you

sell them out at 3 and think you have broken even. You will have to pay tax on the $2,000 "profit" (10 × [5-3]) you made!

2. The tax treatment will be 60 percent long-term and 40 percent short-term. This will apply to gains or losses.

Example
You buy 10 broad-based index LEAPS Calls @ 3 that have just eight months to run. They spurt to 5 two weeks later, and you sell them out there. You have a $2,000 profit and $1,200 (60 percent) is treated as a long-term gain!

Strategic Impact

1. Give serious thought to selling out these instruments at year end. In almost all cases, timing of the sale (for tax purposes), has become irrelevant.
2. This is a way to make a (partial) long-term gain in an up or a down market. It is independent of the time the position is held! If this idea appeals to you, make sure (and then double-check) that the index under consideration is broad-based.

General Considerations

Some of the tax rules can be very beneficial to LEAPS trading. If you monitor a long LEAPS Call (or Put) position, you may be able to take profits as long-term and losses as short-term. As we write this, the difference for most individuals (not subject to the alternative minimum tax) would be only 3 percent. However, that spread could widen with impending changes. The Clinton administration has proposals that could make the difference as great as a reduction from 39.6 percent to 28 percent.

One LEAPS strategy has a very large tax impact. Consider what could happen if you bought stock in, say, April 1994 and wrote an OTM LEAPS covered Call expiring in January 1996. You would have the immediate use of the LEAPS Call premium if you so desired. If the written LEAPS Call were assigned at expiration, you would have a pleasant long-term gain. For most individuals, no tax would be due on that gain until April 1997, three years after you collected the money!

SUMMARY

When you started this book, you might have thought LEAPS were difficult. We hope we have made them easier for you. We know they're easy to understand, compared to the tax law. We think that several of the tax rules relevant to LEAPS trading can add benefits. But we still think that the two most important considerations are:

1. You need to talk about your tax situation with your tax adviser.
2. You should worry first about making the profit, not how much tax will be owed.

CHAPTER 43
PRACTICAL ASPECTS
OF LEAPS

There is the greatest practical benefit. . . .

This is not a strategy chapter. We think we've done enough of them, and we hope that you're now just about ready to enter the world of trading or investing with LEAPS. But there are many practical questions to consider before you do that. We will look at them. Because they cover a very wide range, this chapter will deal with the larger issues first and then with what's left over— one at a time.

Certificateless Society

From the time of the first listed options trading in 1973, options have been a *certificateless society*. That means that you do not get a stock (or any other kind of) certificate when you buy or sell LEAPS. You do get a confirmation from your brokerage house. This is sufficient to prove ownership (of a long or a written position). You should also receive monthly statements from your brokerage. It is obviously very important to keep both of these documents. Whatever you do receive, it is highly desirable to keep your own records. For the brokerage's records it is very important to have any errors corrected immediately. If a phone call does not produce a correction, don't hesitate; write at once. If that doesn't do the trick, give serious thought to changing brokerages. That brings us to our next topic.

Choosing a Brokerage Firm and Choosing a Broker

All brokerage firms are not the same. Many have specific policies about options that are undesirable. Find out about these before you start. The most important is to be sure all the types of trades you want to do will be allowed. As an example, some firms will not allow the sale of uncovered index options (LEAPS or otherwise).

The next angle to check is commissions. Should you use a full-service broker or a discount broker? There are arguments on both sides. What most don't know is that you can often negotiate a discounted commission from a so-called full-service firm. Discount brokers vary in the amount of advice they will give—from zero to a surprisingly large amount.

That brings us to research. If this is an important aspect to you, stay with the brokerage that provides it. Be aware, however, that many investors do their own research. This can be done by subscription or by frequent library trips. At this point we would like to list some outstanding services and sources for research and statistics:

Investor's Business Daily. This daily alternative to *The Wall Street Journal* (*WSJ*) has a host of features that its competitor does not. (We note, that many innovations of *IBD* were later copied by the *WSJ*.) Of foremost importance to you is the 2½ to 3 pages *IBD* sets aside for a large listing of options trades. There is a separate listing here for LEAPS trading. IBD stock tables identify (with a small "o") stocks that have listed options.

Wall Street Journal (WSJ). The WSJ has revised its option tables. In addition to showing the 1,400 most active equity options, a separate listing has the 100 most active equity LEAPS. Index LEAPS are carried and identified on another page as part of a listing of index options trading.

Daily Graphs—Option Edition. This weekly, published by William O'Neill who puts out *IBD*, is invaluable. Although it does not list LEAPS separately, it does provide an almost unbelievable amount of information on options and on the underlying stocks. Indexes are also covered. The only drawback, which is due to the mushrooming number of option stocks, is the omission of many stocks. These are selected each week by the lack of volume. A spot check by your author showed that it was quite rare to leave out a LEAPS stock.

Barron's. We use the word *invaluable* again here. This weekly covers the entire market—stocks, bonds, futures, real estate, etc. It has columns on all of them. "The Striking Price," their option column, is excellent. Beyond all this, there is a statistical section every week that is totally unrivaled. It gives coverage of options and LEAPS as well as an absolutely enormous amount of data from which you can draw inferences that could be of great help in formulating trading and investment decisions.

Standard & Poor's Outlook. This is a weekly published by S&P. It does not have specific option or LEAPS coverage, but it does have a sound and sensible rating system for individual stocks. This includes not only stocks to buy, but stocks to avoid (good for LEAPS Puts). There is commentary from many viewpoints on stock selection. Opinions are also expressed on the entire market as assessed from the fundamental, technical, and economic vantage points.

S&P Stock Guide. This 250+ page, 5" × 8½" compilation is issued monthly by Standard & Poor's. It bears the stamp of their skill and accuracy in the collection of stock data including, among others, price ranges, volume, dividends, earnings, capitalization, and more. Your broker will send you this for a nominal amount.

Value Line. This long-running stock evaluation service is famed for its group rankings, which have been so good over long periods of time that they confound the theorists who say that the market is "efficient" and impossible to beat. The same organization publishes *VL Options Guide,* which is accurate and helpful.

We return to our consideration of brokers. There are many monetary aspects to consider. In addition to commissions, there is the interest rate charged on debit balances in a margin account. Some firms also will pay you interest on credit balances. While it cannot be denied that these are important factors, we believe that service is more important than expense control. Service includes speed and accuracy. This can result in better net prices for you; that is, a better execution may leave you with a lower cost (or higher sales proceeds) than a big discount off a not-so-hot execution. Here we have a somewhat heretical view. You may be very satisfied with your current broker. That doesn't mean that s/he is the right broker for you with options and LEAPS. Two other option areas a brokerage firm might have are very important. These are an options strategist and an options service desk. The strategist answers any and all questions about options and LEAPS, which can range from very esoteric inquiries to telling your broker what the LEAPS symbol is on a particular stock (see Appendix). The strategist will also help your broker select from tactics and tailor a strategy that fits your particular needs. S/he may also publish reports that update option/LEAPS material and that suggest or recommend strategies. While the strategist is for ideas, the service desk is for action. The desks will guide your order through execution. They will select the best market in the case of multiple trading, handle contingent orders (e.g., covered Call writes), and get you quotes.

Example
You want to buy stock and write a LEAPS Call. An options service desk will not worry about the price of either side but only about the net debit involved. You would be willing to take an eighth less on the LEAPS Call if you paid an eighth less for the stock. And the same with an eighth more on either side. A desk handling such an order would not give you an execution on either side unless it could also do the other on your specified terms. People on the desk know how to handle the special problems that can arise with OTC stocks (generally or with LEAPS). When it comes time to sell out (or buy back) a very DIM LEAPS, their experience and expertise are great to have on your side. Obviously these two areas are a big plus for a firm, their absence is a serious negative.

Should You Use Market Orders or Limit Orders?

We think there's a simple answer to this question. It depends on how badly you want to buy (or sell) the stock, LEAPS, or options involved. Sometimes you want to buy, but are afraid to enter a market order. This might be because you are paranoid; it might be because you are justifiably suspicious; or it might be because you are afraid of a moving market. We suggest an "or better" limit order for these cases. If, for example, a LEAPS Call that you want to buy is quoted 17–18 (that is, you can buy at 18; you can sell at 17) and you are fairly desperate to buy, enter an order that says: "Buy at 18¼ OB." The "or better" alerts the exchange floor representative that you are entering an order above the offer (if it hasn't moved in the interim). It tells him or her that it is *not* a mistaken sell order meant to be entered above the current offer. It gives the floor a little leeway in case the market does move, and it prevents you from getting a report at, say 19, on a market order.

Do not overuse this technique. There are some account executives who add the words OB to every order they enter. This merely identifies them as not too bright.

How to Tell When You Are or Are Not Likely to Be Assigned

If a LEAPS Put or Call that you have written becomes DIM, you must be aware of the possibility of an early assignment (that might be good or bad for you, but you should know about it). Here's how to tell (in general). Compare the bid with the ITM amount.

Example
XYZ @ 72
XYZ LEAPS 60 Call quoted 11½–12½
                    or
XYZ @ 72
XYZ LEAPS 60 Call quoted 12½–13½

In the first case you are likely to receive an assignment. In the second, there is extremely little chance of that. How do we know this? Because nobody would be dumb enough, in the second case, to exercise at 60 and sell at 72 (that would net 12), when s/he could get 12½ instead, just by selling out. In the first case, the LEAPS Call is bid at a **discount to parity** and an assignment is likely. Note that we did not say how long until expiration. That's because it's irrelevant. Whether it's one day or many months, anyone who wanted to realize its intrinsic value could easily be moved to exercise. Notice that this method is equally applicable to options. There is a special case that comes into effect at times, most frequently at the time the stock is about to go ex dividend.

Assume XYZ were going to go ex dividend the next day. That means that if you bought the stock today, you would be entitled to the current dividend; if you bought it tomorrow you would not. If the dividend were ¾, you could expect an assignment in the second case as well as the first. Modify the rule to subtract the dividend (when it's imminent) from the bid before you make the comparison. There are other similar exceptions, such as the deadline for tendering a stock. Your broker should assist you in these matters.

What Is Automatic Exercise?

This refers to ITM LEAPS/options on the day before expiration. Sometimes careless customers (or their nonfeasant brokers) neglect to sell or exercise them. Customers are protected by this mechanism. The rules say that unless notified to the contrary, any equity option (LEAPS or other) that is ¾ or more ITM will be exercised on the customer's behalf. For index LEAPS/options, the ITM threshold is ¼. Don't let this lull you into thinking you will not be assigned if the ITM amount is under these levels. You will almost surely be assigned if ITM at all. You should not depend on automatic exercise, but give specific instructions in each case as to what you want done.

Some brokers leave their offices early on Expiration Friday for golfing or other pastimes. If yours is one of them, we say, unequivocally, get another one.

When Is Expiration Day?

This is not a difficult matter, but there is sometimes confusion about it so we will make it explicit. Expiration day is the

Saturday after the third Friday of the month. Expiration day is for legal purposes and for firms to correct errors. The last trading day is the business day preceding expiration (usually a Friday). If you think that's an invariant, come around when Good Friday (a market holiday) occurs on the third Friday. Actually this is the last trading day for equity options and for index options that have a P.M. settlement. The other indexes have their last trading day *two* days before expiration (usually Thursday). Despite this, most refer (erroneously) to that Friday as expiration day. That day does deserve its own name. If it's "out-of-season" we could drop the "R" and name it *"Expiation day."* At all times, we think it should be Judgment Day!

Should You Do 10 LEAPS at a Time?

That's what we did in most of the examples, but they were for educational purposes. As a matter of practice, you should buy (or write) what you can afford. Do not take on more risk than you can afford, either. Still 10 is a convenient number, and many people do that almost automatically. It may be convenient, but when it comes to your dollars, you should seldom do things automatically. You can adjust your purchases up or down depending on the risks involved. There is, however, one very practical argument in favor of the number 10. Most of the option exchanges have a **10 up** rule. This means that quoted markets are good for 10 up, which means 10 on either side of the bid/offer spread. As we go to press, there is not complete uniformity in this matter, but the exchanges are moving in that direction. Soon that will be the case not only for options but for all LEAPS as well.

Example
If a LEAPS Call is quoted 16–17, that means there is a guarantee on the part of the market maker or specialist to sell 10 at 17 or to buy 10 at 16. If you entered an order for 20 LEAPS, you might or might not get a total fill at those prices.

Are LEAPS Traded Elsewhere?

Yes. In Montreal LEAPS trade on the Bank of Montreal; in Toronto, on the Bank of Nova Scotia, Canadian Pacific, Nova Corporation of Alberta, Placer Dome, Royal Bank, and Toronto Dominion. On the European Options Exchange (EOE) in Amsterdam, LEAPS (some as long as five years) trade on AKZO, KLM, Philips NV, Royal Dutch, and Unilever. The same reduced-value LEAPS on the Major Market Index that trade here, also trade on the EOE. All over the world, LEAPS are listed or preparations are being made to list them.

What Does Opening and Closing Mean?

We have distinguished throughout this book between selling out, meaning selling something you own, and writing, meaning selling something you do not own. Formally, these would be labeled, respectively, as selling to close and selling to open. In the same way, initiating a position with a buy order is buying to open and buying back a position is buying to close.

Which Side of a LEAPS Spread Order Should You Enter First?

Neither. The order should be entered as a spread. If the firm involved has a desk, the desk people will execute it that way or give your broker feedback about its execution. "Rolling" orders should also be entered this way.

Example
You want to buy back a written LEAPS Call (quoted 17–18) and write a higher strike (quoted 12–13). You should enter the order as a spread. One way would be:

Buy   10 XYZ LEAPS 60 Call closing
Write 10 XYZ LEAPS 70 Call opening
Net debit 5½

There are several points to note in this example. First, you did not specify the price of either leg, but only the difference. This is like the example cited in the covered write example in the options desk section above. Second, the order specified that the buy was to close and the sell to open. Third, a limit was placed on the debit. The limit was a reasonable one because it could be executed by trading on either the bid or the offer on one leg of the spread and by going halfway in between on the other leg. If you had wanted a more rapid execution, you could have set a 6 limit (offer and bid) or just a market order.

How Do You Know the Other Side Will Deliver?

You do any strategy that includes long LEAPS Calls. You are right, the stock rises, your LEAPS Call goes DIM, and you exercise it (for example, a LEAPS 40 Call with the stock at 90). How do you know that whoever sold that LEAPS Call to you will honor the commitment? We know who was on the other side of that trade. It was The Options Clearing Corporation (OCC). That is the issuer, guarantor, and "other side" to *every* LEAPS/ options trade on all of the options exchanges.

What Books on LEAPS or Options Can We Recommend?

Besides this one, no other book deals specifically with LEAPS. While some of the many options books take up LEAPS, you should be careful since several of them have lots of errors. We can recommend some options books, however. We've already mentioned *Options: Essential Concepts and Trading Strategies* edited by The Options Institute (Homewood, Ill.: Business One Irwin, 1990). Probably the best-known work on this subject is *Options as a Strategic Investment* by Lawrence G. McMillan (Englewood Cliffs, N.J.: Prentice Hall, 1991). Its coverage is extensive but tends to be quite technical. One drawback is the statement in the LEAPS chapter that "LEAPS are nothing more than long-term options." While tautologically true, this characterization misses the essence of LEAPS. Another title you must read before you trade in LEAPS/options is *Characteristics and Risks of Listed Options* published by The Options Clearing Corporation and the options exchanges (Chicago, Ill., 1993). It's legally required and highly informative.

Are There Criteria For LEAPS Listing?

Each options exchange sets its own rules. But there are guidelines from a trade group—the Options CO-OP. These include high recognition of the stock, a minimum stock price of $25, and good volume on both the stock and its existing standard options.

SUMMARY

We have shown you much of the theory of LEAPS trading and investing. There is much to be aware of on the practical side as well.

CHAPTER 44
THE BEST STRATEGY
WITH LEAPS

. . . to learn and propagate the best that is known. . . .

STRATEGY   To Be Determined
OUTLOOK   All
ADVANTAGES   Fits outlook and attitude
DRAWBACKS   Possibly complex
DEGREE OF RISK   What you want

We have looked at many different strategies. Some were designed to maximize leverage; others, to protect profits. We saw how to repair losing positions and how to enhance winning ones. You have been a patient reader, and now you want to go out into the financial world and actualize the knowledge you have acquired. What strategy should you use? Many option texts tell you that such-and-such is "the best strategy." We say unequivocally that there is no such thing. Rather, there is no such *uniform* thing. As we have emphasized repeatedly, people have not only different expectations, but different risk attitudes as well. Even one person will have varying views at various times for the market, for its sectors, and for individual stocks. Also, a given person at different times may be more or less willing to take on risk.

With that said, can we find what strategy is most suitable for a given person at a given time on a specific stock? We think we can do a good job in this respect. We will construct a grid with components of risk-aversion attitude and anticipated movement, noting that our selections are necessarily subjective.

Investment/Trading Style

1. Extremely conservative
2. Conservative

3. Moderate
4. Aggressive
5. Very aggressive

Stock/Sector Outlook

1. Extremely bullish
2. Bullish
3. Neutral
4. Bearish
5. Very bearish

We said we would make a grid, but it would probably be too cumbersome to read. Instead, let's do a tabulation. The first number in the tabulation below is attitudinal, the second is for outlook. The next entry is for the chapter number describing the strategy.

1–1	12	13	14	15	16	31	33			
2–1	10	12	13	14	15	16	30	31	33	
3–1	10	12	15	16	17	30	31	33		
4–1	10	12	15	16	17	18	26	28	29	30	31
5–1	10	12	17	18	26	28	29	30	31	
1–2	13	14	15	16						
2–2	11	12	14	15	16	33				
3–2	12	15	16	17	31	33	34	35	37	
4–2	12	15	16	17	28	29	31	35	37	
5–2	12			17	18	26	28	29	31	35	37
1–3	34									
2–3	11	32	34	36						
3–3	24	25	32	36	37					
4–3	23	24	25	32	36	37				
5–3	23	24	25							
1–4										
2–4	11									
3–4	19	21	34	37						
4–4	19	21	27	37						
5–4	19	21	27							
1–5	19									
2–5	19									
3–5	19									
4–5	19	27								
5–5	19	20	22	28						

We are aware that our two lists are not comprehensive. We think the basic idea is good and just needs a little subjective tinkering. Take a peek, find yourself, and see how to protect, trade, and invest with LEAPS. We've included strategies from Chapters 10 through 37, but we've omitted the others, either because they were not strategies or because they were all-inclusive. Index LEAPS is the prime example here. Note that some strategies appear under more than one heading. Is this contradictory? No. It is because these techniques—while they have one name—really subdivide into different strategies. Ratio writing is a prime example of this phenomenon.

Most entries are in category 4–1, which brings together aggressive and very bullish entries. That's not surprising since the bullish strategies and technique subdivisions outnumber the other stances in this book. One category—#1–4—representing extremely conservative and bearish had no takers. That's sad, but true, in the author's experience. If that description might fit you at times, take another look at some of the techniques discussed in this book. They really can be used in a conservative way.

We want also to say something about size which we have repeatedly mentioned to you. Now we will simply say that it's your money and you can invest it in any way you want. But we want you to be aware that size changes strategy. More precisely, it can change the risk component of the chosen method. Some strategies selected as conservative lose that characteristic when size increases. Writing uncovered Puts is a classic example of a sound strategy degenerating into a dangerous one because of inappropriate size.

Does choosing a strategy with our gridlike approach improve prospects? We think it definitely does—not because there is something magical or mystical in the mechanism, but because it compels you to make both your stance and your perspective explicit. This is the first, all-important step toward discipline. Does this mean that this process will guarantee success? Obviously not, but we think it will place you on the right track toward realizing your investment goals when you use LEAPS.

SUMMARY

Searching for the best strategy is chasing a chimera. "Different strokes for different folks" is the watchword here. Not to mention different strikes for different likes! LEAPS are versatile and can be used in the way you want, whether to limit risk or increase leverage. Explicitly identifying your own attitude along with your expectations is the first step in moving to soundly disciplined investment with LEAPS. In fact, discipline will be the topic of our next chapter.

CHAPTER 45
DISCIPLINE AND THE LEAPS WORK SHEET

Life is always a discipline.

Although we have spoken of discipline many times in this book, most of the references have been general. Now we want to be more specific. You need discipline in all areas of the marketplace. In options trading it is even more essential. One reason, but not the only one, is the essential nature—one might almost say the soul—of options. The best way to describe what happens to options because of their limited life is to turn it around: "Stocks don't expire." By way of contrast, LEAPS do expire, but only after a comparatively long time. That means a double dose of discipline. First, because of the expiration, and second, because you are making a longer-term commitment.

To practice this discipline, we recommend recording your expectations, both initially and as time passes. Most people won't take kindly to that concept. (They may ask themselves, "What am I paying my broker for, anyway?") Whatever you are paying your broker for, your allegiance is, or should be, to yourself and your capital. Still we realize it can be a nuisance. We have devised the LEAPS discipline work sheet to make it easier for you.

The work sheet has several parts: The first three are EYE, CYE, and AYE, acronyms for "Establish your expectations," "Check your expectations," and "Adjust your expectations."

This disciplinary program and work sheet will involve a fair amount of work, but it is for a good cause—the preservation and enhancement of your capital (note the order). There is one way we can reduce the work: We have to follow only the stock and not the associated LEAPS Calls and/or Puts. Thus, for example, if you were involved in writing covered LEAPS Calls, the danger would be the decline in the stock, and you would need to monitor that closely. It would not be requisite to follow the LEAPS Call prices as well.

Before starting our explication, we will recount a highly pertinent narrative. When your author was an options strategist at Drexel Burnham Lambert, he was approached by an account executive who wanted assistance on a highly complex strategy he had devised. It involved several series of Calls (LEAPS were not yet trading). A long succession of conversations ensued over time.

ACCOUNT EXECUTIVE (AE): What do you think of my strategy?

OPTIONS STRATEGIST (OS): To tell you the truth, I think it's needlessly complicated.

AE: Well, that's the way I want to do it.

OS: OK, but it's also dangerous. You might end up losing all your capital. You should. . . .

AE [interrupting]: Don't worry. I know you always talk about discipline, and I always watch the Dow Jones Industrial Average anyway. I'm going to keep a very close eye on it. If it goes under XXX, I'm going to close the whole position.

OS: I think that's a fine idea.

OS [to himself]: Boy, all my talk about discipline has paid off.

* * *

OS: How did you make out on your position when you closed it out?

AE: No. It's still open.

OS: But I thought that if the DJIA went below. . . .

AE: Yes, I know all about it. But it didn't count!

OS: It didn't count?

AE: Certainly not. When it went down 16 points [believe it or not, that used to be a big decline in the market] last week, 12 points was because of the Union Carbide fall. So it didn't count.

OS: The Bhopal disaster was a terrible thing. What about yesterday?

AE: Yeah, I know. It went down 24, but UK was responsible for 21 of those points. So it didn't count either.

OS: Doesn't it count no matter what caused the fall? I think you should stick to what you said and close it out.

AE: No way. Just wait and you'll see how right I am.

We don't think we have to tell the reader the clearly apparent and disastrous end of this true story. But we will emphasize its obvious moral by amending the quotation at the head of Chapter 27 to read: **"Bulls get fat, bears get fat, hogs get slaughtered!"** Establishing a point at which you will take action is commendable, but that is talk, not action. Sticking to your resolution is discipline.

Instead of a free-standing work sheet, ours will have its entries interspersed with explanatory commentary. Because no such discussion can be universally applicable to all LEAPS strategies, we will go through it with the strategy of buying LEAPS Calls. Before starting, we suggest that you go back to Chapter 10 and reread the section on having a clear idea about the stock's expected performance.

EYE—Establish Your Expectations

Record the data: the date, stock price, and LEAPS Call price. It is a good idea to record some other prices as well—at a minimum, one average or index. That could be the Dow Jones Industrial Average, the Standard & Poor 500, or any other measure of the market that has certain characteristics:

_____
1. Date

_____
2. Stock

1. You know (or are willing to learn) about it;
2. You are comfortable with it;
3. It is relatively easy to obtain.

_____
3. Market Index

If you want to go further, you should find a suitable yardstick. That would be a *group* index or average. There are many with options trading and more planned as we write. Options are not necessary here. You could use a Dow Jones Group Index (found in the *WSJ* or *Barron's*) or a Standard & Poor's Group Index (available on your broker's desktop terminal), etc.

_____
4. Group Index

The purpose here is to set a reasonable standard for comparison or indeed for relative strength calculations. For relative strength, simply calculate the percentage increase from the original date for both your selected stock and the group index. Then divide the first by the second and express the result as a percentage.

Now record the expected direction of the stock and the intensity of that move, for instance, "bullish, but mildly so."

5. Outlook

Of course, we know that is what's wanted in a covered Call write. We are preparing you for the generalizing of this work sheet.

Write down your expectation for the stock. This may seem silly to you, but it is not. It is a way of avoiding error that will lead to a loss of capital. Depending on your personality, you can write down something like: "It will more than double in a year" or "It will move to 123⅝ by September 14."

6. Target (*One or More*)

If you are tempted to write something like: "It will go up a lot," we want you to reread the section on expectation in Chapter 10 on buying LEAPS Calls.

Next, record the (approximate) time you think you will hold the position. That is, if you think the stock will be at a specified price in a year, write down the date of one year in the future.

7. Horizon (*One or More*)

Let's take a moment out here. We don't think that you should, or that anybody can, predict price and time so accurately. These are not prognostications; they are intended as your guidelines. The purpose in getting you to quantify and record them is to make you aware of your own thinking. More importantly, it will allow you later to see for yourself if the stock is not performing the way you had expected. Most importantly, it will help produce the determination to take action at that point.

Now that you have an expected price target, select an *out price*. This is a price to get out at, that is, a price that, if reached, will tell you that you are *wrong*. It is obvious that there are wrong prices. If, for example, you start with the stock at 60, expect it to go up, and then it's at 40, it and you are wrong. But it's too late when the stock gets to 40. You have to take action before that or you will lose too much of your investment. What is the right number? Many people feel that it's more than 10 percent. We don't want to impose any number on you. *You* choose the number. Don't be silly about it. As we just saw, waiting for a move from 60 to 40 would not be very smart. So you pick a number that satisfies two requirements:

1. You don't think it will go there.
2. If it did, you will know you are wrong about the stock's target.

We have said that you should watch the stock's move rather than the price of the LEAPS Call, but that's not a rigid rule. If you are more comfortable setting a limit on the LEAPS Call price, that's OK. In fact, you could set a limit on the DJIA, the S&P 500, or a group index you had selected. It doesn't matter which instrument you use. What does matter is that you set a limit beforehand. It matters even more that you stick to the decision to close the position if that limit is breached.

8. Out Price (*One or More*)

Despite our imperative, we recognize that personality plays a large role here. Some might prefer a little more flexibility. We once knew a man who frequently shorted stock (before the days of listed Puts). He set a mental limit to cover the short position—say 60—as an example. But he would not take immediate action then. He waited till the stock rose to 60⅜. His reasoning was something like this: "At 60, that's other shorts getting scared and buying back. At 60⅛, that's the specialist getting short himself (on an uptick). At 60¼, that's a random last desperate cover. But at 60⅜, that's for real!"

We note impassively that he could have simply set a limit of 60⅜ originally. However, as we said, we are aware of the varied reactions of different personality types in the market. It's all right to behave as our old friend did if that's what fits you. What is decidedly not acceptable is to lengthen that process and change it into a rationalization. That ends like the other story—the Bhopal tragedy. In Chapter 40 on LEAPS repair, we quoted the old maxim: "The first loss is the best loss." Now we remind you that the way to get rich in Wall Street is to "cut your losses and let your profits run."

The next step in our regimen is a periodic examination of the position. We will continue to look at only the underlying stock price.

CYE—Check Your Expectations

How frequently should you look at the price? Again, we acknowledge different temperaments here. Some become obsessed and check the price so frequently that their fingers hurt. They suffer not only from carpal tunnel syndrome but what is named *quotron paralysis*. Others are overly nonchalant and never look. We don't want you to do either. What we want is for you to observe the *minimum* evaluation times in this worksheet.

All the times given here are elapsed time from the day the position is taken.

---
9. One week

---
10. One Month

For each time we want you to ask yourself the questions: "Is the stock doing what I expected?" and "Is it near the 'out price'?"

---
11. Evaluation

Warning! Do not lie to yourself. It is your money we are talking about. If the (truthful) answer is positive, go on to the next time period. If it is negative, you must ask yourself another question: "How do you feel about it?"

---
12. Self-Evaluation

We repeat our *warning*. Be honest about your reaction.

Worried	*Nervous*	*Untroubled*	*Complacent*	*Smug*
A	B	C	D	E

A—Prepare to take action. Action can mean closing out the position, partial closure, or remedial measures.

B—Shorten the checking intervals. If there is no improvement go to A.

C—Reread the beginning of Chapter 40 on LEAPS repair. See what happens to those who practice "Hold and Hope." Then go to B.

D—Reread the Bhopal story above. Ask yourself if you want stories like that told about you. Then go to B.

E—Don't trade LEAPS. We're not kidding. If this is the way you behave, you can do better by finding a suitable charity.

Notice! All of these self-evaluations are to be done when, as we said above, the stock is *near* the out price. If the stock violates this price and you do not act (allowing for small, preset variations) you should not read any of A, B, C, D, or E. The only letter for you is F. On second thought, go ahead your way. They say that "experience is the best teacher." We just think it's too bad that you will have to learn such an expensive lesson.

For those who are willing to act on (or even near) a violation, we come to:

AYE—Adjust Your Expectations

We have used "reread" a lot in this chapter. There is a good reason for that. When you find out that you are wrong, it is helpful to have guidance. Here we ask you to reread the sections in Chapter 40 LEAPS repair about changing your expectations from profit to salvage.

There are only three types of adjustments to make:

1. Close the position.
2. Close the position in part.
3. Alter the position.

All of these are fully dealt with in the sections we asked you to go back to. We have interposed the AYE segment because it came in naturally. If it is not applicable to you at this point, go on with CYE.

13. Two Months

This checking process must continue. But if things are going well, the period for evaluations can be lengthened.

14. Every Month

If things are not going correctly, you will have to shorten the period and check more frequently. Our shortest check is one week, and you should go to that. If it's still not good, go to a daily check. Don't forget that these checks are on both the stock *and* your reactions to it.

15. Six Months

If you have gotten this far, very good. That means that the stock hasn't been moving in the wrong direction. Now you should evaluate whether it has been moving rapidly enough to fit your plans. It is hard to be very general here; you may be waiting for a specific event. It may be hard to do it here in an abstract way, but you will know the answer.

16. Greater than Six Months

Continue the checks. We don't know how long a LEAPS position you entered into originally, but time may be running out. If not, good for you! Since you have built up a profitable LEAPS position, you now have more money at risk. This means that you should not let up on vigilance. You should also consider the techniques in Chapter 39 on LEAPS Enhancement. This may appeal to you because of the attraction of greater profits. More important, it should be attractive to you because of the techniques for locking in and otherwise protecting profits.

17. Eight Months Left

This should technically say "eight, seven, or six months left." This is the time when LEAPS convert into ordinary options. That conversion will be a change of symbol. Of considerably more weight is the fact that they will start behaving like ordinary options. We are referring, of course, to time decay. Only you now know what your position is, and only you can decide what to do with it. We simply say that this is another factor to consider in appraising closure or protection.

Final Comments

First, congratulations! We hope you made money. If you didn't, we hope that the work sheet minimized your losses. At the very least, we hope that you adhered to it. If you didn't follow EYE, CYE, and AYE, you may have said BYE to some of your money.

We attempted to go through the work sheet in a general manner. Some LEAPS strategies will require some changes. For example, with combinations you would enter expected ranges, not prices. Index LEAPS strategies need "stock" read as "index." Some LEAPS strategies might need an additional work sheet, for example, LEAPS DCA and reduced-risk trading. Don't let that daunt you. Keeping careful track of your investments is surely a good way of doing business.

Again, this is a suggested minimum—you may want to do more. One obvious addition is constructing a graph. Those who are adept at technical analysis need no instruction here. You don't have to be that complex. If you have never done it before, just record the stock's closing price at any (consistent) interval convenient for you. That could be daily, weekly, etc. If you want to do more, you could make a bar chart. That would show the high, low, and close for each interval you selected. More recondite possibilities are graphing the volume as well and/or the relative strength. All this is up to you.

All that we have asked of you is to practice discipline. Know what you want going in and keep track; if you see that you're not getting it, take appropriate steps. We have made allowance for temperament differences. The one danger here is that giving oneself leeway after the stock breeches its limit can degenerate into doom. It is wise to remember: "Once is happenstance, twice is coincidence, three times is enemy action."

SUMMARY

There is no substitute for discipline in the market, and there is even greater need for it when trading LEAPS. We have used our usual humor in this chapter. We have also done something else not done in any other chapter. We have been harsh, even caustic, in our condemnation of nonadherence to established limits. All this is done for the purpose of first protecting and then enhancing your capital.

CHAPTER 46
A LEAPS SUMMARY

Grow old along with me! / The best is yet to be....

Although this is not a strategy chapter, we think it appropriate to display one of our opening outlines here. Since we always had them in regular type, we will present this one in boldface.

STRATEGY	**Using LEAPS**
OUTLOOK	**Leveraged, protective and imaginative**
ADVANTAGES	**Broadening horizons; time on your side**
DRAWBACKS	**A new approach**
DEGREE OF RISK	**As you please**

We hope that the sentiments expressed here are shared by the reader. Maybe it's time for a last note:

A gentle note to the reader:
Thank you for your patience. We know that this is a difficult subject, and we appreciate your attention.

We have come to the end of our opus. We've enjoyed the dialogue and hope our reader has too. We've tried to be instructive without too much preaching. We do not believe that LEAPS cure all ails, but we do believe that there is a plenum, if not a plethora, of opportunities for investors and traders willing to look at LEAPS.

We've tried to explicate some of these possibilities ranging from the mundane to the miraculous. What is now left to say on the subject? There is really little to add, but we might jog your memory with a synopsis.

We have learned a lot about LEAPS, and we really love them.

- First and foremost, LEAPS have time on their side (and, we hope, on yours) and have large dollar premiums.
- LEAPS are, technically speaking, options, but they are intrinsically different and much safer.
- There is a LEAPS vocabulary in which some common words have a narrow, industry-specific meaning.
- LEAPS have quantifiable determinants that are not so hard to study.
- They are regulated, listed securities traded on national exchanges.
- They have different risk characteristics from options, can increase capital, limit losses, and protect profits, positions, and portfolios.
- LEAPS can be used for leverage, but also for insurance and income.
- LEAPS give you a good deal in the marketplace, even against the experts.

Each LEAPS strategy can be implemented in a manner that is conservative, moderate, or aggressive. Within that manner, you can select and even fine-tune a stance corresponding to your degree of risk-aversion.

For specific strategies we found out that with LEAPS:

- There is more to Call buying than speculation.
- Married Puts allow you to take a position you otherwise wouldn't touch.
- Buying Puts is markedly superior to selling short.
- Writing Puts sensibly is not so dangerous.
- Writing uncovered combinations can make money in a flat market.
- Buying combinations can make profits even when you can't judge direction. They also showed us our first miracle.
- You can average down on a stock position.
- You can do dollar-cost averaging.
- You can substitute LEAPS for stock, either as a substitute for purchase or as a replacement later.

- You can write shorter-term options with lessened risk.
- You can trade stocks back and forth with decreased risk.
- Discipline is all-important, as is a self-imposed limit on size.
- Program trading is an opportunity, not a catastrophe.
- Almost every strategy can be carried over to indexes.

We bid a fond farewell to our heckling cast of characters. They represented the omnipresent negative sentiment on options and LEAPS that is heard so frequently, but they were very helpful to us. They were our unwitting allies. Let's review them briefly:

- Mr. Bigot had a warped view, but inadvertently made the case *for* options.
- Mr. Greedy alerted us to the perils associated with his cognomen.
- Mr. Scoffer led us to realize the difference between what option pros do and what you can do with LEAPS.
- Mr. Skeptic thought he could do just as well without options, but learned better.
- Mr. Smart Alec reminded us that LEAPS strikes start 20 to 25 percent OTM.
- Mr. Wiseacre was very helpful. He led us to the discussion on the overwhelming superiority of protective Puts versus stop orders.
- Mr. Mischief warned us about 100 percent losses with options, but enabled us to counsel against strategies risking a lot more than that.
- Mr. Cynic's comments evolved to a discussion of how the market places very different values on diverse options and LEAPS.
- Mr. Know-it-all learned something he never knew: LEAPS can make miracles.
- Mr. Ares showed us the dangers of trying to make a killing.
- Mr. Doubter thought the world would be simpler without fancy options but paved the way for another LEAPS miracle.

- Mr. Tory kept us on our toes and helped us along the path to reduced-risk equity trading with LEAPS.
- Mr. Miser said what we all would have expected him to say. But he too helped us.
- Mr. Sharp has to be thanked for his implied compliment in thinking we were stealing (from ourselves).

Our thanks to all. Also thanks to our matchmaker who reminded us that finding Mr./Ms. Best Fit is better that looking for Mr. Right.

Now what does the future hold for LEAPS enthusiasts? First, probably more stocks with LEAPS. Second, maybe a still longer life for LEAPS; the CBOE and the ASE have filed with the SEC to trade LEAPS with a life of five years. Third, more widespread trading of LEAPS around the globe. Fourth, some new LEAPS strategies. "There is nothing new under the sun," said the ancient preacher. Without being impious, we think there may be something. This book contains a chapter with a strategy never seen before. The author would be ecstatic if a reader produced others. Finally, there will be more and more converts to LEAPS.

That brings us back to a critic. One of the hecklers mentioned above wasn't given full credit. That was Mr. Skeptic (born-again as Mr. LEAPSman), and he deserves acclaim because he became a LEAPS convert. Like new converts, he became overzealous, but at least, now his heart is in the right place. We hope we have converted you as well. Even if you don't become a LEAPS enthusiast, we would be pleased if you became a LEAPS user. If you do so, we have a final quote to offer you.

Near the beginning of this book we told you that LEAPS were different and better. Throughout we have maintained that the long life of LEAPS transforms them into an instrument that can almost transcend time. Become a LEAPS user and you will never fear that,

... at my back I always hear
Time's winged chariot hurrying near....

APPENDIX

In general, option root symbols are the same as stock symbols. IBM is used to start the symbol for IBM options. The rest is made up of characters that identify the month, strike, and exchange. Over-the-counter (OTC) stocks generally have a four-letter symbol (Amgen = AMGN), but use a separate code for options usually ending in Q (Amgen = AMQ); for LEAPS, still another coding is used. When LEAPS started, the initial L (for LEAPS) was used for LEAPS expiring in 1992. Then Z for 1993, W for 1994 and V for 1995. L will be used again for 1996 LEAPS. The rest of the symbol consists of two letters drawn from the conventional stock symbol. For example, IBM LEAPS started with LIB and went on to ZIB, WIB, and VIB. Not all are as simple as that. Different quotation vendors have widely varying systems of displaying LEAPS quotes, but all use this basic methodology.

For the reader's benefit we present the existing LEAPS alphabetized in three ways:

STOCKS WITH LEAPS

Alphabetically by Stock Name				
		LEAPS Symbols		
Stock	Symbol	1995	1996	Exchange
Abbott Labs	ABT	VBT	LBT	PHLX
Acuson Corp.	ACN	VAU	LAU	PSE
Adobe Systems (ADBE)	AEQ	VAE	LAE	PSE
Advanced Micro Devices	AMD	VAI	LAI	PSE

Stock	Symbol	LEAPS Symbols 1995	LEAPS Symbols 1996	Exchange
		Alphabetically by Stock Name		
AlliedSignal	ALD	VAD	LAL	PHLX
American Barrick Resources	ABX	VBX	LBX	ASE
American Express	AXP	VAX	LAX	ASE
American Home Products	AHP	VAH	LAH	ASE
American Tel. & Tel.	T	VT	LT	CBOE
Amgen Inc. (AMGN)	AMQ	VAM	LMN	ASE
AMR Corp.	AMR	VMR	LAR	ASE
Anheuser-Busch Cos.	BUD	VBD	LBD	PHLX
Apple Computer (AAPL)	AAQ	VAA	LAA	ASE
ASA Ltd.	ASA	VSL	LSL	ASE
Avon Products	AVP	VVP	LVP	CBOE
Baker Hughes	BHI	VBH	LBH	PSE
Bank of Boston	BKB	VKB	LBK	PHLX
BankAmerica	BAC	VBA	LBA	CBOE
BellSouth Corp.	BLS	VBL	LBL	ASE
Blockbuster Entertainment	BV	VBV	LBV	ASE/CBOE
Boeing Co.	BA	VBO	LBO	CBOE
Bristol-Myers Squibb	BMY	VBM	LBM	CBOE
Campbell Soup	CPB	VLL	LLL	NYSE
Centocor Inc. (CNTO)	COQ	VCT	———	CBOE
Chase Manhattan	CMB	VCX	LCM	ASE
Chemical Bank	CHL	VCK	LCK	ASE
Chevron Corp.	CHV	VCH	LCH	ASE
Chrysler Corp.	C	VCY	LCR	CBOE
Chubb Corp.	CB	VCU	LCU	NYSE
Citicorp	CCI	VCP	LCC	CBOE
Coca-Cola	KO	VKO	LKO	CBOE
Columbia Gas	CG	VCS	LCG	ASE
COMPAQ Computer	CPQ	VKP	LKP	PSE
Conner Peripherals	CNR	VCN	LCN	PSE
Consolidated Stores	CNS	VNS	LNS	PHLX
Dell Computer (DELL)	DLQ	VDQ	LDE	PHLX
Delta Airlines	DAL	VDA	LDA	CBOE
Digital Equipment	DEC	VDE	LDC	ASE
Disney (Walt) Co.	DIS	VDS	LWD	ASE
Dow Chemical	DOW	VDO	LDO	CBOE
du Pont (de Nemours)	DD	VDD	LDD	ASE
Eastman Kodak	EK	VEK	LEK	CBOE
Exxon Corp.	XON	VXO	LXO	CBOE

Alphabetically by Stock Name

Stock	Symbol	LEAPS Symbols		Exchange
		1995	1996	
Federal Express	FDX	VFX	LFX	CBOE
Fed'l. Nat'l. M'tge. Assn.	FNM	VFN	LFN	PHLX
Ford Motor	F	VFO	LFO	CBOE
Fruit of the Loom	FTL	VTL	LTL	NYSE
Gap Inc.	GPS	VGS	LGS	CBOE
General Electric	GE	VGE	LGR	CBOE
General Mills	GIS	VGI	LGI	PSE
General Motors	GM	VGN	LGM	CBOE
Georgia Pacific	GP	VGP	LGP	PHLX
Glaxo Holdings plc	GLX	VGX	LGX	ASE
GTE Corp.	GTE	VGT	LGT	ASE
Heinz (H.J.)	HNZ	VHN	LHN	CBOE
Hilton Hotels	HLT	VHL	LHL	PSE
Home Depot	HD	VHD	LHD	PHLX
Homestake Mining	HM	VHM	LHM	CBOE
Intel. Corp. (INTC)	INQ	VNL	LNL	ASE
Int'l. Bus. Machines	IBM	VIB	LIB	CBOE
Int'l. Game Technology	IGT	VGG	LGG	ASE
Johnson & Johnson	JNJ	VJN	LJN	CBOE
K-mart Corp.	KM	VK	LKM	CBOE
Limited Inc.	LTD	VLD	LLD	CBOE
Liz Claiborne	LIZ	VLI	LLI	CBOE
Magna International "A"	MGA	VAG	LGA	CBOE
Marriott Corp.	MHS	VMH	LMH	PHLX
Maytag Co.	MYG	VMY	LMY	NYSE
McDonald's Corp.	MCD	VMD	LMC	CBOE
McGraw-Hill	MHP	VMP	LMP	PHLX
Merck & Co.	MRK	VMK	LMK	CBOE
Merrill Lynch	MER	VME	LME	ASE
Microsoft Corp. (MSFT)	MSQ	VMF	LMF	PSE
Minnesota Mining & Mfg.	MMM	VMU	LMU	CBOE
Mobil Corp.	MOB	VML	LML	CBOE
Monsanto Co.	MTC	VM	LCT	CBOE
Morgan (J.P.) & Co.	JPM	VJP	LJP	PHLX
Motorola Inc.	MOT	VMA	LMA	ASE
NationsBank	NB	VNB	LNB	PHLX
NIKE Inc. "B"	NKE	VNK	LNK	PSE
NYNEX Corp.	NYN	VNY	LNY	NYSE
Oracle Systems (ORCL)	ORQ	VOR	LRO	CBOE
Pacific Telesis Group	PAC	VPC	LPC	PSE
Paramount Commun.	PCI	VPT	LPT	CBOE

		\multicolumn{2}{c}{LEAPS Symbols}	
Stock	Symbol	1995	1996	Exchange
Pepsico	PEP	VP	LPP	CBOE
Pfizer Co.	PFE	VPE	LPE	ASE
Philip Morris	MO	VPM	LMO	ASE
Placer Dome Inc.	PDG	VDG	LPD	PHLX
Polaroid Corp.	PRD	VRD	LRD	CBOE
PPG Industries	PPG	VPP	LP	PHLX
Primerica Corp.	PA	VPA	LPA	PHLX
Proctor & Gamble	PG	VPG	LPR	ASE
Quaker Oats	OAT	VQO	LQO	PHLX
Reebok Int'l.	RBK	VRK	LRK	ASE
RJR Nabisco Holdings	RN	VRJ	LRJ	ASE/CBOE/PHLX
Salomon, Inc.	SB	VSM	LSM	PHLX
Schering-Plough	SGP	VSG	LSG	PSE
Sears, Roebuck	S	VRS	LS	CBOE
SmithKline Beecham plc	SBE	VBE	LBE	PSE
Sprint Corp.	FON	VN	LON	PHLX
SunAmerica	SAI	VSA	LSE	PHLX
Sun Microsystems (SUNW)	SUQ	VSU	LSU	PSE
Synergen (SYGN)	YGQ	VGQ	LYQ	PSE/PHLX
Syntex	SYN	VSY	LSN	CBOE
Telecommunications (TCOMA)	TCQ	VTM	LTE	ASE
Teléfonos de México ADR	TMX	VTE	LMX	*
Tenneco Inc.	TGT	VTG	LNG	ASE
Texaco Inc.	TX	VXC	LTO	ASE
Texas Instruments	TXN	VXT	LTN	CBOE
Time Warner Inc.	TWX	VTW	LTW	PHLX
Triton Energy Corp.	OIL	VOI	LOI	*
UAL Corp.	UAL	VUA	LUA	CBOE
Union Carbide	UK	VCB	LCB	ASE
Unisys	UIS	VUI	LUI	ASE
Unocal Corp.	UCL	VCL	LCL	PSE
Upjohn Co.	UPJ	VUP	LUP	CBOE
U.S. Surgical	USS	VSS	LUS	ASE
U.S. West	USW	VSW	LUW	ASE
USX-Marathon Group	MRO	VXM	LXM	ASE
USX-U.S. Steel Group	X	VXS	LXS	ASE
Wal-Mart	WMT	VWT	LWT	CBOE
Warner-Lambert	WLA	VWL	LWL	ASE
Wells Fargo	WFC	VWF	LWF	ASE
Westinghouse Elec.	WX	VWX	LWX	ASE
WMX Technologies	WMX	VWM	LWM	PHLX

Alphabetically by Stock Name

Stock	Symbol	LEAPS Symbols 1995	1996	Exchange
Woolworth Corp.	Z	VFW	LFW	PHLX
Xerox	XRX	VXR	LXR	CBOE

* Listed ASE/CBOE/PHLX/NYSE

Alphabetically by Option Symbol

Stock	Symbol	LEAPS Symbols 1995	1996	Exchange
Apple Computer (AAPL)	AAQ	VAA	LAA	ASE
Abbott Labs.	ABT	VBT	LBT	PHLX
American Barrick Resources	ABX	VBX	LBX	ASE
Acuson Corp.	ACN	VAU	LAU	PSE
Adobe Systems (ADBE)	AEQ	VAE	LAE	PSE
American Home Products	AHP	VAH	LAH	ASE
AlliedSignal	ALD	VAD	LAL	PHLX
Advanced Micro Devices	AMD	VAI	LAI	PSE
Amgen Inc. (AMGN)	AMQ	VAM	LMN	ASE
AMR Corp.	AMR	VMR	LAR	ASE
ASA Ltd.	ASA	VSL	LSL	ASE
Avon Products	AVP	VVP	LVP	CBOE
American Express	AXP	VAX	LAX	ASE
Boeing Co.	BA	VBO	LBO	CBOE
BankAmerica	BAC	VBA	LBA	CBOE
Baker Hughes	BHI	VBH	LBH	PSE
Bank of Boston	BKB	VKB	LBK	PHLX
BellSouth Corp.	BLS	VBL	LBL	ASE
Bristol-Myers Squibb	BMY	VBM	LBM	CBOE
Anheuser-Busch Cos.	BUD	VBD	LBD	PHLX
Blockbuster Entertainment	BV	VBV	LBV	ASE/CBOE
Chrysler Corp.	C	VCY	LCR	CBOE
Chubb Corp.	CB	VCU	LCU	NYSE
Citicorp	CCI	VCP	LCC	CBOE
Columbia Gas	CG	VCS	LCG	ASE
Chemical Bank	CHL	VCK	LCK	ASE
Chevron Corp.	CHV	VCH	LCH	ASE

		LEAPS Symbols		
Stock	Symbol	1995	1996	Exchange
Chase Manhattan	CMB	VCX	LCM	ASE
Conner Peripherals	CNR	VCN	LCN	PSE
Consolidated Stores	CNS	VNS	LNS	PHLX
Centocor Inc. (CNTO)	COQ	VCT	– – –	CBOE
Campbell Soup	CPB	VLL	LLL	NYSE
COMPAQ Computer	CPQ	VKP	LKP	PSE
Delta Airlines	DAL	VDA	LDA	CBOE
du Pont (de Nemours)	DD	VDD	LDD	ASE
Digital Equipment	DEC	VDE	LDC	ASE
Disney (Walt) Co.	DIS	VDS	LWD	ASE
Dell Computer (DELL)	DLQ	VDQ	LDE	PHLX
Dow Chemical	DOW	VDO	LDO	CBOE
Eastman Kodak	EK	VEK	LEK	CBOE
Ford Motor	F	VFO	LFO	CBOE
Federal Express	FDX	VFX	LFX	CBOE
Fed'l. Nat'l. M'tge. Assn.	FNM	VFN	LFN	PHLX
Sprint Corp.	FON	VN	LON	PHLX
Fruit of the Loom	FTL	VTL	LTL	NYSE
General Electric	GE	VGE	LGR	CBOE
General Mills	GIS	VGI	LGI	PSE
Glaxo Holdings plc	GLX	VGX	LGX	ASE
General Motors	GM	VGN	LGM	CBOE
Georgia Pacific	GP	VGP	LGP	PHLX
Gap Inc.	GPS	VGS	LGS	CBOE
GTE Corp.	GTE	VGT	LGT	ASE
Home Depot	HD	VHD	LHD	PHLX
Hilton Hotels	HLT	VHL	LHL	PSE
Homestake Mining	HM	VHM	LHM	CBOE
Heinz (H.J.)	HNZ	VHN	LHN	CBOE
Int'l Bus. Machines	IBM	VIB	LIB	CBOE
Int'l Game Technology	IGT	VGG	LGG	ASE
Intel Corp. (INTC)	INQ	VNL	LNL	ASE
Johnson & Johnson	JNJ	VJN	LJN	CBOE
Morgan (J.P.) & Co.	JPM	VJP	LJP	PHLX
K-mart Corp.	KM	VK	LKM	CBOE
Coca-Cola	KO	VKO	LKO	CBOE
Liz Claiborne	LIZ	VLI	LLI	CBOE
Limited Inc.	LTD	VLD	LLD	CBOE
McDonald's Corp.	MCD	VMD	LMC	CBOE
Merrill Lynch	MER	VME	LME	ASE
Magna International "A"	MGA	VAG	LGA	CBOE

		LEAPS Symbols		
Stock	*Symbol*	*1995*	*1996*	*Exchange*
McGraw-Hill	MHP	VMP	LMP	PHLX
Marriott Corp.	MHS	VMH	LMH	PHLX
Minnesota Mining & Mfg.	MMM	VMU	LMU	CBOE
Philip Morris	MO	VPM	LMO	ASE
Mobil Corp.	MOB	VML	LML	CBOE
Motorola Inc.	MOT	VMA	LMA	ASE
Merck & Co.	MRK	VMK	LMK	CBOE
USX-Marathon Group	MRO	VXM	LXM	ASE
Microsoft Corp. (MSFT)	MSQ	VMF	LMF	PSE
Monsanto Co.	MTC	VM	LCT	CBOE
Maytag Co.	MYG	VMY	LMY	NYSE
NationsBank	NB	VNB	LNB	PHLX
NIKE, Inc. "B"	NKE	VNK	LNK	PSE
NYNEX Corp.	NYN	VNY	LNY	NYSE
Quaker Oats	OAT	VQO	LQO	PHLX
Triton Energy Corp.	OIL	VOI	LOI	*
Oracle Systems (ORCL)	ORQ	VOR	LRO	CBOE
Primerica Corp.	PA	VPA	LPA	PHLX
Pacific Telesis Group	PAC	VPC	LPC	PSE
Paramount Commun.	PCI	VPT	LPT	CBOE
Placer Dome Inc.	PDG	VDG	LPD	PHLX
Pepsico	PEP	VP	LPP	CBOE
Pfizer Co.	PFE	VPE	LPE	ASE
Procter & Gamble	PG	VPG	LPR	ASE
PPG Industries	PPG	VPP	LP	PHLX
Polaroid Corp.	PRD	VRD	LRD	CBOE
Reebok Int'l.	RBK	VRK	LRK	ASE
RJR Nabisco Holdings	RN	VRJ	LRJ	ASE/CBOE/PHLX
Sears, Roebuck	S	VRS	LS	CBOE
SunAmerica	SAI	VSA	LSE	PHLX
Salomon, Inc.	SB	VSM	LSM	PHLX
SmithKline Beecham plc	SBE	VBE	LBE	PSE
Schering-Plough	SGP	VSG	LSG	PSE
Sun Microsystems (SUNW)	SUQ	VSU	LSU	PSE
Syntex	SYN	VSY	LSN	CBOE
American Tel. & Tel.	T	VT	LT	CBOE
Telecommunications (TCOMA)	TCQ	VTM	LTE	ASE
Tenneco Inc.	TGT	VTG	LNG	ASE
Teléfonos de México ADR	TMX	VTE	LMX	*

Alphabetically by Option Symbol				
		LEAPS Symbols		
Stock	Symbol	1995	1996	Exchange
Time Warner Inc.	TWX	VTW	LTW	PHLX
Texaco Inc.	TX	VXC	LTO	ASE
Texas Instruments	TXN	VXT	LTN	CBOE
UAL Corp.	UAL	VUA	LUA	CBOE
Unocal Corp.	UCL	VCL	LCL	PSE
Unisys	UIS	VUI	LUI	ASE
Union Carbide	UK	VCB	LCB	ASE
Upjohn Co.	UPJ	VUP	LUP	CBOE
U.S. Surgical	USS	VSS	LUS	ASE
U.S. West	USW	VSW	LUW	ASE
Wells Fargo	WFC	VWF	LWF	ASE
Warner-Lambert	WLA	VWL	LWL	ASE
Wal-Mart	WMT	VWT	LWT	CBOE
WMX Technologies	WMX	VWM	LWM	PHLX
Westinghouse Elec.	WX	VWX	LWX	ASE
USX-U.S. Steel Group	X	VXS	LXS	ASE
Exxon Corp.	XON	VXO	LXO	CBOE
Xerox	XRX	VXR	LXR	CBOE
Synergen (SYGN)	YGQ	VGQ	LYQ	PSE/PHLX
Woolworth Corp.	Z	VFW	LFW	PHLX

* Listed ASE/CBOE/PHLX/NYSE

Alphabetically by LEAPS Symbol			
LEAPS Symbol	Stock	Option Symbol	Exchange
LAA	Apple Computer (AAPL)	AAQ	ASE
LAE	Adobe Systems (ADBE)	AEQ	PSE
LAH	American Home Products	AHP	ASE
LAI	Advanced Micro Devices	AMD	PSE
LAL	AlliedSignal	ALD	PHLX
LAR	AMR Corp.	AMR	ASE
LAU	Acuson Corp.	ACN	PSE
LAX	American Express	AXP	ASE
LBA	BankAmerica	BAC	CBOE
LBD	Anheuser-Busche Cos.	BUD	PHLX
LBE	SmithKline Beecham plc	SBE	PSE
LBH	Baker Hughes	BHI	PSE
LBK	Bank of Boston	BKB	PHLX

Alphabetically by LEAPS Symbol

LEAPS Symbol	Stock	Option Symbol	Exchange
LBL	BellSouth Corp.	BLS	ASE
LBM	Bristol-Myers Squibb	BMY	CBOE
LBO	Boeing Co.	BA	CBOE
LBT	Abbott Labs.	ABT	PHLX
LBV	Blockbuster Entertainment	BV	ASE/CBOE
LBX	American Barrick Resources	ABX	ASE
LCB	Union Carbide	UK	ASE
LCC	Citicorp	CCI	CBOE
LCG	Columbia Gas	CG	ASE
LCH	Chevron Corp.	CHV	ASE
LCK	Chemical Bank	CHL	ASE
LCL	Unocal Corp.	UCL	PSE
LCM	Chase Manhattan	CMB	ASE
LCN	Conner Peripherals	CNR	PSE
LCT	Monsanto Co.	MTC	CBOE
LCU	Chubb Corp.	CB	NYSE
LCY	Chrysler	C	CBOE
LDA	Delta Airlines	DAL	CBOE
LDC	Digital Equipment	DEC	ASE
LDD	du Pont (de Nemours)	DD	ASE
LDE	Dell Computer (DELL)	DLQ	PHLX
LDO	Dow Chemical	DOW	CBOE
LEK	Eastman Kodak	EK	CBOE
LFN	Fed'l. Nat'l. M'tge. Assn.	FNM	PHLX
LFO	Ford Motor	F	CBOE
LFW	Woolworth Corp.	Z	PHLX
LFX	Federal Express	FDX	CBOE
LGA	Magna International "A"	MGA	CBOE
LGG	Int'l. Game Technology	IGT	ASE
LGI	General Mills	GIS	PSE
LGM	General Motors	GM	CBOE
LGP	Georgia Pacific	GP	PHLX
LGR	General Electric	GE	CBOE
LGS	Gap Inc.	GPS	CBOE
LGT	GTE Corp.	GTE	ASE
LGX	Glaxo Holdings plc	GLX	ASE
LHD	Home Depot	HD	PHLX
LHL	Hilton Hotels	HLT	PSE
LHM	Homestake Mining	HM	CBOE
LHN	Heinz (H.J.)	HNZ	CBOE
LIB	Int'l. Bus. Machines	IBM	CBOE
LJN	Johnson & Johnson	JNJ	CBOE
LJP	Morgan (J.P.) & Co.	JPM	PHLX
LKM	K-mart Corp.	KM	CBOE

	Alphabetically by LEAPS Symbol		
LEAPS Symbol	**Stock**	**Option Symbol**	**Exchange**
LKO	Coca-Cola	KO	CBOE
LKP	COMPAQ Computer	CPQ	PSE
LLD	Limited Inc.	LTD	CBOE
LLI	Liz Claiborne	LIZ	CBOE
LLL	Campbell Soup	CPB	NYSE
LMA	Motorola Inc.	MOT	ASE
LMC	McDonald's Corp.	MCD	CBOE
LME	Merrill Lynch	MER	ASE
LMF	Microsoft Corp. (MSFT)	MSQ	PSE
LMH	Marriott Corp.	MHS	PHLX
LMK	Merck & Co.	MRK	CBOE
LML	Mobil Corp.	MOB	CBOE
LMN	Amgen Inc. (AMGN)	AMQ	ASE
LMO	Philip Morris	MO	ASE
LMP	McGraw-Hill	MHP	PHLX
LMU	Minnesota Mining & Mfg.	MMM	CBOE
LMX	Teléfonos de México ADR	TMX	*
LMY	Maytag Co.	MYG	NYSE
LNB	NationsBank	NB	PHLX
LNG	Tenneco Inc.	TGT	ASE
LNK	NIKE Inc. "B"	NKE	PSE
LNL	Intel Corp. (INTC)	INQ	ASE
LNS	Consolidated Stores	CNS	PHLX
LNY	NYNEX Corp.	NYN	NYSE
LOI	Triton Energy Corp.	OIL	*
LON	Sprint Corp.	FON	PHLX
LP	PPG Industries	PPG	PHLX
LPA	Primerica Corp.	PA	PHLX
LPC	Pacific Telesis Group	PAC	PSE
LPD	Placer Dome Inc.	PDG	PHLX
LPE	Pfizer Co.	PFE	ASE
LPP	Pepsico	PEP	CBOE
LPR	Procter & Gamble	PG	ASE
LPT	Paramount Commun.	PCI	CBOE
LQO	Quaker Oats	OAT	PHLX
LRD	Polaroid Corp.	PRD	CBOE
LRJ	RJR Nabisco Holdings	RN	ASE/CBOE/PHLX
LRK	Reebok Int'l.	RBK	ASE
LRO	Oracle Systems (ORCL)	ORQ	CBOE
LS	Sears, Roebuck	S	CBOE
LSE	SunAmerica	SAI	PHLX
LSG	Schering-Plough	SGP	PSE
LSL	ASA Ltd.	ASA	ASE

Alphabetically by LEAPS Symbol			
LEAPS Symbol	Stock	Option Symbol	Exchange
LSM	Salomon Inc.	SB	PHLX
LSN	Syntex	SYN	CBOE
LSU	Sun Microsystems (SUNW)	SUQ	PSE
LT	American Tel. & Tel.	T	CBOE
LTE	Telecommunications (TCOMA)	TCQ	ASE
LTL	Fruit of the Loom	FTL	NYSE
LTN	Texas Instruments	TXN	CBOE
LTO	Texaco Inc.	TX	ASE
LTW	Time Warner Inc.	TWX	PHLX
LUA	UAL Corp.	UAL	CBOE
LUI	Unisys	UIS	ASE
LUP	Upjohn Co.	UPJ	CBOE
LUS	U.S. Surgical	USS	ASE
LUW	U.S. West	USW	ASE
LVP	Avon Products	AVP	CBOE
LWD	Disney (Walt) Co.	DIS	ASE
LWF	Wells Fargo	WFC	ASE
LWL	Warner-Lambert	WLA	ASE
LWM	WMX Technologies	WMX	PHLX
LWT	Wal-Mart	WMT	CBOE
LWX	Westinghouse Elec.	WX	ASE
LXM	USX-Marathon Group	MRO	ASE
LXO	Exxon Corp.	XON	CBOE
LXR	Xerox	XRX	CBOE
LXS	USX-U.S. Steel Group	X	ASE
LYQ	Synergen (SYGN)	YGQ	PSE/PHLX
VAA	Apple Computer (AAPL)	AAQ	ASE
VAD	AlliedSignal	ALD	PHLX
VAE	Adobe Systems (ADBE)	AEQ	PSE
VAG	Magna International "A"	MGA	CBOE
VAH	American Home Products	AHP	ASE
VAI	Advanced Micro Devices	AMD	PSE
VAM	Amgen Inc. (AMGN)	AMQ	ASE
VAU	Acuson Corp.	ACN	PSE
VAX	American Express	AXP	ASE
VBA	BankAmerica	BAC	CBOE
VBD	Anheuser-Busch Cos.	BUD	PHLX
VBE	SmithKline Beecham plc	SBE	PSE
VBH	Baker Hughes	BHI	PSE
VBL	BellSouth Corp.	BLS	ASE
VBM	Bristol-Myers Squibb	BMY	CBOE

	Alphabetically by LEAPS Symbol		
LEAPS Symbol	**Stock**	**Option Symbol**	**Exchange**
VBO	Boeing Co.	BA	CBOE
VBT	Abbott Labs	ABT	PHLX
VBV	Blockbuster Entertainment	BV	ASE/CBOE
VBX	American Barrick Resources	ABX	ASE
VCB	Union Carbide	UK	ASE
VCH	Chevron Corp.	CHV	ASE
VCK	Chemical Bank	CHL	ASE
VCL	Unocal Corp.	UCL	PSE
VCN	Conner Peripherals	CNR	PSE
VCP	Citicorp	CCI	CBOE
VCS	Columbia Gas	CG	ASE
VCT	Centocor Inc. (CNTO)	COQ	CBOE
VCU	Chubb Corp.	CB	NYSE
VCX	Chase Manhattan	CMB	ASE
VCY	Chrysler Corp.	C	CBOE
VDA	Delta Airlines	DAL	CBOE
VDD	du Pont (de Nemours)	DD	ASE
VDE	Digital Equipment	DEC	ASE
VDG	Placer Dome Inc.	PDG	PHLX
VDO	Dow Chemical	DOW	CBOE
VDQ	Dell Computer (DELL)	DLQ	PH
VDS	Disney (Walt) Co.	DIS	ASE
VEK	Eastman Kodak	EK	CBOE
VFN	Fed'l Nat'l M'tge Assn.	FNM	PHLX
VFO	Ford Motor	F	CBOE
VFW	Woolworth Corp.	Z	PHLX
VFX	Federal Express	FDX	CBOE
VGE	General Electric	GE	CBOE
VGG	Int'l Game Technology	IGT	ASE
VGI	General Mills	GIS	PSE
VGN	General Motors	GM	CBOE
VGP	Georgia Pacific	GP	PHLX
VGQ	Synergen (SYGN)	YGQ	PSE/PHLX
VGS	Gap Inc.	GPS	CBOE
VGT	GTE Corp.	GTE	ASE
VGX	Glaxo Holdings plc	GLX	ASE
VHD	Home Depot	HD	PHLX
VHL	Hilton Hotels	HLT	PSE
VHM	Homestake Mining	HM	CBOE
VHN	Heinz (H.J.)	HNZ	CBOE
VIB	Int'l. Bus. Machines	IBM	CBOE
VJN	Johnson & Johnson	JNJ	CBOE
VJP	Morgan (J.P.) & Co.	JPM	PHLX
VK	K-mart Corp.	KM	CBOE

Alphabetically by LEAPS Symbol			
LEAPS Symbol	Stock	Option Symbol	Exchange
VKB	Bank of Boston	BKB	PHLX
VKO	Coca-Cola	KO	CBOE
VKP	COMPAQ Computer	CPQ	PSE
VLD	Limited Inc.	LTD	CBOE
VLI	Liz Claiborne	LIZ	CBOE
VLL	Campbell Soup	CPB	NYSE
VM	Monsanto Co.	MTC	CBOE
VMA	Motorola Inc.	MOT	ASE
VMD	McDonald's Corp.	MCD	CBOE
VME	Merrill Lynch	MER	ASE
VMF	Microsoft Corp. (MSFT)	MSQ	PSE
VMH	Marriott Corp.	MHS	PHLX
VMK	Merck & Co.	MRK	CBOE
VML	Mobil Corp.	MOB	CBOE
VMP	McGraw-Hill	MHP	PHLX
VMR	AMR Corp.	AMR	ASE
VMU	Minnesota Mining & Mfg.	MMM	CBOE
VMY	Maytag Co.	MYG	NYSE
VN	Sprint Corp.	FON	PHLX
VNB	NationsBank	NB	PHLX
VNK	NIKE, Inc. "B"	NKE	PSE
VNL	Intel Corp. (INTC)	INQ	ASE
VNS	Consolidated Stores	CNS	PHLX
VNY	NYNEX Corp.	NYN	NYSE
VOI	Triton Energy Corp.	OIL	*
VOR	Oracle Systems (ORCL)	ORQ	CBOE
VP	Pepsico	PEP	CBOE
VPA	Primerica Corp.	PA	PHLX
VPC	Pacific Telesis Group	PAC	PSE
VPE	Pfizer Co.	PFE	ASE
VPG	Proctor & Gamble	PG	ASE
VPM	Philip Morris	MO	ASE
VPP	PPG Industries	PPG	PHLX
VPT	Paramount Commun.	PCI	CBOE
VQO	Quaker Oats	OAT	PHLX
VRD	Polaroid Corp.	PRD	CBOE
VRJ	RJR Nabisco Holdings	RN	ASE/CBOE/PHLX
VRK	Reebok Int'l.	RBK	ASE
VRS	Sears, Roebuck	S	CBOE
VSA	SunAmerica	SAI	PHLX
VSG	Schering-Plough	SGP	PSE
VSL	ASA Ltd.	ASA	ASE
VSM	Salomon, Inc.	SB	PHLX
VSS	U.S. Surgical	USS	ASE

	Alphabetically by LEAPS Symbol		
LEAPS Symbol	Stock	Option Symbol	Exchange
VSU	Sun Microsystems (SUNW)	SUQ	PSE
VSW	U.S. West	USW	ASE
VSY	Syntex	SYN	CBOE
VT	American Tel. & Tel.	T	CBOE
VTE	Teléfonos de México ADR	TMX	*
VTG	Tenneco Inc.	TGT	ASE
VTL	Fruit of the Loom	FTL	NYSE
VTM	Telecommunications (TCOMA)	TCQ	ASE
VTW	Time Warner Inc.	TWX	PHLX
VUA	UAL Corp.	UAL	CBOE
VUI	Unisys	UIS	ASE
VUP	Upjohn Co.	UPJ	CBOE
VVP	Avon Products	AVP	CBOE
VWF	Wells Fargo	WFC	ASE
VWL	Warner-Lambert	WLA	ASE
VWM	WMX Technologies	WMX	PHLX
VWT	Wal-Mart	WMT	CBOE
VWX	Westinghouse Elec.	WX	ASE
VXC	Texaco Inc.	TX	ASE
VXM	USX-Marathon Group	MRO	ASE
VXO	Exxon Corp.	XON	CBOE
VXR	Xerox	XRX	CBOE
VXS	USX-U.S. Steel Group	X	ASE
VXT	Texas Instruments	TXN	CBOE

* Listed ASE/CBOE/PHLX/NYSE

INDEX

A

Aggressive; *see* Style, investment/trading
All-or-none thinking, 96, 247
Aristotle, 11
Assigment(s), 15, 38, 54, 58, 60, 63, 65–66, 70, 73–74, 77, 100–101, 109, 111, 125–26, 131, 139–40, 144, 167, 169, 199–200, 210, 243, 278–79
  compared to exercise, 30
  higher probability of, 204–7
  of index options, 220–22, 225, 230–31
  of OTM, 81–84
  and taxes, 268, 272
At the money (ATM) 33, 49–50, 66–67, 83–84, 104, 127, 159, 165, 179–80, 184, 195, 199–200, 204, 206, 226, 245, 254
  averaging down with,179
  Call write, 128
  defined, 30
  LEAPS index Put purchase, 228
  Put purchase, 150
  Put write, 66
  ratio write, 168 170

B

Backwardation, 11
Barron's, 16, 224, 276
Black-Scholes Equation, 24, 31
Breakeven (B/E) point, 100, 131, 172–73, 176, 178–79 , 253
Breakeven Point, Strategic (SBE), 239

C

Characteristics and Risks of Listed Options, 282

Collateral, 10, 56, 65, 67–69, 75, 110, 112, 125, 166, 168–69, 175, 200, 226
  additional, 128, 160
  initial 41, 65, 67, 111, 127–27, 135, 139, 143, 175, 200–201
  requirements 41, 67, 82, 84, 143
  Treasury securities as, 70
Commissions, 5, 8, 15, 89–90, 104, 116, 275–77
Conservative; *see* Style, investment/trading
Contango, 11

D

Daily Graphs—Option Edition, 275
Deep in the money (DIM) 55, 88, 101–3, 110, 132, 161, 204, 223, 228, 245, 277, 282
  Calls, averaging down, 209
  Calls, DCA 184
  Calls as stock replacement, 198
  Calls as stock surrogate, 195–97, 206
  defined, 30
  LEAPS index Calls as portfolio substitute, 228
  Put better than short sale, 132
Deep out of the money (DOOM); *see* Far out of the money
Delta, 25–27, 116, 159–62, 164, 179–81, 199–200, 217, 264
  negative, 26
  non-constant. 25
  for Puts, 26
Determinants 9–10, 23, 26, 29, 31, 34, 105, 224, 299
Discipline 183, 186–87, 286–97, 300
Discount, buying stocks at, 185
Discount, LEAPS trading at, 223–24, 230

Discount broker, 275
Discount to parity, 279
Diversification, 51–53, 68–69, 102,
    197 197
Dividend(s) 8, 9, 23, 26, 27, 29, 34 97, 98,
    101, 119, 121, 196, 276, 279
    ex, 27
    expected 26
    impact 29
    as payment for Put, 97
    predicted 38
Dow Jones Industrial Average, 264,
    289, 290
Drexel Burnham Lambert 289

E

Enhancement, 4, 20, 53, 61, 75, 81, 86–
    87, 123, 191, 223, 235–50, 251, 255,
    284, 288, 295, 297
Exchange Hotlines, 16
Exchanges
    American Stock Exchange (ASE), 14,
        232, 301
    Chicago Board Options Exchange
        (CBOE), 3, 12–14, 100, 195,
        232, 301
    European Options Exchange (EOE), 281
    New York Stock Exchange (NYSE), 12–
        14, 20
    Pacific Stock Exchange (PSE), 14
    Philadelphia Stock Exchange (PHLX),
        14, 232
Exercise, automatic, 279
Exercise price; see Strike(s)
Exercise Settlements
    AM , 220
    closing, 220
    opening, 220
    PM, 220
Exercise styles 221
    American, 221, 229
    European. 221, 224, 227
Exercising LEAPS Calls or Puts 16, 220,
    230, 267
Expiration, 12, 15, 37, 40, 46–49, 53, 56,
    63, 65, 72–73, 80, 81, 86, 93–94, 99–
    102, 109, 112, 117, 128, 130–32, 135–
    36, 142–45, 148, 150, 154, 172–74,
    201, 204–8, 210, 215–16, 220–21,
    231, 235, 264, 266, 279–80, 288

Expiration—*Cont.*
    closing prior to, 105–6, 112, 136, 224–
        25, 246
    date 12, 72, 180
    day 266, 279–80
    Friday 46, 117, 220, 264, 279
    matching, to expectation 36, 53, 66,
        110, 121
    month 15, 33, 46, 207
    system for conventional options 206
    and taxes 267–68, 270–72
    Thursday 264
    time remaining until 9, 23–24, 26, 36,
        40, 42, 75, 105, 151, 196, 207, 214,
        223, 238–39, 253, 278
    week 186 264

F

Fair Value; see Theoretical value
Far out of the money (FOM) 23, 50, 103,
    123, 132, 181
    defined, 30
    Put write, 160
    uncovered Call write, 165
Federal Reserve Board, 42
Future(s), 9 11, 263, 276

G

Gamma, 25–26
GNMA (Ginnie Mae) options, 13
Group Index, 290–92
    Dow Jones, 290
    Standard & Poor's, 290

H

Hedge, 13, 19–20, 184, 188–89, 191
    covered write as, 57
    LEAPS OTM covered write as, 96
    perfect, 116
Horizontal Spread; see LEAPS Strate-
    gies, Calendar Spread

I

In the money (ITM) 33, 49–50, 67, 89,
    102, 104, 110, 112, 123, 131–32, 135,
    154, 161, 179, 199–200, 204, 206,

In the money (ITM)—*Cont.*
208, 226, 230, 238–39, 246–47, 249, 254, 278–79
defined, 30
In-the-money amount, 220
Index Arbitrage; *see* Program Trading
Index LEAPS, 13–14, 52,186, 219–32, 279–80, 286, 296
automatic exercise of, 279
for DCA, 186
definition and strategies, 219–32
and discipline, 296
spreads 229
and taxes, 271–72
Index
Bank, 221
Beta, 13
Biotech, 221
Gaming, 13
Gold/silver, 13
International, 13
Oil, 221
Technology, 13
Indexes
broad, 221, 228, 232, 271–72
industry, 13, 221
market, 221
narrow, 12, 221, 271
sub-, 221
Index options, 5, 12, 206, 219—21, 275
collateral for, 42
definition, 219–20
exercises/assignments, 231
expirations, 279–80
strategies for, 221
and taxes, 271–72
Industry Group 51, 52, 187, 223
Insurance, LEAPS as, 13, 19, 91, 96, 226, 229
Interest rate(s) 8, 10, 29, 30, 38, 39, 55, 105, 106, 116, 117, 224, 226
discount, 29
mortgage, 29
prime, 29
risk-free, 9, 23, 29, 30, 38 39, 69
Internal Revenue Service (IRS), 92, 266, 269
Wash Sale, 181–82, 201, 269
Intrinsic value, 12, 30, 88, 95, 100, 102, 121, 131, 135, 154, 201, 220, 224–25, 253, 279

Investor's Business Daily, 275
In the money (ITM), 33, 50, 89, 102–4, 110, 112, 123, 131–32, 161, 179, 195, 199–200, 204, 206, 220, 226, 230, 239, 246–47, 249, 254
and automatic exercise, 279
covered call write 103
defined, 30
and discount to parity, 278–79
protective Put, 88–91
Put write, 66–67
qualified covered calls, 269–70

L

Last trading day 15–16, 271, 280
LEAPS, reduced-value, 231–32 281
LEAPS discipline worksheet, 288
LEAPS money generator 77–79, 84
LEAPS Strategies
Affirmative Action (Sell Half Position, Write LEAPS Straddles), 209–11
Averaging down with LEAPS, 178–82, 299
Bear(ish) Call Spreads, 134–36
Bear(ish) Put Spread, 130–33, 246, 256
Better to Marry Rich, 97
Bull(ish) Spreads With LEAPS Calls, 99–107, 112, 134, 238–39, 244–46, 253–55
Bull(ish) Spreads With LEAPS Puts, 108–13, 134–36
Buying Index LEAPS Straddles and Combinations, 227
Buying LEAPS Calls, 21, 36, 40, 46–53, 58, 67–68, 103, 148, 161, 197, 199, 212, 235–40, 251–54, 266, 299
Buying LEAPS Index Calls, 222–23
Buying LEAPS Index Puts, 223–25
Buying LEAPS Married Puts, 92–98, 247, 256, 267, 270–71, 299
Buying LEAPS Puts, 20,116–24, 128, 132, 164, 239–41, 254, 266, 299
Buying LEAPS Straddles and Combinations, 148–55, 212, 215, 239, 247, 257, 299
Buying Married Index LEAPS Puts, 227
Buying Protective Index LEAPS Puts, 226

LEAPS Strategies—*Cont.*
Buying Protective LEAPS Puts, 86–91, 98, 121, 188, 247, 256–57, 300
Calendar Spread, 203
Covered Call Writing, 54–67, 69, 71–72, 76, 101–3, 125, 171, 174, 188–89, 206, 241–45, 254–55, 265, 270, 272–73
Dollar Cost Averaging (DCA), 183–97, 209, 229, 249, 296, 299
Dollar Cost Averaging (DCA) With Index LEAPS, 228–29
Fences, 87, 91, 165, 188–92, 198, 249
Index Fences, 228
Ratio Spreading 174–77, 248
Ratio Writing, 166–73, 248, 286
Ratio Writing/Ratio Spreading With Index LEAPS ,228
Reduced-Risk Trading, 212–18, 296, 301
Replacement Therapy, 198–202, 210, 226, 228, 245, 249, 257
Replacement Therapy With Index LEAPS, 228
Surrogate Therapy, 195–98, 203, 205–6, 228, 249
Surrogate Therapy With Index LEAPS, 228
Synthetic Short, 164–65, 190–91, 244, 248
Synthetic Short With Index LEAPS, 227
Synthetic Stock, 159–63, 201, 248
Synthetic Stock With Index LEAPS, 227
Systematic Covered Writing, 77
Time Is of the Essence (Long LEAPS/Write Shorter-Term), 203–8, 229, 238, 249
Time is of the Essence With Index LEAPS, 229
Writing Covered Calls With Index LEAPS, 225–26
Writing Covered Combinations, 80–85
Writing Covered Straddles, 72–78, 81, 84
Writing LEAPS Puts, 63–72, 77–79, 199, 217, 221–22, 245, 255, 269–69, 286, 299
Writing Uncovered Calls, 125–29, 164–65, 171, 173, 247–48, 256
Writing Uncovered Combinations, 142–47, 247, 258, 299
Writing Uncovered Index LEAPS Calls, 226

LEAPS Strategies—*Cont.*
Writing Uncovered Index LEAPS Puts, 221–22, 226
Writing Uncovered Index Straddles and Combinations, 221, 227
Writing Uncovered Straddles, 138–41, 144–45, 147, 247, 258
LEAPS symbols, 16
Leverage, 19–20, 40, 46, 49–51, 53, 68, 102, 104, 107, 116–17, 124, 130, 133–34, 159–60, 162, 164–65, 174–75, 178–79, 195, 197, 212, 223, 232, 237, 241, 284, 287, 298–99
Long(er)-dated options, equivalent to LEAPS, 282
Long(er)-dated options, LEAPS as more than 4, 282
Long-term (tax aspect), 92–93, 266, 268, 272–73
Long-term profit, 123, 267, 272
Longer-term investments 19, 212

M

Margin, 15, 41–42, 62, 65, 82, 139; *see also* Collateral
initial 76, 82, 118, 127
maintenance 126
minimum, 41, 64, 127,221
Put, 76, 82
requirement, 64, 143, 258
stock on, 41, 61–62, 65, 67, 70, 75, 82, 102, 118, 196–97
Margin account, 42, 61–62, 104, 176, 276
Margin call, 118–19, 127
Margin interest, 41, 62, 65, 82, 104, 176, 276
Mark-to-the-market, 271
Miracle, 154–55, 208, 212, 215, 236, 299–300
Moderate; *see* Style, investment/trading

N

New York Times, The, 34

O

OEX; *see* S&P 100 Index
Open Interest, 13

Options / Essential Concepts and Trading Strategies, 282
"Options for the small investor," 214
Options as a Strategic Investment, 282
Options Clearing Corp., The (OCC), 14, 282
Options Institute, 214
Order(s)
  "or better," 278
  closing, 74, 151, 155, 239–42, 244–46, 252–55, 257, 281
  contingent, 277
  limit, 225, 264, 277
  market, 29, 90, 277–78, 282
  opening, 253, 281
  rolling, 281
  spread, 281
  stop(-loss), 90, 300
Other People's Money (OPM), 236–39
Other People's Money, 239
Out of the money (OTM), 33, 47–50, 83, 89, 95, 109–10, 112, 135, 144–46, 149, 161, 172, 176, 179, 184, 188, 195, 197, 199, 203–6, 213, 226, 228, 238, 248, 272, 300
  amount for margin, 42, 82, 122, 143, 200–201
  in bull call spread, 103–4
  Call buying, 49, 53
  Call writing, 58, 62, 96, 103–4, 254, 270
  defined, 30
  Put purchase, 122–23
  Put write, 66–67, 69
Outlook, stock/sector/market, 4, 21, 71, 88, 128, 136, 138, 142, 186, 229, 235, 285
  change in, 112, 127, 136, 171, 240, 258
  recording, 295

P

Position Limit, 15
Program Trading 29, 186, 263–65, 300
Protection, LEAPS for 6–7, 13 19–20, 57–58, 61,76. 84–91, 92–93, 95–98, 120–21, 162, 165, 188–89, 191–91, 198, 205–6, 211–12, 214, 217–18, 226, 232, 247, 254, 256–57, 271, 279, 284, 296–300
Put and Call Brokers and Dealers Association, 12

Put buying, superior to short selling, 118–20

Q

Qualified Covered Calls, 269–70

R

Random Walk Theory, 25
Range
  annual, 34, 39, 146
  breakeven, 144–46
  calendar year, 46
  expected, 28, 296
  projected, 28
Repair, 4, 40, 53, 59, 107, 123, 147. 161, 222, 251–58, 284, 293–94
  of fences, 191
Return
  annual(ized) 55, 57, 66, 76, 82, 128, 145
  period 55, 65, 76, 82, 140, 200
  as secondary, 67
Risk
  attitude toward, 6, 36, 56, 66, 84, 184, 238, 284
  lower with LEAPS, 6, 23, 49, 53, 71, 98, 103, 132–33, 161–62, 173, 208, 299
  unlimited, 120, 125–28, 164, 168
  zero-, positions, 97, 237, 239,
Risk aversion, matching strategy to, 21, 36, 48, 67, 70, 197, 222, 299
Roll(ing), 74, 75, 93, 226, 236, 239, 243, 245, 254, 281
  diagonal, 255
  down, 254
  out, 255
  up, 239, 242, 243, 246, 250

S

S&P 100 Index, (OEX), 206, 220–21
  composition of, 219
  exercises of, 220
  introduction, 12
  LEAPS, 231–32
S&P 500 (SPX), 12–13, 219, 220, 263, 292
  LEAPS (SPL), 13
  LEAPS (SPX), 232

Sage, Russell, 11
Scalping, 18, 49, 212, 214, 218
SEC, 10, 12, 301
Size, 53
  changes strategy, 286
  correspond to stock, 50
  inappropriate, 40, 51, 102, 107, 123,
      175–76, 212, 217–18, 222, 227,
      248, 286, 300
Spread(s)
  defined, 99
  index LEAPS, 229
  margin for, 42, 110–11
  must go in Margin Account, 42, 104,
      176; *see also* LEAPS Strategies
  time, 203
  vertical, 203
Square root of time, 24 27
Standard & Poor's Outlook, 276
Standard & Poor's Stock Guide, 34, 276
Standard deviation, 9
Strangle, 80
Strike(s), strike price, striking price, 9,
      12, 20, 23, 25, 30, 34, 53, 135, 139,
      142–45, 148, 287
  creation of, 33, 89, 238, 300
  fewer for LEAPS, 33, 235, 241
  matching to expectation, 48–50, 121–
      22, 146, 184
  OTM, advantage of, 58, 62, 81, 122,
      128, 144–46, 160, 169, 189
  separation between, 100–101, 103–4,
      109–11, 131, 225, 227, 238,
The Striking Price, 276
Style, investment/trading, 21, 162, 284;
      see also Risk aversion
Supply and demand, law of, 10, 23, 26, 29

T

Tax rules
  holding period, 92–93, 123, 181,
      267–70
  offsetting positions, 269

Tax rules—*Cont.*
  60/40 treatment, 272
  substantial reduction of risk of loss
      test, 269
  treatment of married Puts, 91–93, 95,
      98, 270–71
Thales, 11
Theoretical Value 24, 31, 34–35, 38–
      39, 172
Time decay, 37, 153, 204, 265, 296
Time value, 30, 88, 95, 100, 102, 121,
      123, 131, 135, 154, 201, 208, 220,
      224–25, 253, 279
Time, square root of, 24, 27
Treasury securities, 18, 29, 38, 50–51,
      69–70, 179, 181, 196–97, 199
  bonds, 38
  issues, 69
Triple Witching Hour, 264
Tulip Bulb Craze,11, 13

V

Value Line, 276
VL Options Guide, 276
Volatility, 9, 10, 23, 27, 31, 38
  annual(ized), 27
  approximation of, 28
  average, 27
  estimate of, 27
  expected, 39
  forecast, 31
  historic, 31
  implied, 31
  individual, 31
  projected, 29, 34, 39
  as standard deviation, 9
Voltaire, 245

W

Wall Street Journal, The, 275
Weidman, Jerome, 239

Time Decay of 2- and 3-Year Options

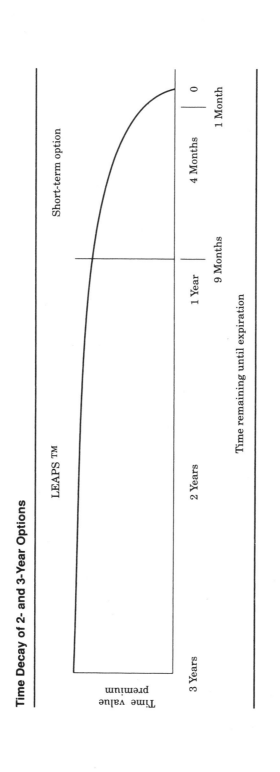